The Cherokees

INDIANS OF THE SOUTHEAST

Series Editors

Theda Perdue
University of Kentucky

Michael D. Green
Dartmouth College

Advisory Editors

Leland Ferguson
University of South Carolina

Charles Hudson
University of Georgia

Mary Young
University of Rochester

The Cherokees

A Population History

BY RUSSELL THORNTON

with the assistance of
C. Matthew Snipp and Nancy Breen

UNIVERSITY OF NEBRASKA PRESS
Lincoln and London

Acknowledgments for the use of previously published material
appear on page xvi.

First printing of paperback edition: 1992
Most recent printing indicated by the last digit below:
10   9   8   7   6   5   4   3   2   1

Library of Congress Cataloging-in-Publication Data
Thornton, Russell, 1942–
The Cherokees: a population history/by Russell Thornton,
with the assistance of C. Matthew Snipp and Nancy Breen.
p.   cm.–(Indians of the Southeast)
Includes bibliographical references.
ISBN 0-8032-4416-9 (alk. paper)
ISBN 0-8032-9410-7 (pbk.)
1. Cherokee Indians–Population. I. Snipp, C. Matthew.
II. Breen, Nancy. III. title. IV. Series.
E99.C5T48   1990   89-77142
305.8'975–dc20   CIP

For
Watt, Wallace, Walter, and W. G. Thornton
and for
all the Cherokees,
East, West, and everywhere

For God said, if the Cherokees be destroyed and become extinct, then that will be the destruction of the whole world. This is the word of the forefathers of our own land.

Keetoowah Society of
Cherokee Indians

Cherokee blood, if not destroyed, will win[d] its courses in beings of fair complexions, who will read that their ancestors became civilized under the frowns of misfortune, and the causes of their enemies.

John Ridge

Contents

Illustrations

Series Editors' Foreword

One of the questions confronting contemporary Native Americans and federal policymakers is Who is an Indian? It is not easy to answer. What makes a person an Indian? Is it ancestry, enrollment, culture, or self-image? Many people whose names do not appear on the rolls of federally recognized tribes find satisfaction in defining themselves as Indian, but the material benefits that accrue to those who are officially enrolled make the issue a sensitive one for native peoples and for the United States government. Who decides legitimacy—individuals, Indian tribes, the states, or the federal government? In *The Cherokees: A Population History*, Russell Thornton narrows the focus to a single people, the Cherokees, and demonstrates how a changing population has made defining *Cherokee* very difficult.

Thornton's demographic history chronicles the epidemics suffered by the Cherokees and the population losses caused by war and removal. But he also deals with recovery and growth. The Cherokee population was never static; it changed frequently in number, location, and definition. According to Thornton, the Cherokees never have been a totally unified, homogeneous population. In the early historical era, they lived in the southern Appalachians in independent villages with little political cohesion; being Cherokee merely meant belonging to a matrilineal Cherokee clan into which whites and blacks as well as other native peoples were sometimes adopted. In the nineteenth century the Cherokees began to disperse—most to Indian Territory but others to Texas, Arkansas, California, and other regions—although some remained in the East. Intermarriage with whites and a growing nationalism forced a redefinition of Cherokee. Geographical distance, lawsuits, and civil wars further complicated the issue, and the current popularity of "Cherokee grandmothers" and the United States Census Bureau's decision to permit racial self-identification have made a consensus on who is a Cherokee virtually impossible. Thornton's analysis of the Cherokee population is an important contribution to the scholarly, official, and popular debates.

Theda Perdue
Michael D. Green

Acknowledgments

This book began in a conversation I had with Theda Perdue, now of the University of Kentucky, during a 1985 Newberry Library conference on American Indian history held at the Smithsonian Institution, Washington, D.C. As coeditor, with Mike Green of Dartmouth College, of a series on southeastern Indians newly inaugurated by the University of Nebraska Press, she suggested the topic. I responded with enthusiasm, and we briefly discussed some pertinent issues. In the following three years I had several discussions with Theda and Mike by mail and telephone, and in person during visits with Theda at Clemson University and with Mike at Dartmouth College and at various professional meetings we attended. Both Theda and Mike were generous enough to read drafts of my manuscript and offer criticisms, comments, and suggestions. I thank them sincerely for their varied contributions. I also thank anonymous reviewers for reading drafts, as well as Nancy Breen, then of the United States Bureau of the Census, and C. Matthew Snipp, then of the University of Maryland, coauthors of chapter 7 and the Appendix. They also provided the data on the Cherokees in the 1980 United States census that are presented in chapter 7 and the Appendix.

I wrote the manuscript under various grants from the University of Minnesota and other institutions. During the 1985–86 academic year I had a sabbatical leave from the University of Minnesota, a Bush Foundation Supplemental Fellowship in conjunction with it, and a small travel grant from the College of Liberal Arts of the University of Minnesota. I spent parts of 1986 and 1987 in the Department of Anthropology of the National Museum of Natural History at the Smithsonian Institution under a Smithsonian Institution Fellowship, and that is where this book began. During May 1986 I was a visiting distinguished lecturer in the Graduate Group in Demography of the University of California, Berkeley, under that University's Chancellor's Distinguished Visiting Lectureship Program. Finally, during the summer of 1987 I held a research grant from the Graduate School of the University of Minnesota to finish the manuscript, and I completed it after I moved from the University of Minnesota to the University of California, Berkeley, in 1988.

Various parts of the book have been presented at professional meetings, conferences, and lectures during the past several years. These included the 1983 annual meetings of the American Society for Ethnohistory in Albuquerque, a 1986 symposium on the Cherokees at Western Carolina University in Cullowhee and the Eastern Cherokee reservation, North Carolina, a 1987 conference entitled "Toward a Quantitative Approach to American Indian History" at the Newberry Library, Chicago, a 1987 lecture at the University of Oklahoma in Norman and a 1989 colloquium at the Graduate Group in Demography at the University of California, Berkeley. I thank discussants and participants for their comments on my presentations.

I am grateful to Gloria DeWolfe of the Department of Sociology at the University of Minnesota for the many hours she spent at the word processor preparing various drafts of the manuscripts and for her comments, insights, and suggestions.

Finally, I thank Melissa Meyer, my wife, for reading and commenting on the entire manuscript and for continued support in all my endeavors.

Introduction

This book is a population history of a great American Indian people of what is now the United States. It traces the Cherokees as a physical population from their first contacts with Europeans and Africans to their existence today.

The Cherokees were and are a demographically amorphous population. Their origins remain a mystery, and a controversial one. Scholars have long argued the issues and have arrived at plausible hypotheses, but no one knows for sure how the Cherokees came into being, where they originated, or even when they first arrived on their traditional lands in the Southeast. Demographically defining today's Cherokees is equally perplexing. They now (1990) encompass some 8,500 to 9,000 enrolled members of the Eastern Band of Cherokees in North Carolina, some 90,000 in the Cherokee Nation of Oklahoma, and about 7,500 in the United Keetoowah Band of Cherokee Indians in Oklahoma. The population also includes the 232,344 self-reported Cherokees in the 1980 United States census and those who will self-identify as Cherokee in the 1990 census. Many other people—whites, blacks, and others—have some degree of Cherokee ancestry but are not identified as Cherokees, at least for the census. In the twentieth century it is appropriate to consider the Cherokees as different populations rather than as a single people—diverse populations defined by separate locations and criteria.

The story I tell is often not a happy one—certainly not for the first several centuries after the Europeans and Africans arrived on Cherokee lands. More often than not it deals with misfortune, tragedy, sorrow, and death. It is the story of the Cherokees' struggle with demographic change as Europeans and Africans arrived upon American Indian land, colonized the original people, and supplanted Cherokees and other native populations. The demographic changes for the Cherokees, as for other American Indian peoples, included drastic population reduction, massive relocation, and eventual population confusion as they met, traded, fought, prayed, and intermingled with Europeans, Africans, and others.

The story is also one of survival, perseverence, and hope as the Cherokees confronted their new demographic situation. They met the challenges head on and adapted to them, and eventually they prospered. In doing so, however, the Cherokees became very different populations: heterogeneous and impossible to define clearly. They were not destroyed and they did not become extinct, but they were forever altered. The main forces of demographic change, as woven into their history, were geographical dispersion and miscegenation. Today the Cherokees struggle with their own physical identity: eventually Cherokee blood did "win[d] its courses in beings of fair complexions," as John Ridge, a Cherokee, predicted. Yet other Cherokees resemble their native forebears more closely than they resemble the European invaders.

In tracing this population history I also tell something of the social and cultural histories of the Cherokees, since the three intertwine, but only as much as is necessary to understand their history as a physical population. My story is not a general history of the Cherokees.[1]

I draw upon not only original information on the Cherokees, but numerous secondary sources as well—published works in the scholarly disciplines of history, anthropology, archaeology, physical anthropology, sociology, geography, and demography.

OVERVIEW

The story begins with Cherokee origins. In chapter 1 I briefly discuss the emergence of the Cherokees as a distinct American Indian population and consider Cherokee lands and population size before first contact with Europeans, probably in 1540. Included is a section on techniques for assessing aboriginal American Indian population sizes and an estimate of the aboriginal Cherokee population.

In chapter 2 I consider the numerical declines and recoveries of the Cherokee population during the eighteenth century, giving attention to Old World pathogens brought by Europeans and Africans, which became "the frowns of misfortune" for the Cherokees. Pathogens included particularly *Variola major,* which causes smallpox in humans, and I describe various epidemics of smallpox. I also discuss the effects of warfare on the Cherokee population, particularly the "Cherokee War" of 1760 and the American Revolution: these were in many respects "the causes of their enemies." Finally, I examine the shrinking Cherokee lands during the eighteenth century and the first emigrations of Cherokees from the Southeast.

Chapters 3, 4, and 5 cover Cherokee population history during the nineteenth century. In chapter 3 I examine Cherokee population growth during the first decades of the century and further Cherokee emigration from the Southeast, then detail the Cherokee population in 1835 and consider the massive Cherokee population relocation —the Trail Where We Cried (Trail of Tears)—and resulting population losses. Chapter 4 describes the separate Cherokee populations in the mid-nineteenth century, then discusses the devastating effects of the Civil War on the Cherokee population, along with the Cherokee freedmen (former slaves) and the "adoption" of Delawares and Shawnees into the Cherokee tribe. Finally, the size and geographic distribution of the Cherokees toward the end of the nineteenth century are described in chapter 5, as are other demographic and related characteristics of Cherokees and numbers of non-Cherokees on Cherokee lands in North Carolina and Indian Territory.

Chapter 6 examines the twentieth-century Cherokees. I discuss population growth and changing demographic characteristics during this century and examine the biological mixing of Cherokees with non-Cherokees. Also considered are issues of defining the Cherokees as a distinct segment of the United States population, including procedures of census enumerations, Bureau of Indian Affairs requirements, and criteria for tribal membership. The chapter additionally discusses the United Keetoowah Cherokees, "mixed" and "traditional" Cherokees, primarily in Oklahoma at midcentury, and the "Red-Black Cherokees," a distinct group of Cherokee-black mixture.

Chapter 7, written with Nancy Breen and C. Matthew Snipp, examines Cherokee populations today, both the total Cherokee population and North Carolina Cherokees, Oklahoma Cherokees, California Cherokees, and Cherokees elsewhere, including further discussion of the Red-Black Cherokees and considerations of current tribal enrollments. After this we discuss the "Cherokee grandmother" phenomenon—the large number of individuals who have or claim some Cherokee ancestry. Finally, we consider the question, "Who is Cherokee?" and look at the likely demographic future of Cherokees as distinct American Indian tribes and as a subpopulation of the total United States population.

The Conclusion briefly discusses implications for the demographic future of other American Indians, drawn from records on Cherokees and other native peoples.

A technical appendix written with C. Matthew Snipp and Nancy Breen focuses on procedures for enumerating American Indians in the United States censuses, particularly the 1980 census, with special reference to the recent Cherokee population "growth."

CHAPTER 1

Aboriginal Lands and Population

The Cherokees say they and other human beings were created after plants and animals were made. Plants and animals were told by the creator—the Cherokees do not know who he or she was—to stay awake for seven nights and watch the world. Most could not do so. Of the plants, only the spruce, cedar, pine, holly, and laurel trees were able to watch so long: that is why they are now green all year. Of the animals, only the owl, the panther, and a few others were able to stay awake: that is why they see at night and prey on those who must sleep. Human beings were then created: "At first there were only a brother and sister until he struck her with a fish and told her to multiply, and so it was." Seven days afterward the girl had a child; another came seven days later, then another, and so forth, and the human beings "increased very fast until there was danger that the world could not keep them. Then it was made that a woman should have only one child in a year, and it has been so ever since" (Mooney [1900] 1982:240).

The Cherokees also have a migration story, perhaps telling of the first arrival of human beings in the Western Hemisphere. It was recorded about 1717 by Alexander Long, a Carolina trader. It may refer to a journey across Beringia, the land once joining present-day Alaska and Siberia, and through the ice-free corridors of what is now Canada, and then to a separation of those who became the Cherokees from other migrants. Thus the people's movement toward the "sone setting," as expressed in the story below, could be explained by a south-southeast movement to "warmer wether." (The reference to bringing "coren and pease pumpkins and muskmelons" and "writting" seems improbable.) In any event, the story is as follows:

Four oure coming here we know now noething but what was had from our ancestors and has brought it down from generation to generation//the way is thus were belonged to another land far distant from heare//and the people increased and multiplied so fast that the land could not hold them soe that they were forst to separate and travele to look out for another countray//they travelled soe four that they came to a countray that was soe could that [obscure here] . . . yet goeing still one they came to mountains of snow and ice the prestes held a council to pass these montains//and that they believed there was warmer wether one the other sid of those mountains because it lay near the sone setting which was beleved by the whol assembly wee were forst to make raccits [snowshoes] to put on our ould and yonge//and passed one our journey and at last found our our soe fare gone over these mountains till we lost sight of the same and went thrues darkness for a good space and then . . . the sone again and goeing one we came to a countray that could be inhabited and there we multiplaid so much that we over spread all this maine, we brought all manner graines such as coren and pease pumpkins and muskmelon as for all sorte of wild frute wee found here naturally growing//as we were one our jrnay over these mountains we lost a vast quantitie of people by the onseasonable could and darkness that we went thrue//when wee come one this maine first wee were all one languige//but the prid and ambeshun of some of the leading men that caused . . . amonst the traibes//they separated from one and other and the languige was corrupted//moreover we are tould by our ancestors that when wee first came on this land that the prestes and beloved men was writting but nott one paper as you doe but one white deare skins and one the shoulder bones of buflow for severall yeares but the . . . of the young people being so grate thatt they would nott obey the priest nor . . . but lett thire minds rone after hunting of wild beasts that the writing was quite lost and could not be recovered againe Soe much for thire comeing on this maine. (Quoted in Corkran 1952:27)

The Cherokees do not now know when or how some humans first became Cherokees. Almost certainly they had their origins in an ancient time, distinct from the present, when things were not as they are now. The Cherokees think they may even have emerged from the ground after other human beings were created, for it is said there is another world under the surface, identical except that the seasons are different. According to the Cherokees, "The streams that come down from the mountains are the trails by which we reach this underworld, and the springs at the heads are the doorways by which we enter it, but to do this one must fast and go to water and have one of the underground people for a guide" (Mooney [1900] 1982:240).[1]

Some scholars have asserted that this is where the name Cherokee came from—given them by their neighbors. The scholars have argued that *Cherokee* means "cave people," for the Cherokees are said to have come from under the ground (see, for example, Reid 1970:3) and also lived in a mountainous land full of caves. The nineteenth-century anthropologist James Mooney stated:

> Cherokee, the name by which they are commonly known, . . . seems to be of foreign origin. . . . It first appears as Chalaque in the Portuguese narrative of De Soto's expedition, published originally in 1557, while we find Cheraqui in a French document of 1699, and Cherokee as an English form as early, at least, as 1708. The name has thus an authentic history of 360 years. There is evidence that it is derived from the Choctaw word choluk or chiluk, signifying a pit or cave, and comes to us through the so-called Mobilian trade language, a corrupted Choctaw jargon formerly used as the medium of communication among all the tribes of the Gulf states, as far north as the mouth of the Ohio. (Mooney [1900] 1982:15–16)

The eighteenth-century trader James Adair asserted that the name came from the (apparently Cherokee) word *chee-ra*, meaning (sacred) fire, forming *cheera-tahge*, or "men possessed of the divine fire" (Adair [1775] 1930:237). Probably the name is from the Creek *chilokee*, "people of a different speech," as John W. Swanton has stated; perhaps it is the name from which the form Chalaque was derived (Swanton [1939] 1985:49–50). The anthropologist John Witthoft supported this interpretation, based on his work with Eastern Cherokee "informants": "The name came from the Creek, Celokokalke, 'people of another language' (celokalki, 'Cherokees')." He asserted, "The Creek name by which the Cherokee were first known to Europeans became the general name for them in the Southeast, and was soon accepted even by the Cherokee themselves; names for other tribal groups have come into existence after a similar fashion" (Witthoft 1947:305).

The Cherokees commonly called themselves Tsalagi (Tsaragi) or, in the plural, Ani-Tsalagi (Ani-Tsaragi), perhaps "corrupted" to form the name Cherokee or perhaps derived from the same word as Cherokee. According to James Mooney, their proper name for themselves was Yunwiya or, in the plural, Ani-Yunwiya. It means, more or less, "the people," "the real people," or "the principal people": Mooney says, "The word properly denotes 'Indians,' as distinguished from people of other races, but in usage it is restricted to mean members of the Cherokee tribe, those of other tribes being designated as Creek, Catawba, etc., as the case may be." On ceremonial occasions the name frequently used was Ani-Kituhwagi, or "people of Kituhwa"— in the plural, Ani-Kituhwa—signifying the Cherokees' descent from the inhabitants of the ancient village of Kituhwa (Kittowah) (Mooney [1900] 1982:15).[2]

Today the Cherokees, in their own written language, refer to themselves as ᏣᎳᎩ : Tsa-la-gi; in the plural, ᎠᏂᏣᎳᎩ : A-ni-Tsa-la-gi. Of course, in English they call themselves Cherokee, the name perhaps eventually derived from the Creek word discussed above, and perhaps through corrupting Tsalagi.

FIRST CHEROKEES IN THE SOUTHEAST

Scholars differ on where the Cherokees came from and when they arrived on their traditional lands in the Southeast. The archaeological record of human occupancy of the Southeast goes back to at least 10,000 B.C. (see Muller 1978:283; Canouts and Goodyear 1985:181), but this does not mean the Cherokees, or even their very distant ancestors, were there that early. Cherokees, as Cherokees, did not exist nearly so far back in time, nor did they necessarily emerge from the first or even from early occupants of the Southeast. The Cherokees as a more or less distinct American Indian people seem to be at the very most only one or two thousand years old. They may have developed from other American Indian peoples already in the Southeast, or they may have migrated there from another region.

Migration

Some scholars, particularly anthropologists, have contended that the Cherokees, or those who became the Chero-

kees, arrived on their new lands in the Southeast from the north or
northeast, or even the northwest. This migration might have been
in relatively recent times—say a few centuries ago—or in more ancient times, a thousand or so years ago, the Cherokees having been
driven south by their linguistic kinsmen the Iroquois. As evidence,
scholars have cited the Cherokees' linguistic similarity to the Iroquois, an American Indian people to the north, and their dissimilarity
to other American Indians of the Southeast (Lounsbury 1961; Haas
1961). These scholars have also cited as evidence the many migration
legends contained in the oral traditions of the Cherokees, as well as
in legends of other American Indian peoples that might pertain to the
Cherokees—for example, the Delawares and the Wyandots (Hurons)
(Mooney [1900] 1982:17–23).

According to a Cherokee tradition, they originated in the East,
toward the rising sun, then began a westward migration lasting many
years (Mooney [1900] 1982:20). Arriving on their present home in
the Southeast, the tradition goes, "they found it possessed by certain 'moon-eyed people,' who could not see in the daytime. These
wretches they expelled" (quoted in Mooney [1900] 1982:22). John
Witthoft's informants stated that the Cherokees came from the
southwest. One informant, Will West Long, "recognized two basic
groups of Cherokee: the original group, from which his people split
off before migration, called *anigaduwagi*, 'confederated people'; and
the Cherokee who came to the East, *onaselagi*, 'they separated from
the bunch'" (Witthoft 1947:304).[3]

Emergence

Other scholars, particularly archaeologists, have contended that the Cherokees, as Cherokees, developed on their traditional southeastern lands from pre-Cherokee populations of American Indians who had been there at least a thousand years, if not a
great deal longer. Some have even maintained that the Cherokees
built pre-Columbian mounds in the Southeast (Thomas 1891, [1894]
1985:718–21). As evidence of this antiquity, these scholars have cited
the apparent linguistic divergence between the Cherokees and the
Iroquois of possibly as long as 3,500 to 3,800 years ago (Lounsbury
1961:11). They also have cited the archaeological record of the Southeast. It indicates, according to some, that the Cherokees emerged in
the Southeast as "the end product of a long, continuous, and multi-

linear development" (Dickens 1979:28; see also Lewis and Kneberg
1946:4–20, 1958:156). One archaeologist argued for a trilineal development of Cherokee culture in the Southeast, dating from A.D. 1000,
as reflected in three early archaeological phases, primarily based on
mound construction and ceramic forms: Early Etowah, Hiwassee
Island, and Early Pisgah. According to Roy S. Dickens, Jr. (1979:12,
fig. 3), the sequence of phases was Early Etowah (A.D. 1000) to Late
Etowah/Wilbanks (A.D. 1250) to Early Lamar (A.D. 1450) to Late
Lamar Variations (A.D. 1650); Hiwassee Island (A.D. 1000) to Early
Dallas (A.D. 1250) to Late Dallas (A.D. 1450) to Overhill (A.D. 1650);
and Early Pisgah (A.D. 1000) to Late Pisgah (A.D. 1250) to Early Qualla
(A.D. 1450) to Late Qualla (A.D. 1650). These lines continued to well
into the 1800s, Dickens argued, reflected in (as I discuss in chaps. 2
and 3) three Cherokee divisions at that time: Lower Cherokee, Overhill Cherokee, and Middle Cherokee (Dickens 1979:12, fig. 3, 28;
also Dickens 1976; Keel 1976).[4]

Issues of the Cherokee origins and migration are not yet settled,
but most contemporary scholars favor the archaeological view of
early Cherokee development in the Southeast (Fogelson 1978:10).

ABORIGINAL LANDS AND POPULATION

However and whenever the Cherokees first became
the Cherokees, it seems they were occupying southeastern lands
at the time Europeans made their first recorded penetration there
in 1539–43, during the expedition of Hernando de Soto.[5] De Soto
may have first encountered the Cherokees in the province of Chalaque (also Xalaque or Chelaque); this was originally thought to have
been north of present-day Savannah, Georgia, but some contemporary scholars think it was somewhere west of Charlotte, North Carolina (Hudson, Smith, and DePratter 1984:73). First contact between
De Soto and the Cherokees, however, might have occurred when
he arrived at the village of Guasili, probably near present-day Marshall, North Carolina (Swanton [1946] 1979:110; Hudson, Smith, and
DePratter 1984:74; also Swanton [1939] 1985).[6] This was likely on
May 29, 1540 (Hudson, Smith, and DePratter 1984:74). According
to a report of the expedition, the Cherokees gave De Soto and his
men three hundred little dogs and some corn as food, in addition to
some *tamemes*, or Indians, to carry their loads. After spending some
time gambling with dice, De Soto and his expedition left on May 31.

Next the expedition passed the Cherokee town of Canasoga, probably near present-day Hot Springs, North Carolina, where they were given baskets of mulberries (Hudson, Smith, and DePratter 1984:74). They left the town shortly thereafter and eventually left Cherokee territory as well.

James Mooney ([1900] 1982:14) asserted that lands claimed by the Cherokees extended from the Ohio River southward to present-day central Georgia, and from what are now the states of Tennessee, Kentucky, and Alabama to the Wabash River. Certainly not all of this area was "settled" by the Cherokees at any one time, and much of it may be considered merely "lands claimed" or "hunting territory." As Mooney ([1900] 1982:14) noted, American Indian tribes often had no fixed boundaries, and lands claimed by the Cherokees were also claimed by other tribes.

Cherokee lands can best be described as the part of eastern North America that makes up the core of the southern Appalachian highlands. This area may be subdivided into five zones: the southern Appalachian mountain system, primarily high mountains; the Piedmont plateau, primarily "upland"; the Appalachian valleys and ridges, parallel mountain ridges; the Cumberland plateau, an escarpment sloping to the southeast and rising to the northeast from its southern edge; and the interior lowlands, a low plateau (Goodwin 1977:6–16). The core area of Cherokee settlement—about 40,000 square miles, or some 103,600 square kilometers—covered most of the southern Appalachian mountain system and parts of the central portions of the Appalachian valleys and ridges and the Piedmont plateau (Goodwin 1977:9, fig. 2, 11, fig. 3). River basins and systems included within these areas are the New River system, the South Fork of the Holston River basin, the Watauga River basin, the Nolichucky River basin, the French Broad River basin, the Big Pigeon River basin, the Little Tennessee River basin, the Hiwassee River basin, the tributaries of the Upper Savannah River system, and the Coosa River and its affluents (Goodwin 1977:20–25).

Encompassed within this area were various natural vegetation zones: the southern Appalachian forest of oak and chestnut; the southern Piedmont mixed forests of pines and hardwoods; the Cumberland mixed forests of, for example, beech, basswood, dogwood, chestnut, buckeye, sugar maple, birch, maple, hemlock, and pine; and the lowland forests of oak, hickory, maple, tulip trees, honey locust, mulberry, and cedar (Goodwin 1977:16–20).

Anthropologist Alfred L. Kroeber indicated a total Cherokee

area larger than these 103,600 square kilometers; he asserted that their area encompassed 134,400 square kilometers, or about 52,000 square miles. Recent scholarship, however, indicates that the early (sixteenth-century) Cherokees may have occupied a smaller territory than the Cherokees used later. As Charles Hudson (pers. comm.; also Hudson 1987:84) has noted, "They appear to have been pretty much in the mountains. They were absent from the lower Little Tennessee River, and we are now thinking they may have been absent from the northern corner of Georgia." One possibility is that the Cherokees expanded after the European entrada and came to occupy lands abandoned by their aboriginal neighbors.

Nevertheless, the Cherokees did eventually cede some 125,000 square miles—325,000 square kilometers—to the United States of America (Royce [1887] 1975:256), giving *some* indication of the extent of the Cherokee domain recognized by the United States government at different times.

Aboriginal Population

A key issue in American Indian history, as well as in the history of non-Indian Americans, is the size of the aboriginal population in the area of the United States (indeed, in the whole Western Hemisphere). This is important because the number of American Indians here about 1492 gives some indication of the nature and complexity of aboriginal Indian societies and cultures. Generally, scholars argue that larger numbers indicate more elaborate and complex societies and cultures and smaller numbers less elaborate and complex ones. Thus, knowing the number of aboriginal American Indians tells us something about social and cultural life at that time in history. Similarly, having the information, we can infer changes in—perhaps simplification of—societies and cultures that occurred before accurate descriptions of American Indians and their ways of life emerged. Furthermore, although evidence indicates a depopulation of American Indians after European and African arrival, we do not know how great the depopulation was. Its magnitude, of course, depends on how many Indians were here at the time of initial contact.

Despite the importance of aboriginal population size, we do not know how many American Indians were here about 1492. Perhaps we will never know. We have, however, developed various estimates derived by various methods.

Estimating Aboriginal American Indian Populations

Twentieth-century scholars, myself included, have used a variety of methods to arrive at American Indian population estimates. I have summarized and discussed the methods and resulting estimates elsewhere (Thornton 1987a:17–22).

As summarized, the method used must encompass four separate issues: the estimates' scope, the data used to derive the estimates, the techniques used to evaluate the data for the estimates, and the techniques used to derive the estimates.

Scope.   The scope of the estimate refers to the particular geographic area encompassed. Some scholars have estimated the aboriginal population of the total Western Hemisphere; others have made estimates for its regions, subregions, or specific tribes. In some estimates—for example, those by James Mooney (1910, 1928) and Alfred L. Kroeber (1939) for North America—broad geographic areas are further subdivided into both subregions and specific tribes.

Data.   Scholars have also based their estimates on a wide variety of data and information. This has included such *ethnohistorical* sources as figures or estimates reported by Europeans for tribal populations; *archaeological* data derived from excavations; *physical anthropological* data derived from skeletal remains; *ecological* evidence as to how many people "could have been supported" in an area; *demographic* information such as mortality rates from epidemics; and information on the *social structure* of native societies—their "complexity."

Data evaluation.   Scholars have often not accepted any type of data at face value but have assessed accuracy. This has been done, for example, by comparing one source of data with another, by comparing data from two or more points in time to see if they "make sense," by checking data against known historical events, by assessing the credibility of the person or method supplying the data, and by checking the data against scientific facts about human populations generally.

Techniques for estimation.   Given particular types of data, various techniques have been used to estimate population size. The simplest technique I have termed the *ethnohistorical method;* one may simply rely on ethnohistorical reports and use one's own judgment to arrive at an estimate. Another technique involves *subpopulation projections* whereby information about a subpopulation is projected to a larger population, or similarly, one may make a *subareal projection* by using information about the population of a subarea to estimate the population of a larger area. *Ecological projections* involve, for example, estimating population size from indirect information about characteristics such as village size, number of villages, or even house size or number of houses. In *carrying-capacity projections*, which have often been used to make population estimates, one ascertains how many people could have been supported in an area based on resources accessible to them as well as on the level of technology available to exploit the resources. Finally, there are *depopulation projections*. Using this technique, one might project known rates of depopulation backward in time to arrive at an earlier population size. Or one might use depopulation ratios, say those from epidemics, to establish an earlier population size. (Typically these assume—generally incorrectly—no population recovery between epidemics.) Or one might simply fit known population sizes to a mathematical curve.

Given these techniques, some scholars have asserted that the land that became the United States teemed with millions and millions of American Indians in 1492 (for example, Dobyns 1966, 1983). Others have contended there were far fewer—perhaps only a few million (for example, Mooney 1928; Ubelaker 1976a, 1988; Thornton and Marsh-Thornton 1981). A reasonable number I recently arrived at for the conterminous United States area is at least over 5 million (Thornton 1987a: 32).

Whatever their aboriginal population, American Indians declined to only 250,000 or less by about 1900, surely due to both increased American Indian death rates and decreased birthrates following the arrival of Europeans and Africans. Changes in death rates and birthrates both resulted primarily from the introduction of such Old World diseases as smallpox, measles, cholera, diphtheria, scarlet fever, the plague, malaria, and various forms of influenza and venereal disease into the relatively disease-free pre-Columbian population. They also resulted from wars and genocide, removals and relocations, and destruction of native ways of life (see Thornton 1987a). (After 1900 the American Indian population began to increase: it was enumerated at 1,366,676 in the 1980 United States census [U.S. Bureau of the Census 1984: 2, table A].[7])

Cherokee Population Size about 1650

The Smithsonian Institution anthropologist James Mooney in 1910 and 1928 did the now-classic estimates of early American Indian population sizes. Mooney estimated sizes of American Indian tribes at what he considered to be the date of each tribe's first extensive European contact. According to him, dates of such contact ranged from 1600 to 1845, depending on the geographic area of the United States.[8] He estimated the Cherokee population at 22,000 in 1650, "the beginning of regular white colonization," as he expressed it (Mooney, 1928:7–8). According to another Smithsonian Institution anthropologist, Douglas H. Ubelaker (1976b:260), however, the source of the estimate is not clear.

Ubelaker (1976b:260) further noted that Mooney commented about the sources of his information on the Cherokees in a 1907 article prepared for the *Handbook of American Indians North of Mexico* (Hodge 1907–10): "With the exception of an estimate in 1730, which placed them at about 20,000, most of those up to a recent period gave them 12,000 or 14,000, and in 1758 they were computed at only 7,500. The majority of the earlier estimates are probably too low, as the Cherokee occupied so extensive a territory that only a part of them came in contact with the whites" (Mooney 1907:247).

After examining Mooney's unpublished notes on file in the National Anthropological Archives at the Smithsonian Institution, Ubelaker elaborated upon Mooney's sources: "His notes refer to estimates of 500 men in 1708 by Nathaniel Johnson, 4,000 warriors and 11,210 souls in 1715 by a trade commission report, 10,000 souls in 1720 (also attributed to Johnson), and 20,000 in 1730 (no source given)." He concluded: "Mooney's comments in the *Handbook* indicate he considered all of these estimates too conservative and guessed the original figure must have been around 22,000" (Ubelaker 1976b:260).

Thus the "classic" estimate of Cherokee aboriginal population is not only for the year 1650 but is apparently derived almost entirely—and subjectively—from the reports of Europeans having contact with the Cherokees in the eighteenth century. Recently Peter M. Wood (1989:63; see also Wood 1988:35) criticized Mooney's estimate of the Cherokees and estimated them at between 30,000 and 35,000 in 1685. This number seems excessive for that time, however; it was derived simply by "doubling" a post–smallpox epidemic population (in

1697) estimated at 16,000 in 1700, assuming a 50 percent mortality rate and no population recovery during the fifteen-year period.

Earlier Population Size

Even disregarding Wood's estimate and assuming that Mooney's figure of 22,000 Cherokees for 1650 is correct, there may have been greater or fewer numbers of Cherokee before that date. In general, however, Mooney's population estimates for other American Indian tribes are considered to be extremely conservative by contemporary scholars, *if used as an indication of aboriginal American Indian population sizes* (for example, Ubelaker 1976a; Thornton 1978, 1987a:26–29; Thornton and Marsh-Thornton 1981). Moreover, Mooney estimated that the *total* American Indian population of the Gulf states region, in which he included the Cherokees, was only 114,400 at the year 1650 (Mooney 1928:9). Contemporary scholars have estimated the aboriginal population of the approximate area as considerably larger: one estimate set it at 204,400 (Ubelaker 1988:261, table 1); another estimate set the population size at at least 473,616, or more than four times Mooney's estimate (Ubelaker 1976a:664, table 2).[9]

Using Mooney's 22,000 population figure and a Cherokee area of 134,400 square kilometers (about 52,000 square miles), Alfred L. Kroeber, in his classic *Cultural and Natural Areas of Native North America* (1939:141, table 7), arrived at an aboriginal Cherokee population density of 16.30 per 100 km^2 (actually 16.37 people per 100 km^2). Recently, however, Douglas Ubelaker (pers. comm.) argued for a Cherokee population density of 24 per 100 km^2, or a total population of 25,000 for the land area he used, which was only the "core" area of Cherokee settlement, slightly more than 100,000 square kilometers (about 40,000 square miles).

Certainly the exact size of aboriginal Cherokee territory is unknown and, as I stated earlier, may have been smaller than Cherokee territory after the sixteenth century. Only somewhat over 100,000 square kilometers is probably a little small, however; 120,000 square kilometers (about 46,000 square miles) seems more reasonable. Applying Ubelaker's population density of 24 per 100 km^2 yields a total population of 28,800. This also may be a little low; 25 per 100 km^2 is probably more likely.

What we know about the aboriginal Cherokee environment indicates an abundant food supply. The Cherokees had various wild food plants at their disposal, producing vegetables, fruits, nuts, and seeds; for example, pigweed (amaranth), varieties of *Smilax*, arrowhead, cattail, blueberries, mulberries, raspberries, and blackberries, grapes, acorns, walnuts, hickory nuts, and chestnuts. In addition, they had a variety of cultivated foods, particularly maize (corn), beans, squash, gourds and pumpkins, and sunflowers. The Cherokees also had access to abundant animal life, including deer, buffalo, bears, opossums, raccoons, rabbits, squirrels, wild turkeys, pigeons, trout, catfish, bass, and various shellfish (Goodwin 1977:49–81).

Such a food supply seemingly could easily have supported a far larger number of people than Kroeber's 16.30 (16.37) per 100 km^2 and perhaps somewhat more than Ubelaker's 24 per 100 km^2. Using 25 people per 100 km^2 and an area of Cherokee settlement of 120,000 square kilometers yields a population size of 30,000. The Cherokees may not have been so numerous, but they easily could have been. (It is doubtful that there were more than 30,000.)

It is likely the Cherokees experienced some depopulation before any significant European contact. George R. Milner noted:

> When De Soto traversed the Southeast in 1539–1543, the Spanish encountered areas of high population density and complex socio-cultural systems. European penetration of the interior was infrequent, brief and geographically restricted for more than a hundred years following the famed De Soto Entrada. By 1700, English and French adventurers, traders, missionaries, and soldiers had entered this region in numbers, and many wrote of their encounters with the Indians. Accounts dating from this period describe areas of low population density. Although a number of continuities in artifact style and site organization were present, socio-cultural systems very different from those encountered previously by De Soto were described. (Milner 1980:40)

Milner (1980:43–44; see also Smith 1984:77) pointed out, however, that even the chroniclers of De Soto's expedition recorded the possible existence of an epidemic disease in the Southeast, perhaps stemming from Lucas Vázquez de Ayllón's landing on the coast of present-day South Carolina in 1521, or his attempt to "settle" that coast in 1526. Moreover, the historian Charles Hudson noted that the De Soto expedition moved with some ease through Cherokee territory. This, according to Hudson, means the Cherokees had been weakened by smallpox or some other European disease (Hudson 1976:112).

The first smallpox epidemic in the United States area may have occurred from 1520 to 1524. It perhaps centered in the Florida area and in the Southwest, although we do not know its exact geographic extent (Dobyns 1983:15, table 1). There may even have been an earlier smallpox epidemic in the Southeast, as epidemiological theory suggests: the first reported New World smallpox epidemic was on the island of Hispaniola (present-day Dominican Republic and Haiti) in 1507. After De Soto's visit, the Cherokees were probably soon confronted with European diseases, either directly or as spread to the Cherokees by other American Indian tribes. Possible epidemics in the general geographic area of the Cherokees after De Soto and up to 1650 include influenza (1559), typhus (1586), and bubonic plague (1612–19); there was possibly also a severe epidemic of an unknown disease from about 1564 to 1570 (Dobyns 1983:19, table 3, 20, table 4, 21, table 6, 23, table 9; see also Milner 1980).

Such possible epidemics suggest there may have been significant depopulation of the Cherokees by 1650, the date for Mooney's estimate of 22,000. Perhaps some recovery did occur by 1650: depopulation does not necessarily lower a group's size for an extended period, and populations *can* recover losses in a very short time (see, for example, Thornton 1989). Nevertheless, it seems probable that the Cherokees numbered more than 22,000 before 1650. As we shall see in chapter 2, Cherokee population—despite periods of gains as well as losses—declined to about 16,000 by 1800. Assuming Mooney's figure of 22,000 for 1650 is correct, this represented a net decline of 6,000 during 150 years. Projecting this same rate of decline *backward* 150 years to 1500 produces a population size of 28,000 for that year. Actually, however, the rate of decline may have been greater from 1500 to 1650 than from 1650 to 1800. As we saw above, epidemics of smallpox, influenza, typhus and bubonic plague *could have* infected the Cherokees during that time; if so, they might well have significantly reduced population size. This reduction could have been more significant than the reduction by disease from 1650 to 1800, since epidemiological theory suggests that initial epidemics of a disease are more severe than later ones and cause greater population losses. It is possible that the decline from 1500 to 1650 was not 6,000, but 8,000 or even 10,000. If so, this would yield an aboriginal population size for the Cherokees of 30,000 or more.

CHAPTER 2

Pathogens and Wars: The 1700s

Although the Cherokees surely encountered a few other Europeans, and Africans, after Hernando de Soto in 1540, there is little certain information until over one hundred years later. In 1673 the Virginian James Needham and Gabriel Arthur probably made contact with the Cherokees, as likely did Henry Woodward in 1674: Woodward referred to them as the "Chorakee" Indians on the headwaters of the Savannah River (Swanton [1946] 1979:11).

These dates marked the beginning of an increasing contact of the Cherokees with Europeans and Africans. This contact included the capture and selling of Cherokees as slaves, possibly by the year 1681 (Goodwin 1977:86): during that year "a permit was issued for the exportation of several 'Seraquii' slaves, probably Cherokee captured by the Savannah Indians" (Crane [1929] 1959:40). In 1684 a treaty (or agreement) was made at Charleston between the Cherokees and the government of the colony of South Carolina, supposedly to protect the Cherokees against their enemies the Catawbas, the Congarees, and the Shawnees, who had captured a number of Cherokees and carried them off to be sold into slavery (Thomas 1903:103; see also Mooney [1900] 1982:31; Swanton [1946] 1979:111). (Charleston by this time was an active center of traffic in Indian [and black] slaves, the traffic having begun, according to Thomas [1903:95], only four years after the town's founding in 1670.[1]) Despite this treaty, nine years later, in 1693, the Cherokees again sent a delegation to Charleston "to complain that the Catawbas, Congarees, and Savannahs had been preying on them and selling the captives to the English for slaves in violation of trading regulations" (Perdue 1979:29; see also Halliburton 1977:7). They were informed that the prisoners were gone and could not be returned. According to one historian, John Phillips Reid (1976:27), most Cherokee slaves were exported, a few to the northern colonies, most to the West Indies.

European-Cherokee contacts intensified before long, perhaps dating from 1690 when the trader James Moore journeyed over the Appalachian Mountains to, as he put it, "make new and further discovery of Indian Trade" (quoted in Crane [1929] 1959:40). Contemporary historians assert that Moore really led a hostile attack on the Cherokees (see, for example, Reid 1976:24). According to Starr and Mooney, an Irishman named either Alexander or Cornelis Dougherty first established trade relations with the Cherokees and in 1690 was the first white man to marry a Cherokee (Starr [1922] 1967:24; see also Mooney [1900] 1982:31). Goodwin (1977:86; see also Reid 1976:36) said this was incorrect: "Actually, and according to his own admission, [Cornelis] Dougherty did not contact the Cherokee until 1719, at which time he established permanent residence in the Valley Towns and remained there until his death." And Malone (1956:6) asserted that the first trader to live in Cherokee country may have been Eleazar Wiggan, noted to be there in 1711. It thus seems unlikely that extensive trade between the Cherokees and the Europeans had been established as early as 1690.

In any event, by about the end of the century trade relations between the Cherokees and the Europeans were established, perhaps in 1698 by William and Joseph Cooper (Reid 1976:37). The Cherokees exchanged deerskins and other commodities, including some Indian slaves (Thomas 1903:96; Perdue 1979:19), for firearms and ammunition, hatchets, metal tools and kettles, decorations, cloth, salt, and rum. Before many more decades had passed, the Cherokees were dependent on trade goods; they admitted "they could not live without the English" (quoted in Crane [1929] 1959:117).

Little, however, is known about the Cherokees at this time, particularly from a demographic standpoint. It is not until the early decades of the eighteenth century that we may really begin to examine the Cherokees as a population from records kept by the Europeans. By the beginning of that century the European colonists were making increased inroads into Cherokee territory. Many of their experiences were recorded, and many reports on the Cherokees were conveyed; as a result, we can now begin to trace in detail their population history.

CHEROKEE POPULATION SIZE ABOUT
1700 TO 1720

Whatever the exact aboriginal population size of the Cherokees, they had likely experienced depopulation by the early eighteenth century. Douglas Ubelaker (pers. comm.) estimated Cherokee population at 22,000 in 1700, down significantly from his estimate of 25,000 during 1500 to 1600. Peter Wood (Wood, Waselkov, and Hatley 1989:38, table 1) estimated even more severe depopulation: from 32,000–35,000 in 1685 to only 16,000 in 1700. According to James Mooney (1907:247), in 1715 their number was officially reported as 11,210, a figure listed in a trade commission report (Ubelaker 1976b:260; also Crane [1929] 1959:131–32n. 91; Wood 1989:61). Most other reports shortly after this time placed total Cherokee population at 10,000–12,000 about 1720 (see Fernow 1890:273–75; Goodwin 1977:111, table 16; Anderson and Lewis 1983:354, 355, 509). Some reports were expressed as the number of Cherokee men rather than the total Cherokee population; in these instances the number given is about 3,500–3,800 (Goodwin 1977:111, table 16; Anderson and Lewis 1983:232, 355, 509). These figures, when multiplied by a typical ratio of one man for each three persons in the total Cherokee population (see, for example, Fernow 1890:275; Goodwin 1977:111, table 16),[2] yield a population of 10,500–11,500, also for about 1720. Extrapolating backward to about 1700 and assuming some depopulation from 1700 to 1720 would put the Cherokee population closer to Wood's estimate than to Ubelaker's for the turn of the century.

If severe depopulation did occur during the latter 1600s or early 1700s—and it probably did (see, for example, Smith 1984)—it was perhaps largely a result of smallpox introduced to this hemisphere by the Europeans. One smallpox epidemic among the Cherokees during this period has been established, and smallpox seemingly was present in surrounding areas at various times. For example, Henry Dobyns (1983:15, table 1) noted a 1665–67 smallpox epidemic that raged from Florida to Virginia, and "in 1691 smallpox is said to have caused death, blindness, and disfigurement to the Illinois Indians living near the mouth of the Illinois River" (Stearn and Stearn 1945:32–33). Claimed Cherokee lands stretched virtually as far as the Illinois River; moreover, we know that the Cherokees sometimes fought the Illinois Indians, journeying westward to do so. Very possibly, then, the Cherokees could have contracted smallpox at this time. Also, as John Duffy (1951:332) noted, an epidemic that started in Jamestown, Virginia, in 1696 gradually spread into the Carolinas, killing many whites and even more Indians. Duffy, citing Stearn and Stearn (1945:33), goes further to assert that the infection probably spread as far west as the lower Mississippi valley, since the tribes there were also attacked. John Phillip Reid (1976:30) argued that the Cherokees were exposed to smallpox about this time, experiencing their first smallpox epidemic in 1698, and that their population had decreased measurably. Similarly, Peter Wood (1989:63) noted that the first documented smallpox epidemic to reach the Cherokee settlements arrived in 1697. It is possible that influenza accompanied this epidemic along the Gulf coast and in the Southeast (Dobyns 1983:19, table 3), and the Cherokees could have suffered from it as well.

Unknown population losses from warfare, though perhaps minor at this particular time, may be added to probable Cherokee depopulation from epidemic disease. Wars were fought both with other American Indian peoples and with European colonizers. After about 1700 the Cherokees used firearms, which were introduced to them at this time (Mooney [1900] 1982:32). The Cherokees fought with the Catawbas, the Shawnees, and the Congarees, with the Illinois, and with the Creeks. They also fought with the Iroquois: John Reid (1976:30) asserted that, after depopulation from the smallpox epidemic of about 1698 the Cherokees were "an attractive target for the Iroquois who had defeated most of their enemies in the north and were looking for new conquests." The Cherokees fought the Tuscaroras, particularly from 1711 to 1713, since the Cherokees sided with South Carolinians in the Tuscarora War, which drove the Tuscaroras northward from the Southeast to join the Five Nations. The Cherokees then joined the Yamassees against the English in 1715, after which there was probably some slight population decline (Goodwin 1977:107). In 1716 they attacked a Kaskaskia (Illinois) Indian village (Anderson and Lewis 1983:55), probably on the Mississippi River, and probably shortly after the Kaskaskias had suffered an epidemic of an unknown disease (Blasingham 1956:383). Warfare would have reduced Cherokee population directly through deaths and perhaps indirectly as the sex imbalance caused by so many Cherokee males going off to war reduced the birthrate (Goodwin 1977:107). As James

Adair ([1775] 1930:229) noted, "In every Indian country, there are a great many old women on the frontiers, perhaps ten times the number of men of the same age and place."

EARLY CHEROKEE DIVISIONS AND TOWNS

Not only are we able to get estimates of Cherokee population for the early eighteenth century, we can get a description of Cherokee divisions and towns as well.

Cherokee Divisions

At this time the Cherokees reportedly were divided into broad divisions named after the locations of Cherokee towns but generally denoting linguistic and subcultural differences. One division was in the south lands, the Lower Towns, situated along rivers in what is now South Carolina; another was to the north, the Upper or "Overhill" Towns, in what are now eastern Tennessee and extreme northwestern North Carolina. In the center were the Middle Towns; however, it is said the British considered this last area two separate divisions. To the west were the Valley Towns, in present-day extreme southwestern North Carolina and northeastern Georgia. In more or less the center of the area, but to the east, were the Middle Towns, along a portion of the Little Tennessee River and its tributaries, in the western part of what is now North Carolina. A northern and eastern portion of the Middle Town area was sometimes designated as the "Out Towns," since the area was geographically isolated from the main body of the Cherokees (see, for example, Goodwin 1977:38–40).[3] (See map 1.) According to some archaeologists, as discussed in chapter 1, these three main divisions—Lower, Overhill, and Middle Cherokee towns—may be traced back to original divisions in the emergence of the Cherokees. Roy Dickens believes the Lower Towns may be traced to the Early Etowah archaeological phase, the Overhill Towns to the Hiwassee Island phase, and the Middle Towns to the Early Pisgah phase (1979:12, fig. 3). (This may not necessarily be so, however: possibly these divisions developed at different times; e.g., the Cherokees may have moved into the Overhill area very late, after the Creeks withdrew.)

James Adair, writing in the late eighteenth century, said the Chero-

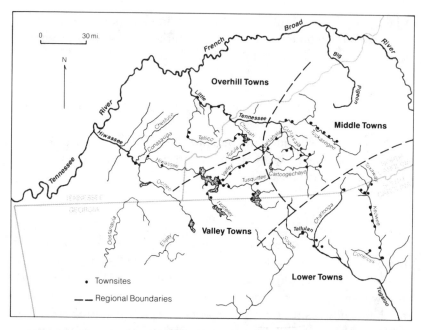

1. Cherokee divisions about 1700. After Goodwin (1977:45, fig. 6).

kees made two linguistic divisions of their country: Ayrate, or "low," and Ottare, "mountainous." He noted, "The former division is on the head branches of the beautiful Savanah river and the latter on those of the easternmost river of the great Mississippi" ([1775] 1930:237–38). James Mooney argued, however, that Adair's classification was far from perfect: "As is usually the case with a large tribe occupying an extensive territory, the language is spoken in several dialects, the principal of which may, for want of other names, be conveniently designated as the Eastern, Middle, or Western" (Mooney [1900] 1982:16).

Early Cherokee Towns

Mooney (1907:248) listed 169 Cherokee towns occupied at one time or another; other sources list 160 (see Smith 1979: 47). It is estimated the Cherokees were living in at least 60 separate towns, perhaps a few more, in the early 1700s (see, for example, Goodwin 1977:38, 44, 153–56). In 1715, according to Mooney (1907: 247), the Cherokees had 19 Upper Towns with a total population of 2,760; 30 Middle Towns with a population of 6,350; and 11 Lower

Towns with a population of 2,100. This totals 60 separate towns and a population of 11,210, with an average town size of 187. Yet, a report from this time asserted that the Cherokees lived in 72 villages (and had a total of 10,000 men) (Anderson and Lewis 1983:55). How many more towns—if any—the Cherokees occupied before this period is perhaps now only a matter of speculation. Conceivably they could have occupied a larger number; as we saw above, their population may have been reduced before the second decade of the 1700s. If they did occupy more towns, it was likely not many more, given the archaeological record of the Cherokee lands.

A 1721 census listed the Cherokee as living in 53 separate towns, ranging in size from 62 to 622, with a total population of 10,434 and an average town size of 197 (Fernow 1890:273–75; also Goodwin 1977:108–9, table 15). (See table 1.)

Cherokee towns were near water—along rivers, streams, or lakeshores or by springs. Houses might be clustered together or stretched out along rivers or streams, depending on the topography of the land, with larger settlements at the junction of two rivers or at the mouths of major streams (Goodwin 1977:42). Goodwin has argued that the pre-European pattern was characterized by clusters of houses, whereas after European arrival the houses were more often scattered. This changed pattern in settlements supposedly occurred from 1670 to the mid-1770s, when the Cherokees had to relocate many towns away from their traditional settlement regions (Goodwin 1977:41, 82). It probably became more pronounced, as we see below, after the European invasions of 1760 and 1776, since scattered settlements were less vulnerable to invasion. Other reasons Goodwin proposes for the change include the introduction of European technology, commercial trade with the Europeans and the establishment of trade routes, disease, and population decline. Not only did the pattern of Cherokee towns change after European contact, the nature of the houses forming them apparently changed too: Goodwin writes, "When the pioneers first visited the Southern Appalachian mountain tribes, scattered towns consisted of simple rectangular, or square, huts supported by a frame of locked poles, covered with bark, and weatherproofed with a mixture of white clay and earth (e.g., talc), or sap and cane. During the pre-contact period, the posts were wide apart (6–8 inches) and filled with sap or cane, whereas after European contacts the Indians bound the posts as close together as possible in an effort to insure greater security" (1977:112).

Table 1. Cherokee Towns in 1721

Town	Population			
	Men	Women	Children	Total[a]
Cattojay	48	51	39	138
Changee	80	60	60	200
Charraway	70	71	35	176
Chattoogie	30	40	20	90
Checlokee	71	71	77	219
Cheowhee	30	42	42	114
Cowyce	78	78	102	258
Cunnookah	89	59	54	202
Eascenica	44	42	48	134
Eastatoe	150	191	281	622
Echie	55	50	44	149
Echoce	44	30	36	110
Echotee	59	97	65	221
Elojay	56	70	65	191
Elojay	30	39	47	116
Elojay ye little	58	50	64	172
Erawgee	43	49	41	133
Great Euphusee	70	72	60	202
Kewokee	168	155	137	460
Kittowah	143	98	47	288
Little Euphusee	70	125	54	249
Little Terrequo	50	56	48	154
Little Tunnissee	12	30	20	62
Mougake	57	31	42	130
Nookassie	53	50	39	142
Noonnie	61	56	60	177
Oakenni	57	52	75	184
Old Eastatoe	40	50	34	124
Quannisee	37	31	36	104
Sarrawotee	40	55	50	145
Settequo	77	123	73	273
Stickoce	97	90	95	282
Stickoce	42	30	30	102
Suoigella	50	65	60	175
Suskasetchie	150	140	145	435
Tarrahnie	72	11	7	90

Table 1. Continued

Town	Men	Women	Children	Total[a]
		Population		
Tarrassee	33	38	24	95
Taseetchie	36	44	45	125
Taskeegee	60	62	64	186
Taskeegee	70	69	75	214
Terrequo	100	125	116	341
Timotly	42	68	42	152
Tockaswoo	50	60	60	170
Tomotly	124	130	103	357
Toogellon	70	66	68	204
Tookarechga	60	50	45	155
Tookareegha	77	114	36	227
Torree	59	60	69	188
Tuckoe	34	33	27	94
Tunnissee	160	193	190	543
Turrurah	60	40	22	122
Wattogo	64	59	53	176
Wooroughtye	30	20	12	62
Total	3,510	3,641	3,283	10,434

Source: Fernow (1890:273–75).
[a] As Goodwin (1977:108–9, table 15) pointed out, the census listed by Fernow incorrectly gives the number of women at 3,595, children at 3,274, and total at 10,379, assuming the town figures are correct. However, he incorrectly listed the number of women at 56, the number of children at 48, and the total at 154 for the town of Suoi-gella; yet his total population figure for the entire census is correct at 10,434.

European Trails

By the early eighteenth century European colonists had established routes into Cherokee territory, in large part as a result of competition between the British and French for the flourishing trade system. These trails linked colonial coastal settlements with key Cherokee towns. One trail, from Fort Henry, Virginia, led south and west and, after forking, to the Middle, Valley, and Overhill towns. Two trails led north: one from Charleston crossed the Lower Towns and extended into the Middle Towns and Valley Towns; one from Fort Moore (Savannah) led north also, but to the Lower Towns and Valley Towns. All three trails linked with one another at various points and via other trails to form a network across Cherokee territory.

Trails not only brought the Cherokees more trade goods, particularly guns, cloth, and rum, but also increased the number of traders and brought more conflict with the Europeans and, as we will see in more detail below, epidemic disease. All of these would, at least initially, more or less follow the network of trails and waterways. Goodwin (1977:101), for example, argued that the distribution of guns into Indian lands followed the major trade routes rather closely. The Lower Towns seemed well supplied by 1715 and in 1716 the Upper Towns and Middle Towns demanded an equal share of the munitions trade. The pattern of Cherokee settlement along waterways and the trails to their towns would have thus overlaid the Cherokees with a net or web of disease as Europeans moved throughout their territory.

CHEROKEE POPULATION ABOUT 1730S

By about the 1730s the Cherokees appear to have grown somewhat in population, though it would have been difficult for them to increase as much as most estimates indicated. Mooney (1907:247) noted they were estimated at 20,000 in 1729; many, but not all, other estimates from this time place them at from about 4,000 to 6,000 "warriors" (Goodwin 1977:111, table 16; Anderson and Lewis 1983:60, 61, 237, 336). James Adair, who published *History of the American Indians* in 1775 and typically is regarded as a reliable source for southern Indians of that time, estimated that the Cherokees "amounted to upwards of six thousand fighting men" in about 1735 (Adair [1775] 1930:238). When multiplied by a typical ratio of one "warrior," as opposed to man, for each four persons in a total population (see, for example, Krzywicki 1934:318; Cook 1976:4–6), these estimates give a Cherokee population range of 16,000 to 24,000.

These figures may be more nearly correct than others for earlier periods. Goodwin stated that the estimate of 6,000 warriors and close to 20,000 in total population was probably the most accurate of the early counts because observers during the earlier colonial period could not determine the Indian population accurately because of

Indian-white hostilities, the inaccessibility of many Indian towns, and individual and group biases, among other problems (1977:107–10). It is doubtful, however, that the Cherokee population approached 20,000.

That there was population gain is perhaps reflected in an increase in Cherokee towns beyond the fifty-three reported for 1721. Although one map for 1730 listed fifty-two towns, a modern map compiled from various sources lists fifty-nine about 1721–30 (Smith 1979:47–48, 51–56, tables 1–4). However, European contact with the Cherokees was limited in 1721, and some towns may not have been known at that date. (Also, the number of towns does not necessarily correspond to population size.)

During the 1730s, nevertheless, the Cherokees probably suffered an epidemic of smallpox, causing significant depopulation. In 1738, again according to Adair, smallpox "was conveyed into Charleston [South Carolina] by the Guinea-men ["Guinea negroes," according to Samuel Cole Williams, editor of the 1930 edition of Adair's book], and soon after among them, by the infected goods" (Adair [1775] 1930:244). It was possibly spread to the Cherokees by traders during the summer of 1739 (see Williams in Adair [1775] 1930:244, n. 118). It may have arrived from Florida: Goodwin writes that the British colonists had persuaded 900 Cherokees to help them fight the Spanish in 1739, and the Cherokees returned from this expedition to the Florida settlements with smallpox (1977:103).

According to the Cherokee "magi" and "religious physicians," however, it was a plague inflicted upon them because of "the adulterous intercourse of their young married people, who in the past year, had in a most notorious manner, violated their ancient laws of marriage in every thicket,"[4] and the Cherokee chiefs claimed their people had been poisoned by bad rum brought in by the traders (Adair [1775] 1930:232, 244, n. 118).

In any event, reports indicated that thousands of Indians died in the tribe's worst epidemic (Goodwin 1977:103). It was said that after becoming infected and seeing themselves disfigured, "[a] great many killed themselves; . . . some shot themselves, others cut their throats, some stabbed themselves with knives, and others with sharp-pointed canes; many threw themselves with sullen madness into the fire, and there slowly expired, as if they had been utterly divested of the native power of feeling pain" (Adair [1775] 1930:245).

Adair described the death of a Cherokee man:

When he saw himself disfigured by the small pox, he chose to die,
that he might end as he imagined his shame. When his relations
knew his desperate design, they narrowly watched him, and took
away every sharp instrument from him. When he found he was
balked of his intention, he fretted and said the worst things their
language could express, and shewed all the symptoms of a desperate person enraged at this disappointment, and forced to live and
see his ignominy; he then darted himself against the wall, with all
his remaining vigor,—his strength being expended by the force of
his friends opposition, he fell sullenly on the bed, as if by those
violent struggles he was overcome, and wanted to repose himself.
His relations through tenderness, left him to his rest—but as soon
as they went away, he raised himself, and after a tedious search,
finding nothing but a thick and round hoe-helve, he took the fatal
instrument, and having fixed one end of it in the ground, he repeatedly threw himself on it, till he forced it down his throat,
when he immediately expired.—He was buried in silence, without
the least mourning. (Adair [1775] 1930:245–46)

Adair ([1775] 1930:244) concluded that in a year the epidemic reduced the Cherokees "almost one-half." If this was true and the population range above is correct, then the Cherokees numbered some
8,000 to 12,000 after the epidemic. It is probable that the Cherokee
population was considerably less than 20,000 before the epidemic
and that it was reduced by less than 50 percent (see, for example,
Englund 1974:48–49). Wood (1989:38, table 1) listed the Cherokees
as numbering 9,000 by the beginning of the 1740s. It is probable that
many Cherokee settlements were abandoned because of population
loss, particularly those in Georgia, on the Chattooga, Tugaloo, and
Chattahoochee rivers (Goodwin 1977:103).

CHEROKEE POPULATION ABOUT
1740 TO 1800

The Cherokees seem not to have fully recovered the
population losses dating from the 1738–39 smallpox epidemic until
after the end of the century. Most reports during these many decades
place Cherokee population in the same 8,000 to 12,000 range, though

some estimates, seemingly incorrect, are as high as 20,000 to 24,000 (see Adair [1775] 1930:239; Goodwin 1977:111, table 16; Anderson and Lewis 1983:60–61, 64, 69, 85–86, 174, 219, 237, 238, 241, 255, 273, 282, 325–326, 336, 341, 377, 415–15, 509). Shown in table 2, for example, are estimates of the number of Cherokee "warriors" (and men), reported from 1740 to 1783, obtained from William T. Anderson and James A. Lewis's *Guide to Cherokee Documents in Foreign Archives* (1983). As I have shown, an approximate population size for the Cherokees may be obtained from estimates of warriors reported in the table by multiplying their numbers by four (or by three for estimates of men). There is, however, an undoubted time lag in some of the estimates; they come from correspondence, and the actual "information" may have been obtained a year or so earlier. This seems to be the case for the estimates of 1740 and 1741. Both seem to refer to the population before the smallpox epidemic or in its early stages. The figures for 1742 clearly show the effects of the epidemic (even more so, perhaps, since they refer to numbers of men, not warriors). Perhaps the Cherokee population had recovered somewhat by the second smallpox epidemic, about 1760, but it is difficult to tell

Table 2. Estimates of Numbers of Cherokee "Warriors," 1740 to 1783

Date	"Warriors"
1740	5,000
1741	4,000
1742	3,000[a]
1742	"4,000"[b]
1746	6,000
1747	3,000
1756	2,000
1757	5,000
1760	2,000[a]
1764	2,700
1765	3,000
1773	3,000
1783	3,000

Note: Estimates are as reported in documents in Anderson and Lewis (1983).
[a] Cherokee men rather than "warriors."
[b] Forty towns with 100 men each.

from these figures. It is clearer that some population gain followed it, with estimates of the number of warriors falling around 3,000. Mooney (1907:247) nevertheless asserted that the Cherokees "suffered a steady decrease during the wars with the whites, extending from 1760 until after the close of the Revolution." If this was so, then they would have subsequently had rapid population gain, since Mooney ([1900] 1982:80) stated that they numbered about 20,000 at the end of the century.

Certainly there were Cherokee population gains and losses during this period, but the picture is so muddled that it is not possible to say with any accuracy what they were. Any population gains probably were short-lived, as the Cherokees were reexposed to epidemics and subjected to almost constant warfare. Conversely, the overall depopulation effects of both disease and warfare may have been overestimated (see, for example, Englund 1974:54–55), particularly if population losses were followed by gains within a short time.

During this period the number of Cherokee towns appears to have definitely declined. A map supposedly drawn by the Cherokees listed over fifty towns in about 1750; documents in 1751 and 1755 listed only thirty-nine (see Smith 1979:51–56, tables 1–4). A modern map compiled for 1755–62 lists forty-four Cherokee towns (Smith 1979:49), and a 1775 report listed forty-three (Bartram [1791] 1958:235–36; Goodwin 1977:111, table 16). Other sources about this time give the number of towns as thirty-nine, forty-one, and forty-two for the years 1775, 1776, and 1781 (Smith 1979:51–56, tables 1–4). Whatever the numbers, Cherokee towns seem clearly to have declined from over sixty reported early in the century. (This does not necessarily indicate population loss, however; it may reflect population concentration.)

Both population loss and the declining number of towns were due not only to other episodes of smallpox and other diseases, but also to war and rum. All of these not only caused Cherokee deaths but perhaps led to relatively low numbers of births for certain periods. Conversely, Cherokee birthrates may have risen for a time following population losses, producing periods of rapid population gain when coupled with low levels of mortality.

Smallpox and Other Disease

In 1759–60, smallpox struck the Cherokees again. Early in 1760 an Augusta, Georgia, correspondent wrote with reference to the Cherokee town of Keowee (on the Keowee River in northwestern South Carolina [see Smith 1979:48, map 2, 49, map 3, 50, map 4, 51, table 1, 52]): "The late accounts from Keowee are that the Small-Pox has destroyed a great many Indians there; that those who remained alive, and have not yet had that Distemper, were gone into the Woods, where many of them must perish as the Catawbas did," and the August 13, 1760, *Pennsylvania Gazette* reported that "we learn from Cherokee country, that the People of the Lower Towns have carried smallpox into the Middle Settlement and Valley, where that disease rages with great violence, and that the People of the Upper Towns are in such Dread of the Infection, that they will not allow a single Person from the above named Places to come amongst them" (quoted in Duffy 1951:338).

In addition to smallpox at this time, it is possible, though by no means probable, that the Cherokees suffered from measles, influenza, or both. An epidemic of measles may have infected southeastern tribes from 1759 to 1760; an epidemic of influenza probably occurred among American Indians in 1761 (Dobyns 1983:17, table 2; 19, table 3). Mortality may have been high, since they had had little, if any previous exposure to measles and therefore lacked immunity to it, and recovery from influenza does not confer immunity to it.

Two decades later, nevertheless, smallpox is said to have struck a dissident group of Cherokees, the Chickamaugas, yet again: "In the spring of 1780 a company of immigrants made the first settlement on the present site of Nashville. Enroute, on passing the Chickamauga towns on the Tennessee River, they were attacked by the hostile Cherokee. The Cherokee Indians captured a boat on which were twenty-eight persons, among whom was a man named Stuart, and his family, who were infected with the smallpox. As if in retribution, smallpox broke out among the Chickamauga causing the death of many" (Stearn and Stearn 1945:46). Similarly, a letter on March 18, 1780, from Savannah, where a "congress" was being held between the Cherokees and other Indians and the newly appointed superintendent of Indian affairs for the Atlantic district, Thomas Brown, reported that the "Cherokees have gone home from fear of a smallpox epidemic, which cost them 2,500 men earlier" (Anderson and Lewis 1983:169).

Another episode of smallpox may have struck the Cherokees only a few years later—in 1783 (Stearn and Stearn 1945:49), possibly accompanied by influenza (Dobyns 1983:19, table 3). It is said that the Cherokees suffered severely from it and that it "broke their last remaining resistance to the advancing settlement of their lands" (Stearn and Stearn 1945:49).

Warfare

Also an important influence on the size of the Cherokee population were conflicts both between the Cherokees and other American Indian tribes and with European colonizers, later Americans. Often the Cherokees sided with one of the European countries against other American Indians.

The Cherokees were not considered particularly warlike during the early 1700s; in fact, some tribes considered them cowards. But they became caught up in the struggles between European colonizers for American Indian land. Also, there was a sharp depopulation of surrounding American Indian tribes, particularly those toward the southeast coast, because of war, disease, and the slave trade (see, for example, Nash 1982:121–30; Wood 1988, 1989). James Axtell (1981:50) quoted John Lawson's observation of Carolina Indians in the early 1700s: "Lawson said that due to smallpox and rum 'there is not the sixth savage living within two hundred Miles of all our Settlements, as there were fifty years ago.'" Meanwhile the Cherokees, at least, maintained a relatively large population into the 1700s, in part because of a greater isolation but also because of an alliance with the English (see Nash 1982:234–35). Seemingly as a result, the Cherokees not only became warlike but emerged as a dominant military force during the 1700s. Malone (1956:4) asserted: "Cherokee fighting powers increased with experience, and by the eighteenth century all Indian intruders had been driven from Cherokee domains. The warriors had acquired particular skill with the more modern weapons, the gun and the knife." Nash noted that the nature of Cherokee tribal organization changed during this period, and warriors began to take the lead in tribal councils. He further pointed out that by the 1760s "the Cherokees made 'warring and warriors an unambiguous part of the good life' and gave the war chiefs new and coercive political authority over the nation" (Nash 1982:241–42). It seems likely as well that the other Indians simply died out faster, thus giving the Cherokees dominance over the area.

Although the Cherokees may have shared a common early background with the Iroquois and other Five Nations Indians to the north, the Cherokees and the Iroquois were bitter enemies by the time of the first history written about them. During the eighteenth century the Cherokees and the now Six Nations Indians—the Tuscaroras having joined the Five Nations—attacked one another repeatedly. Conflicts with the Illinois Indians also continued, and the Cherokees sometimes journeyed on the Wabash River to attack them (see Anderson and Lewis 1983:45, 50, 60, 122). The Cherokees fought the Creeks on numerous occasions and suffered population losses: for example, the Creeks destroyed two Cherokee towns in 1750 and five towns in 1752 (Smith 1979:48). The Cherokees also fought the Chickasaws and are said to have suffered a severe defeat at Chickasaw Old Fields in 1769 (Swanton [1946] 1979:112). They also fought the Catawbas, the Shawnees, the Alabamas, and other Indians on sporadic occasions.

Conflicts between the Cherokees and the European colonists are what really seem important to Cherokee population history during the period, however, particularly the "wars" of 1760–61 and 1776.

The 1760–61 War

In many ways the 1760–61 war may be seen as the culmination of the struggle between Britain and France as France sought to extend her dominance in the Southeast. In 1714 the French built Fort Toulouse, north of present-day Montgomery, Alabama: "From this central vantage point they had rapidly extended their influence among all the neighboring tribes until in 1721 it was estimated that 3,400 warriors who had formerly traded with Carolina had been 'entirely debauched to the French interest,' while 2,000 more were wavering, and only the Cherokee could still be considered friendly to the English." Moreover, from then until 1763—the date of the final French withdrawal—the "Indian wars" are said to have resulted from the French-English struggle for "territorial and commercial supremacy, the Indian being simply the cat's-paw of one or the other." Although allied with the English during this period, the Cherokees favored the French: "It required every effort of the Carolina government to hold them to their allegiance" (Mooney [1900] 1982:35).

In 1756 England formally declared war with France, though the actual conflict may be traced to 1754 when the French captured an English post, near present-day Pittsburgh, which became Fort Duquesne. Afterward the English negotiated treaties with the Cherokees against the French and their Indian allies (Mooney [1900] 1982:39).

Conflicts between the Cherokees and their English "allies" soon developed, nevertheless, particularly during a joint effort against the Shawnees in 1756. Some Cherokee allies were slain by Virginians, and the Cherokees began to attack Carolina settlements. Tensions escalated further, and the Carolina governor declared war against the Cherokees in November 1759 (Mooney [1900] 1982:41–42). Efforts at reconciliation were made, but to no avail, and war began in earnest the following summer, in June 1760.

During the ensuing war the Cherokees were devastated by the English, especially by English troops under Colonels Montgomery and Grant. Montgomery, with over 1,600 men, marched through Cherokee territory twice in 1760, destroying many of their towns (Anderson and Lewis 1983:101). He is said to have first "surprised" a Cherokee village, Little Keowee, "killing every man of the defenders"; he then destroyed the Lower Towns, "burning them to the ground, cutting down the cornfields and orchards, killing and taking more than a hundred of their men, and driving the whole population into the mountains before him" (Mooney [1900] 1982:43). Montgomery next moved north to the Middle Towns and Upper Towns. Here he was more or less defeated by the concentrated forces of the Cherokees.

In 1761 Colonel Grant and 2,600 men, including some Chickasaws and Catawbas, dealt another blow to the Cherokees, burning fifteen Middle Towns to the ground, as well as all the plantations, and destroying some 1,400 acres of Cherokee crops (Anderson and Lewis 1983:257). All told, Grant drove some 5,000 Cherokees (men, women, and children) into the woods and mountains to starve. Before long the rest of the Cherokee population fled to what western towns and Overhill settlements remained, where there was barely enough food for a third of the total Cherokee tribe (Goodwin 1977:105). Adair noted in this regard: "The Cherokee had a prodigious number of excellent horses, at the beginning of their late war with us; but pinching hunger forced them to eat the greatest part of them, at the time of that unfortunate event" (Adair [1775] 1930:242). The Cherokees were also cut off from most of their trade goods: the only ones reaching them came from the French. As Gary Nash (1982:256) noted: "The desperate shortage of trade goods forced the Cherokees back to ancient customs—fashioning clothes from deer and bear skins and tipping their arrows with bone points instead of trader's brass."

By the end of the war, according to Adair, there were only some 2,300 Cherokee warriors, which he stated was "a great diminution for so short a space of time: and if we may conjecture for futurity, from the circumstances already past, there will be few of them alive, after the like revolution of time" ([1775] 1930:239).

The War of 1776

By the beginning of the Revolutionary War, the Cherokees were more or less firmly on the side of the British against the "Americans," as were most other American Indian tribes in the Southeast. Along with the British and some Tories, the Cherokees attacked Charleston in June 1776 and other colonial settlements as well. Then the colonists began to mount their own attacks on the Cherokees.

Eventually several thousand "American" troops reportedly were sent to "destroy the Cherokees" (Anderson and Lewis 1983:323, also 320), attacking them from several quarters. According to James O'Donnell, "The plan . . . agreed upon by the Carolinas and Virginia, Georgia being unable to participate, called for South Carolina to destroy the Lower towns, the two Carolinas to level the Middle and Valley towns, and Virginia to lay waste the Overhill towns" (1973:43–44).

General Griffith Rutherford attacked from North Carolina. He destroyed thirty-six Cherokee towns, all those on the Oconaluftee and Tuckasegee rivers, on the "upper part" of the Little Tennessee River, and on the Hiwassee River to the junction of the Valley River and below. He also destroyed Cherokee cornfields and "killed or carried off" livestock (Mooney [1900] 1982:49). The Cherokees then retreated to the Smoky Mountains.

Colonel Andrew Williamson of the South Carolina militia soon attacked the Lower Towns with over 1,000 troops. Supposedly he "burnt every town, and destroyed all the corn from the Cherokee line to the Middle settlement." Generals Rutherford and Williamson then joined forces to attack the Middle Towns: "For two weeks the combined armies scorched the Middle settlements, leaving no habitations or food." On the heels of these attacks, Colonel Christian and his Virginians marched toward the Overhill Towns. The Cherokees, in response, "fled into the mountains, leaving behind in their villages, horses, cattle, dogs, hogs, and fowls as well as between forty and fifty thousand bushels of corn and ten or fifteen thousand bushels of potatoes" (O'Donnell 1973:45, 47, 48). Soon the Americans, hoping to dissuade the Creeks from joining the British, spread word that the Cherokees saw "their towns burned, their corn cut down, and their people driven into the woods to perish" (Anderson and Lewis 1983:156).

The effects upon the Cherokees, in James Mooney's words, were "well nigh paralyzing":

> More than fifty of their towns had been burned, their orchards cut down, their fields wasted, their cattle and horses killed or driven off, their stores of buckskin and other personal property plundered. Hundreds of their people had been killed or had died of starvation and exposure, others were prisoners in the hands of the Americans, and some had been sold into slavery. Those who had escaped were fugitives in the mountains, living upon acorns, chestnuts, and wild game, or were refugees with the British. From the Virginia line to the Chattahoochee the chain of destruction was complete. For the present at least any further resistance was hopeless, and they were compelled to sue for peace. (Mooney [1900] 1982:53)

Eventual Peace

Conflicts did not end here, despite a peace treaty, but continued to one degree or another until 1794, as many of the Cherokees moved their settlements down the Tennessee River to Chickamauga Creek and below it and many others moved westward.

Chickamauga settlements were eventually burned, those at Chickamauga Creek in 1782; most Chickamaugas then moved even farther to the south (Malone 1956:38–39). Other Cherokee settlements were destroyed as well. By the end of 1782 the Cherokees "had been reduced to the lowest depth of misery, almost indeed to the verge of extinction." They had seen their towns "laid in ashes and their fields wasted," their warriors killed, their women and children "sickened and starved in the mountains." As if this were not enough, "to complete their brimming cup of misery the smallpox again broke out among them in 1783" (Mooney [1900] 1982:61). (It was probably at Chickamauga that the 1780 smallpox epidemic began.)

The conflict did not stop here but continued for another decade, despite a treaty made with the new United States government in 1785. Most of these hostilities were centered in the Valley Towns on the Hiwassee River and in the towns of the Chickamaugas (Mooney [1900] 1982:63). The Chickamaugas had by now separated from the other Cherokees "because the upper Cherokees would no longer take any part in their Hostilities against the white People & moreover often discovered [disclosed] their designs" (quoted in Malone 1956:39).

In 1788 a Cherokee town on the Hiwassee was burned, and many inhabitants were killed in the river while they were trying to escape; then several towns on the Little Tennessee were burned and some of their inhabitants were killed (Mooney [1900] 1982:65). Atrocities continued on both sides for a number of years. In one instance the Americans supposedly beheaded Cherokee women and children who were planting crops; in another instance the Americans attacked women and children on their way to South Carolina to buy corn (Anderson and Lewis 1983:653, 656).

In 1792 most of the Chickamaugas were living on the lower Tennessee River in villages then known as the Five Lower Towns:

> Running Water, the most northerly of the five, consisted of a hundred huts and was a "common crossing place for the Creeks." Three miles below was Nickajack, which contained about forty houses. Long Island village, "which comprehends an island called the Long Island in the Tennessee, and a number of huts on the south side," consisted of about a dozen houses and was located five miles below Nickajack. Farther on was Crow Town, considered "the lowest town in the Cherokee nation," which had about thirty inhabitants. Fifteen miles south of Running Water was Lookout Mountain Town, located on the creek of the same name. Containing eighty huts, it was situated in a valley about three miles wide next to Lookout Mountain. (Malone 1956:39)

William Blount, governor of the "territory south of the Ohio," reported that "these five towns contained approximately three hundred warriors, in addition to various groups of hostiles such as Shawnees, Creeks, Northern Indians, and 'white Tories' " (Malone 1956:39).

Two years later, in 1794, these Chickamauga villages were devastated by Major James Ore: Nickajack and Running Water were destroyed, with many Indians killed and numbers of prisoners taken (Malone 1956:45).

On November 7 and 8, 1794, a conference was held at Tellico blockhouse: reportedly "the result was satisfactory; all differences were arranged on a friendly basis and the long Cherokee war came to an end" (Mooney [1900] 1982:79).

Issues and hostilities continued despite the conference, particularly with a group of Chickamauga Cherokees who, in about 1782, had moved to across the Ohio River to settle in a town on Paint Creek, near Shawnee friends and allies. About 1787 these Cherokees reportedly numbered some "seventy warriors" (Mooney [1900] 1982:79). In this same year, about 1787, the Chickamauga town was attacked and burned "by increasingly powerful Kentuckians." The Indians then moved to two townsites near the mouth of the White River in present-day southern Indiana (Tanner 1978:99).

Further conflicts continued, but other treaties were eventually negotiated, the final one in 1798.

CHEROKEE POPULATION AT CENTURY'S END

By the end of the eighteenth century most Cherokees still clung to their traditional, though now greatly reduced, lands in the Southeast of what had by then become the United States. Mooney ([1900] 1982:81) concluded: "The close of the century found them still a compact people (the westward movement having hardly yet begun) numbering probably about 20,000 souls." This population figure is clearly too high. Ubelaker (pers. comm.) believes they numbered only 18,000; I suggest below that there were even fewer.

Cherokee Land Cessions

During the 1700s, as war and peace alternated, the Cherokees made various cessions of land, under treaties dating from 1721 to 1798. As compiled by Charles C. Royce in his *Cherokee Nation of Indians* ([1887] 1975:2–3), the Cherokees made sixteen separate cessions of land during this century, under thirteen treaties. (See table 3.) The first was the treaty of 1721 with South Carolina, ceding a tract of Cherokee land in South Carolina lying between the Santee, Saluda, and Edisto rivers. The last was a treaty of October 2, 1798, with the United States, under which three separate tracts were

Table 3. Eighteenth-Century Cherokee Land Cessions

Cherokee Treaty	Cession	Square Miles
Treaty of 1721 with South Carolina	Tract in South Carolina between Santee, Saluda, and Edisto rivers	2,623
Treaty of November 24, 1755, with South Carolina	Tract in South Carolina between Wateree and Savannah rivers	8,635
Treaty of October 14, 1768, with British superintendent of Indian affairs	Tract in southwestern Virginia	850
Treaty of October 18, 1770, at Lochaber, South Carolina	Tract in Virginia, West Virginia, northeastern Tennessee, and eastern Kentucky	9,200
Treaty of 1772 with Virginia	Tract in Virginia, and West Virginia, and eastern Kentucky	10,917
Treaty of June 1, 1773, with British superintendent of Indian affairs	Tract in Georgia, north of Broad River	1,050
Treaty of March 17, 1775, with Richard Henderson and others	Tract in Kentucky, Virginia, and Tennessee	27,050
Treaty of May 20, 1777, with South Carolina and Georgia	Tract in northwestern South Carolina	2,051
Treaty of July 20, 1777, with Virginia and North Carolina	Tract in western North Carolina and northeastern Tennessee	6,174
Treaty of May 31, 1783, with Georgia	Tract in Georgia, between Oconee and Tugaloo rivers	1,650
Treaty of November 28, 1785, with United States	Tract in western North Carolina	6,381
Treaty of July 2, 1791, with United States	Tract in western North Carolina and eastern Tennessee	4,157
Treaty of October 2, 1798, with United States	Tracts in Tennessee, between Hawkins's Line, Tennessee River, and Chilhowee Mountain, and between Clinch River and Cumberland Mountain	952
	Tract in North Carolina, between Pickens's and Meigs's lines	587

Source: Royce ([1887] 1975:2–3, 256).

ceded: a tract in Tennessee between "Hawkins's Line," the Tennessee River, and Chilhowee Mountain; a tract in Tennessee between the Clinch River, and the Cumberland Mountains; and a tract in North Carolina between "Pickens's Line" and "Meigs's Line." In the inter-

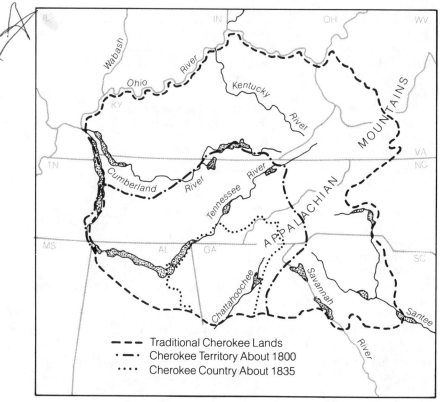

2. Shrinking Cherokee lands. After Mooney ([1900] 1982: pl. 111).

vening years other treaties entailed land cessions in North and South
Carolina, Virginia, West Virginia, Tennessee, Kentucky, and Georgia.
All told, 82,277 square miles of land in the Southeast were ceded.[5]
   Nevertheless, even "after repeated cessions of large tracts of land,
. . . they remained in recognized possession of nearly 43,000 square
miles of territory, a country about equal in extent to Ohio, Virginia,
or Tennessee" (Mooney [1900] 1982:81). (See map 2.) About half of
this territory lay in Tennessee, with the rest virtually equally in
Georgia and Alabama, though a small portion lay in the extreme
southern corner of North Carolina. As to Cherokee towns, "The old
Lower towns on Savannah river had been broken up for twenty years,
and the whites had so far encroached upon the Upper towns that
the capital and council fire of the nation had been removed from the
ancient peace town of Echota to Ustanali, in Georgia. The towns on
Coosa river and in Alabama were almost all of recent establishment,

peopled by refugees from the east and north. The Middle towns, in North Carolina, were still surrounded by Indian country" (Mooney [1900] 1982:81–82).

Population Size

Mooney's assertion of 20,000 Cherokees and Ubelaker's of 18,000 at the end of the eighteenth century seem high, both from the perspective of population estimates of a few decades earlier and those for the early 1800s shown in the next chapter. A figure of not over 16,000 seems more nearly correct. Also, by this time groups of Cherokees were in the West, beyond the Mississippi River, forming a new life there: the division and relocation of the Cherokee population had both already begun and would accelerate in the first decades of the following century. They have continued until today.

First Movements Westward

It is not possible to specify when the first Cherokees crossed the Mississippi River: as Mooney wrote, "There was probably never a time in the history of the tribe when their warriors and hunters were not accustomed to make excursions beyond the great river." Perhaps the initial emigration occurred not long after the first Cherokee treaty with South Carolina in 1721. Then a group of Cherokees led by Yunwi-usgaseti ("dangerous man"), "foreseeing the inevitable end of yielding to the demands of the colonists, refused to have any relations with the white man, and took up their long march for the unknown West." Some initial communications between the emigrant group and the main body of Cherokees took place as the emigrants journeyed toward the Mississippi River, but communication soon ceased after they crossed: "Long years afterward a runner came from the west that they were still living near the base of the Rocky Mountains" (Mooney [1900] 1982:99–100).

According to Helen Hornbeck Tanner, from the mid-1700s to about 1795 the Cherokees were constantly involved in Indian affairs of the Ohio valley, away from their homeland. Involvement often was only through trips or contacts, but sometimes there were longer-term relocations whereby the Cherokees joined the Shawnees, the Delawares, and the "Mingoes" (groups of Iroquois from New York and Canada) who were joining the already established Wyandots (Hurons) in the Ohio area. For example: "By 1755, a body of Cherokees were living on the Ohio river at the mouth of the Kentucky river, reportedly at the behest of the Six Nations," and "by 1783, Cherokees had joined the Mingo and Wyandot in a sprawling community on the upper Mad river of Ohio, near present Zanesfield" (Tanner 1978:94, 95, 99).

Other subsequent "westward emigrations" occurred. I have already mentioned the movement of the Chickamaugas north of the Ohio River in 1782. Another movement took place shortly thereafter. A group of Cherokees who had fought on the British side in the Revolutionary War asked permission of the Spanish governor at New Orleans to relocate west of the Mississippi River to what was then Spanish territory (Mooney [1900] 1982:100). The request was granted by the governor of Louisiana, Don Esteban Miró, and it seems probable that some Cherokees settled in the Arkansas country in 1783 (Washburn 1910:129; Englund 1974:65). According to a report in Anderson and Lewis (1983:663), the application was from two Cherokee chiefs on behalf of 1,800 warriors. In 1785 some Cherokees, reportedly dissatisfied with the terms of the Hopewell Treaty of that year, were said to have journeyed the Tennessee, Ohio, and Mississippi rivers to the St. Francis River in Spanish territory (now eastern Arkansas). They first formed a settlement on the St. Francis, but then moved to a better site on the White River and were joined by later emigrants (Foreman 1930:29).

In 1794 some Cherokees under their chief, the Bowl (Bowles),[6] fled—with some white prisoners—from their towns on the Tennessee River, traveling down that river and then down the Ohio and the Mississippi as far as the mouth of the St. Francis River. They then went up the St. Francis—their prisoners were released to journey down the Mississippi to New Orleans—and settled permanently. (In 1804 Meriwether Lewis reported two Cherokee towns on the St. Francis. He asserted that they could raise 250 warriors [Everett 1985:104]. This would have made a total population size of approximately 1,000.) As we shall see, "others joined them from time to time, attracted by the hunting prospect, until they were in sufficient number to obtain recognition from the government" (Mooney [1900] 1982:100).[7]

Demographic Heterogeneity

A kind of demographic heterogeneity had by this time developed in the Cherokee population, which continues today: it was the result of a biological mixing with non-Indian populations—primarily whites, but also with blacks. The mixing with whites was a result of unions formed primarily between Cherokee women and "white men, chiefly traders of the ante-Revolutionary period, with a few Americans from the back settlements" (Mooney [1900] 1982:83), perhaps the trader Dougherty, for example.[8] Traders apparently had a relatively easy time forming unions with Cherokee women. Reportedly there were no Cherokee laws governing marriage or adultery: "Cherokee men had nothing to say about their women's behavior" (Reid 1976:141).

Children of such unions suffered no social stigma; it has even been asserted, albeit probably incorrectly, that "the Cherokee desired children begotten by white men much above those by native husbands." In any event, such children "presented no legal or social complications, for it mattered little among the Cherokees who was the father" (Reid, 1976:141), since they traced descent matrilineally. Other mixing of whites and Cherokees perhaps resulted from the incorporation of whites, sometimes as captives, into the tribe. For example, about a dozen French deserters were adopted in 1755 into Cherokee families that had lost men in the wars (Corkran 1962:62), and Chickamauga Cherokees apparently kept a "Miss Thornton, taken by Otter Lifter" (quoted in Halliburton 1977:12–13) in 1794.[9]

Cherokees not only had contacts with whites, they also had contacts with blacks, perhaps even before De Soto's expedition. As Theda Perdue (1979:36) stated: "When the black slaves in Lucas Vazquez de Ayllón's ill-fated colony on the Pedee River revolted in 1526, some of the rebels fled to the Indians, and it is at least possible that the Cherokees saw the Africans as their offspring." Black slavery had also been "introduced" to the Cherokees by the late 1700s, primarily by English traders (see, for example, Halliburton 1977:3–19), and soon some prominent Cherokee men were slaveholders (Mooney [1900] 1982:83; also Halliburton 1977:11). In time the European institution of slavery "replaced" slavery as known among the pre-European Cherokees, who had held "slaves" or *atsi nahsa'i*—primarily captives obtained through warfare (Perdue 1979:4). As with Cherokee-white contact, Cherokee-black contact produced mixed-blood offspring, at least in a biological sense. Since the Cherokees traced their descent along female lines, a child of a Cherokee mother and a non-Cherokee father was considered fully Cherokee, although children of Cherokee-black unions increasingly were not accepted unequivocally.[10]

By the end of the eighteenth century the Cherokees had also more or less incorporated other American Indians into their population, including some Delawares, some Natchez, some Creeks, and some Chickasaws (see, for example, Anderson and Lewis 1983:24, 56, 158, 318, 424). Some of this was in response to the depopulation of other American Indian tribes (and perhaps also to Cherokee depopulation). John Lawson noted in his *New Voyage to Carolina* (1709), with reference to Carolina Indians in the early 1700s: "Although there is nothing more coveted amongst them, than to marry a Woman of their own Nation, yet when the Nation consists of a very few People (as nowadays it often happens) so that they are all of them related to one another, then they look out for Husbands and Wives amongst Strangers" (quoted in Axtell 1981:94).

This mixing with whites, blacks, and other American Indians continued—even accelerated—in the nineteenth century.

CHAPTER 3

Resurgence and Removal:
1800 to 1840

The first few decades of the nineteenth century were characterized overall by a resurgence in the Cherokee population, though decline occurred in the initial decade. The Cherokees had formally settled the "war" issue with the new United States federal government late in the eighteenth century, so major population losses from warfare no longer occurred. Losses came from a smallpox epidemic in the first years of the century: As R. Palmer Howard noted, "In 1806 a severe [smallpox] epidemic prompted the Cherokee chiefs to engage a white physician who was paid $150 for his services, a large sum at the time" (1970:73). And there were subsequent, probably relatively minor epidemics of smallpox and other diseases. Nevertheless, the Cherokee population began to increase by about the end of the first decade. But resurgence was short-lived: the five years of their forced removal from the Southeast to Indian Territory—from about 1835 to 1840—inflicted serious population losses.

CHEROKEE POPULATION TO 1835

The first good population figures for the nineteenth-century Cherokees are for the years 1808–9, the result of the so-called Meigs census conducted by Colonel Return J. Meigs. The census enumerated 12,395 Cherokees in the East: 6,116 males and 6,279 females (plus 583 slaves and 341 whites) (see Evans 1981:61; Thornton 1984:295, table 1). To this we may add an estimated 1,000 Cherokees already west of the Mississippi River, giving 13,395.

As we saw, however, Mooney asserted the Cherokees numbered

about 20,000 at the end of the eighteenth century, and Ubelaker estimated 18,000. Another estimate, in 1801, by John De Lacy places them at 5,000 "warriors," which, when multiplied by the typical ratio of one warrior for every four people, also gives a total population of 20,000 (see Anderson and Lewis 1983:702). But were these figures even nearly correct, several population trends would have occurred. The Cherokee population would have to have grown extremely rapidly during the last decade or so of the eighteenth century, since population figures for the early 1780s are considerably below 20,000, as we saw. Or the population would have to have undergone a very sharp decline during the first decade of the nineteenth century, assuming the Meigs census is reasonably correct. Some decline resulted from the 1806 smallpox epidemic, but it probably was not enough to reduce the population by so many thousands. There was an 1801–2 smallpox pandemic among American Indians, but it centered on the plains and probably did not spread to the Cherokees. The Cherokees did not experience any other known major epidemic diseases at this time, nor did surrounding American Indian peoples (see, for example, Dobyns 1983:155–23, tables 1–9). And the Cherokees engaged in no major wars. Of course the Meigs census could have grossly underestimated the Cherokees in 1808–9, but this seems doubtful in light of subsequent censuses discussed below. Another explanation is that there were far more Cherokee emigrants west of the Mississippi than the estimated 1,000. This is very possible, but it seems unlikely there were enough to make the various estimates and censuses compatible. Probably the Cherokees numbered considerably fewer about 1800 than Mooney's estimate of 20,000 or even Ubelaker's of 18,000. Only 16,000 is a reasonable figure, I think, for their population at that date. It is also likely that the Cherokees were somewhat reduced by the 1806 smallpox epidemic, and it is probable the population west of the Mississippi River numbered more than the estimated 1,000, as we shall see below. Thus the Meigs census enumerating 12,395 Cherokee in the East could have been correct.

Population in the 1820s

The Cherokees reportedly numbered 17,000 about 1820 (Morse [1822] 1970:364, 367, table 1). Approximately 11,000 of these were in the East, and 6,000 were west of the Mississippi River, though this 6,000 figure may be too high (see Englund 1974:67–68).

Jedediah Morse ([1822] 1970:152; see also Evans 1981:61) asserted that 3,000 Cherokees emigrated westward in 1818. Records indicate that though 2,190 Cherokees enrolled to remove to the West from 1817 to 1819, after the treaty of 1817, only 1,102 actually went (Baker 1977:152). Morse ([1822] 1970:152; Evans 1981:61) also claimed that the new emigrants joined 3,000 already there. If this was so, then there likely were more than 1,000 Cherokees in the West in 1808–9, and the total Cherokee population for that period would be larger than the 13,395 reported above.

About this time the Cherokees were plagued by various diseases, including "consumption," measles, and smallpox. For example, Elias Boudinot asserted in 1823, regarding "consumption", that "perhaps the 'Cherokee Nation is destined to fall by this Instrument of Death'" (Howard 1970:73). And Howard (1970:73) noted that measles also occurred in epidemics. Smallpox struck the Cherokees yet again in 1824, especially near the Valley Towns of North Carolina and in the hills of Tennessee (Howard 1970:73). The missionary Moody Hall reported:

> The Small Pox is raging to an alarming degree within 1-½ miles of the Valley Town mission. We have heard that it is spreading very fast, & is now within 20 miles of Calhoun [Tennessee]. Owing to the ignorance & inattention of the Indians it is probable that it will spread generally thro' the country & that 1000 will die with it. In our little Town where it first appeared in the nation, 27 have died; all that had it except one. . . . [Should we obtain from Tennessee] the matter for the cow pox I shall use all my influence to have all the Cherokees inoculated. The Old Conjuror has appointed a great Phys[ic] dance, (as in the case of the measles) promising that all who join him, shall not be afflicted with the disease.
>
> The Christians all say that they think more of a short sincere prayer, than of their seven days fasting & drinking physic. (Quoted in Malone 1956:135–36)

In 1826 the Cherokee population in the East was reported at 13,963, but the actual date for the figure was 1824 (see Sturtevant 1981:91, n. 9). Another report stated:

> A correct Census of the Nation was taken last year (1825) by order of the National Council to ascertain the amount of property and taxable individuals within the Nation. [The correctness of this

may be relied on, and] [T]he result proved to be 13,583 native
Citizens—147 white . . . men married with Indians and 73 white
women d[itt]o and African Slaves 1,277 to which if we add 400
Cherokees who took Reservations in North Carolina and [who
are] not included in the Census, and who have since merged again
among us—the Cherokee Nation will contain 15,280 [= 15,480]
inhabitants. There are a few instances of African Mixture with
Cherokee blood . . . but that of the white may be as 1 to 4—occa-
sioned by intermarriage which has been increasing in proportion
to the march of civilization. (Sturtevant 1981:81)

At that time there were, some say, only an additional 3,500–4,000
Cherokees in the West. If so, the total population would have been
about 17,713 (see Thornton 1984:295, table 1). (If Morse was correct
that the Western Cherokees totaled 6,000 in about 1820, then the
Cherokee population in 1826 would have been larger than 17,713,
perhaps about 20,000.)

In 1828 the Cherokee national newspaper, the *Cherokee Phoenix*,
reported the Eastern Cherokee population at 14,972; adding 3,750
for the West in 1826 (3,500–4,000) gives a total population of some
18,722 (see Thornton 1984:295, table 1). (Here again, if Morse was
correct the population would have been 20,972.)

Population in 1835

A census of the Eastern Cherokees (sometimes called
the Henderson Roll) was conducted in 1835: it enumerated 16,542
Cherokees (see National Archives of the United States 1960, Record
Group 75, T496; also Tyner 1974). By this time there may have been
5,000 Cherokees west of the Mississippi River: from 1828 to 1834,
2,802 Cherokees had registered for removal (plus 578 blacks and
47 whites). Nevertheless, by 1834 only 1,171 Cherokees (plus 293
blacks) had actually emigrated, according to official records (see Baker
1977:18–50). In at least one instance potential emigrants changed
their minds because of reports that cholera had spread among emigrants of other southeastern Indians who were also "encouraged" to
relocate to the West. Howard (1970:74) noted: "Widespread were the
tales of the tribulations and many deaths from cholera during the removal of other southeastern tribes. . . . Reports of cholera in the
spring of 1834 reached the assembly camp of the Cherokees who had

enrolled with the Superintendent of Removal, Benjamin F. Currey. To his dismay, more than half the enrollees changed their mind." Those who subsequently emigrated in 1834—457 Cherokees, according to Howard—suffered greatly: "A few died from measles and accidental drowning in the first weeks. Then cholera struck before they reached the Arkansas River. . . . By April 15th, the cholera epidemic was at its height. Fifty emigrants and a physician died from this affliction and 31 from other causes before they reached Dwight Mission in the Cherokee Nation on May 10th, 1834. Within the year, half the remainder of this party died" (Howard 1970:74).[1] Adding these 1,171 emigrants to the 3,500–4,000 estimated above yields a total of about 5,000 in the West. If this was correct—it may not have been, since some of the emigrants died—the total Cherokee population then becomes 21,542 (see Thornton 1984:295, table 1). The increase therefore could have been from as few as 13,395 in 1808–9 to about 21,542. This represents substantial growth during the period but is not impossibly high (see, for example, Englund 1974:77–78). (But if one again uses Morse's 6,000 figure for 1820, the total becomes 24,713: 16,542 plus 6,000 plus 1,171 other migrants west by 1834.)

Characteristics of 1835 Population

The Cherokee census of 1835 was conducted under the auspices of the United States War Department; it gathered a variety of information on the Eastern Cherokees. The census was conducted by state, using special agents for each state: Tennessee, Daniel Henderson; Alabama, Rezin Rawlings; North Carolina, Nathaniel Smith; and Georgia, C. J. Nelson and George W. Underwood. Using data from this census, one can present a brief demographic profile of the Eastern Cherokees at that time.

The census enumerated 16,542 Cherokees in the East. As shown in table 4, of the total 16,542, 8,946 lived in the Georgia area, 3,644 in the North Carolina area, 2,528 in the Tennessee area, and 1,424 in the Alabama area. There were slightly more females than males: the sex ratio (number of males per 100 females) was 98.9. The Cherokees comprised 2,637 households, yielding an average "family" size of over six individuals. They lived in about forty towns and villages and on isolated farms and settlements (Malone 1956:119). As also shown in table 4, the total number of farms recorded was 3,120, owned by 2,495 individuals: 224 had two, 77 had three, 33 had four, 17 had

Table 4. Summary of 1835 Cherokee Census

| | State Area | | | | |
	North Carolina	Georgia	Alabama	Tennessee	Total
Indians	3,644	8,946	1,424	2,528	16,542
Slaves	37	776	299	480	1,592
Intermarried whites	22	68	32	79	201
Farms	714	1,735	259	412	3,120
Acres cultivated	6,906	19,216	7,252	10,692	38,134

Sources: Hewes (1978:6, table 1); McLoughlin and Conser (1977:685); National Archives of the United States, 1960, Record Group 75, T496.

five, 8 had six, 1 had seven, 1 had nine, and 1 had thirteen (Malone 1956:138). The Cherokees had 38,134 acres under cultivation at this time.

Full-Bloods in 1835

The overwhelming majority of the population were listed as full-bloods. In an analysis of this census, William McLoughlin and Walter Conser (1977:693) found: "The census of 1835 indicates that 12,776 of the individuals listed or 77.27 percent were fullbloods; 1,391 individuals or 8.40 percent were halfbloods; 1,469 or 8.87 percent were 'quadroons,' one-quarter Cherokee: 897 individuals or 5.55 percent had no racial status indicated in the census."[2] This stood in marked contrast to a report at that time that half of the 1809 Cherokee population was of mixed blood (see Morse [1822] 1970:152; also McLoughlin and Conser 1977:693–94). Moreover, 69.5 percent of Cherokee families were composed entirely of full-bloods, 12.6 percent comprised full-bloods and mixed-bloods, and 17.9 percent had no full-bloods. McLoughlin and Conser (1977:680) concluded that the full-bloods did not live in isolated pockets in the mountains but were scattered throughout the nation, though they were concentrated in a few states and areas. Table 5 shows the percentage of the various "blood" categories by state. Thus the North Carolina area had a larger percentage of full-bloods in its Cherokee population than any of the other areas, followed by Georgia, Alabama, and Tennessee. High proportions of full-bloods were found in "the mountainous region of the Great Smokies on the border between North Carolina and Tennessee and extending somewhat into northwestern Georgia and northeast-

Table 5. 1835 Cherokee Population in State Areas,
by Percentage of Mixture

| | State Area | | | |
Mixture	North Carolina	Georgia	Alabama	Tennessee
Full-bloods	88.9	81.0	61.3	56.8
Half-bloods	2.5	5.9	14.9	21.0
Quarter-bloods	6.2	7.5	13.5	14.5
Mixed "Negro"	0.5	0.01	0.3	1.2
White intermarriage	0.5	0.7	2.2	2.9
Mixed Spaniards	0.0	0.5	0.7	0.0
Mixed Catawbas	0.0	0.01	3.3	0.5
Total	98.1	95.6	96.2	96.9

Source: McLoughlin and Conser (1977:688, table 7).

ern Alabama" and "in the southern and southwestern part of the
Cherokee nation where its borders touched those of the Creek and
Chickasaw nations" (McLoughlin and Conser 1977:686). The 1835
census also counted only 201 intermarried whites in the Cherokee
population of 1835 (National Archives of the United States, 1960,
Record Group 75, T496),[3] and "there were only sixty 'mixed negroes'
—Cherokee-black—within the nation or .036 percent of the total
population. Similarly, the percentages for mixture with the Catawba,
'Catawby,' Indians, with Spanish ancestry . . . are extremely small"
(McLoughlin and Conser 1977:694–95).

Slaves in 1835

As reflected in the 1835 Cherokee census, the Cherokees had 1,592
"black slaves" (see table 4), an increase over previously reported numbers: 583 in 1809, 1,277 in 1826, and 1,038 in 1828 (McLoughlin and
Conser 1977:681, table 1). Slavery did not permeate the Cherokee
tribe but was concentrated in the hands of a very few: only 7.4 percent of tribal members held slaves. Slaveholders were concentrated in
the more mixed-blood Cherokee communities and among the more
mixed-blood families: only 1 percent of the all-full-blood families
owned slaves; 10.8 percent of the mixed families and 30.4 percent
of the no-full-blood families did (McLoughlin and Conser 1977:691,
695). This, of course, was because the more mixed-blood families
were wealthier and engaged in plantation agriculture. Numbers of

slaves also varied by state area: there were only 37 in the North Carolina area, but 299 in the Alabama area, 480 in the Tennessee area,
and 776 in the Georgia area (National Archives of the United States,
1960, Record Group 75, T496).

CHEROKEE REMOVAL:
THE TRAIL OF TEARS

Population gains during the initial decades of the
nineteenth century were short-lived; they ended not long after 1835
during the forced removal of large numbers of Cherokees from the
Southeast into the northeastern part of what was designated Indian
Territory, now northeastern Oklahoma. The removal was such an
ordeal for the Cherokees and caused them so much suffering that they
named it Nunna daul Tsuny, literally "the Trail Where We Cried." It
has become known as the Trail of Tears. The removal occurred despite the "success" the Cherokees had in adapting their society and
cultue to Euro-American pressures.

Background

As described in chapter 2, Cherokee lands had shrunk
decidedly during the eighteenth century, so much that by the beginning of the nineteenth century they totaled only a little over 40,000
square miles. (Not all of this was in the Southeast; some was in
Arkansas Territory). As shown in table 6, further land cessions were
made in the initial decades of the nineteenth century. According to
Charles C. Royce, the Cherokees in the Southeast ceded 23,988.25
square miles of land from 1804 through 1819. At this point, they remained in possession of only 12,316 square miles in the Southeast
(Royce [1887] 1975:256). Their southeastern lands now encompassed
only the territory where the present states of North Carolina, Tennessee, Georgia, and Alabama more or less converge. (See map 2.)
Coinciding with this loss of land, but due to a variety of other
factors as well, particularly relocations during the wars of the previous century, the Cherokee settlement pattern had changed by this
time. On the one hand, the pattern of the location of Cherokee towns
had changed. As mentioned earlier, only the North Carolina Middle
Towns remained relatively intact by this time. The Cherokee Lower

Table 6. Nineteenth-Century Cherokee Eastern Land Cessions

Cherokee Treaty	Cession	Square Miles
Treaty of October 24, 1804, with United States	Tract in Georgia, known as Wafford's Settlement	135
Treaty of October 25, 1805, with United States	Tract in Kentucky and Tennessee, west of Tennessee River and Cumberland Mountain	8,118
Treaty of October 27, 1805, with United States	Tract in Tennessee of one section at Southwest Point	1.25
Treaty of January 7, 1806, with United States	Tract in Tennessee and Alabama, between Tennessee and Duck rivers	6,871
Treaty of March 22, 1816, with United States	Tract in northwest corner of South Carolina	148
Treaty of September 14, 1816, with United States	Tract in Alabama and Mississippi	3,433
Treaty of July 8, 1817, with United States	Tract in northeastern Georgia	583
	Tract in southern Tennessee	435
	Tracts in northern Alabama, between Cypress and Elk rivers, and above mouth of Spring Creek on Tennessee River	?
Treaty of February 27, 1819, with United States	Tract in northern Alabama	1,154
	Tracts in Tennessee	2,408
	Tract in North Carolina	1,542
	Tract in Georgia	837
Treaty of December 29, 1835, with United States	Tract in Alabama, Georgia, North Carolina, and Tennessee, being all remaining lands east of the Mississippi River	12,316

Source: Royce ([1887] 1975:2–3, 256).

Towns on the Savannah River had been dispersed, and the Cherokees had removed both their capital and their council fire from Echota to Ustanali because of a general encroachment of whites into the Upper Towns. As a consequence, the Cherokees had established new towns in Alabama and on the Coosa River as "refugee settlements" for tribespeople arriving from the east and the north.

The traditional Cherokee village pattern was also, if not broken up, at least modified. Douglas C. Wilms noted that by the 1830s Cherokee towns consisted of loose clusters of homesteads strung out over great distances and separated by surrounding woodland. He also asserted that nineteenth-century Cherokees viewed surrounding woodland as necessary to the functioning of a homestead: "Here, hogs and cattle could forage and small game could be hunted or trapped. Moreover, the woodland was a source of fuel, wild fruits and nuts, as well as building and fencing materials." This importance was reflected in Cherokee laws, which allowed individuals to clear and use as much land as they desired as long as they did not come nearer than a quarter of a mile to a neighbor. The dispersed pattern probably developed when the deerskin trade with Europeans altered the traditional social structure (Wilms 1974:51). The adoption of European farming techniques after the demise of the fur trade probably accelerated the pattern. In fact, at this time many Cherokees lived on isolated farms rather than in towns, whatever their pattern. It was even stated in the initial issue of the *United Brethren's Missionary Intelligencer* that "at present only that portion of the Cherokee nation, which is confessedly the most indigent and degraded continues to live in towns. The greater and more respectable part live on their plantations, and thus acquire those habits of industry and sobriety" (quoted in Morse [1822] 1970:155). Despite this tendency, Cherokee towns continued to exist in 1835, though perhaps modified from the earlier pattern as more variation appeared: towns continued, and perhaps even larger ones developed, but at the same time many Cherokees began to live on farms. In analyzing the 1835 Cherokee census, McLoughlin and Conser (1977:690–91) stated: "Using the various placenames for Cherokee settlements indicated by the census takers as they moved through the nation, the census yields a total of 129 'communities' (or Cherokee settlements) varying in size from one family with nine persons to 110 families with 830 persons; there was an average of twenty families per community."

At this same time the Cherokees were becoming formally organized more or less as a "state." In 1817 they created a bicameral legislature (Malone 1956:74–90), and ten years later, on July 26, 1827, they held a constitutional convention at New Echota (in what is now Georgia, where the Cherokee capital was situated after moving westward from Echota) and developed a national constitution. Charles R. Hicks was elected principal chief; John Ross was the new assistant chief (Mooney [1900] 1982:112–13). This could be said to have created the Cherokee Nation—the Eastern as opposed to eastern Cherokees having come into existence in 1813, as we see below, with the formal creation of the Western Cherokees.

At about this time, 1815, gold was discovered in the Cherokee Nation, in the upper Georgia area—ironically, by a Cherokee boy. In

1828 more gold was discovered, near present-day Dahlonega, Georgia, and, as Mooney ([1900] 1982:116) said, "the doom of the nation was sealed." Late in the same year the state of Georgia enacted legislation to "annex" Cherokee lands within its borders, to take effect on June 1, 1830. Eventually these Cherokee lands were "mapped out into counties and surveyed by state surveyors into 'land lots' of 160 acres each, and 'gold lots' of 40 acres, which were put up and distributed among the white citizens of Georgia by public lottery, each white citizen receiving a ticket." The 1828 legislation also extended the legal jurisdiction of Georgia over the Cherokee area: "All laws and customs established among the Cherokee were declared null and void, and no person of Indian blood or descent residing within the Indian country was henceforth to be allowed as a witness or party in any suit where a white man should be dependent." Soon "bands of armed men invaded the Cherokee country, forcibly seizing horses and cattle, taking possession of houses from which they had ejected the occupants, and assaulting the owners who dared make resistance" (Mooney [1900] 1982:117–18).

Meanwhile, the United States Congress passed the Indian Removal Act, on May 28, 1830 (see Prucha 1975:52–53). It provided for the exchange of American Indian lands in any United States state or territory, but especially in the southern United States, for lands west of the Mississippi River and for the removal of American Indians to western lands. President Andrew Jackson used the act very effectively to remove southern tribes and relocate them onto lands west of the Mississippi,[4] thus securing Indian lands east of the river for settlement by the expanding non-Indian population of the United States. (At this time, 1830, the total population of the United States was 12.87 million. Its total area was 1,754.6 thousand square miles; only 632.7 thousand square miles could be considered "settled," that is, occupied by two or more persons per square mile [Alterman 1969:209].)

Now subjected to continued harassment by Georgia and Georgians and pressure from the United States government to cede remaining lands and move west of the Mississippi, the Cherokee Nation in the Southeast resisted as best it could. It even took several cases to the United States Supreme Court, winning an important case involving the missionary Samuel A. Worcester, who resided on Cherokee lands with tribal permission. When he was arrested by the Georgia militia for refusing to take an oath supporting the laws of Georgia, Worcester and the Cherokee Nation maintained that Georgia had no right to interfere, since the Cherokees were a sovereign nation with a definite territory. The United States Supreme Court agreed with Worcester and the Cherokees—they ordered the state to release the missionary. Georgia refused. President Jackson is said to have replied, with reference to the chief justice: "John Marshall has made his decision; now let him enforce it" (quoted in Mooney [1900] 1982:120).

Three years of turmoil followed. A treaty between the Cherokee Nation and the United States government was eventually signed, not by the principal officers of the Cherokee Nation, but by such members of the numerically small "treaty party" as Major Ridge, Elias Boudinot, Stand Watie, and John Ridge. In this 1835 Treaty of New Echota, the Cherokees ceded their southeastern lands to the United States in exchange for lands in Indian Territory and $15 million. The formal leaders of the tribe under John Ross, now principal chief, protested strongly, but to no avail.

Westward Migrations

During these events of the early nineteenth century, some Cherokees had voluntarily moved to the West, though often with the encouragement of the United States government, beginning from about 1806 to 1809 (McLoughlin 1984:36; also McLoughlin, 1975). Most who emigrated joined Cherokees who had moved there in the previous century.

This encouragement produced a "removal crisis" for the Cherokees during the period 1806–9, whereby some groups wanted to move but others wanted to stay (see McLoughlin, 1975). In response, the agent for the Cherokees, Colonel Meigs, "tried to coerce the tribe into total removal to the West" (McLoughlin 1984:36). In 1808 Colonel Meigs "was instructed by the Secretary of War to use every effort to obtain their consent to an exchange of their lands for a tract beyond the Mississippi" (Mooney [1900] 1982:101). A group of traditional Eastern Cherokees became interested in the proposal, thinking it might be a way to escape the encroaching non-Indians:

In that year, 1808, the eastern nation, having already become divided, under the designation of "Upper and Lower towns," sent deputations to Washington as representatives of both parties, who submitted a proposition to the President of the United States for a formal and final separation of the tribe, by "establishing a division line between the Upper and Lower towns." The one party desiring to remain east of the Mississippi, and begin the "establishment of fixed laws and regular government," and become "cultivators of the soil." The other party expressed their anxiety to remove west of the Mississippi, and select a country there, which they would accept in exchange for their portion of the country east. (*New American State Papers* [1789–1860] 1972, 12:255–56)

Moreover, United States president Jefferson authorized those wanting to emigrate to send an "exploring expedition" west. He promised also that "when this party had 'found a country suiting the emigrants and not claimed by other Indians,' the United States would 'arrange with them the exchange of that, for a just portion of the country they leave, and to a part of which, proportioned to their numbers, they have a right'" (*New American State Papers* [1789–1860] 1972, 12:256).

In 1809, at government expense, a delegation of southern Cherokees made a trip to the Arkansas and White rivers to inspect the land. Their view of the land was favorable; a number stayed, "and settlements were immediately commenced, under sanction of the promise made by the President" (*New American State Papers* [1789–1860] 1972, 12:256). This group perhaps numbered about 300 and may have been led by Chief Tahlonteeskee (Everett 1985:38). (Reportedly, Cherokees in Arkansas numbered 2,000 in 1811 [Everett 1985:112]. There may have been more.) In the winter of 1811–12 an earthquake along the St. Francis River caused much flooding. At this time those Cherokees who had located there in earlier years fled to join the new immigrants in the territory between the Arkansas and White rivers (Starr [1922] 1967:38–39; also Washburn 1910:22). In addition to these, other Cherokees in the East intended to remove. Despite their apparent eagerness to migrate, however, they did not do so because funds were lacking: "The matter was held in abeyance for several years, during which period families and individuals removed to the western country at their own expense until, before the year 1817, they numbered in all two or three thousand souls" (Mooney [1900] 1982:102).

Whatever the numbers of Cherokees west of the Mississippi River, they had increased to such an extent that an agent, Major William L. Lovely, was assigned to them. Lovely also reported other Indians in the area besides Cherokees: Choctaws, Delawares, Miamis, Pawnees, and Quapaws (Everett 1985:38–39). These were in addition to the Osage Indians indigenous to the area, part of whom were still there.

By 1813 the Cherokees here had also established themselves as a more or less formal, separate group and had become the Arkansas, or Western Cherokees, as opposed to simply western Cherokees (Mooney [1900] 1982:102; Washburn 1910:22). According to Emmett Starr, the newly created formal group of Cherokees established a capital in 1813 at Takatoka's village, Takatoka being the principal chief of the Western Cherokees from 1813 to 1818, having succeeded the Bowl (John Bowles) (Starr [1922] 1967:39, 26).

Late in 1817 another treaty with the Eastern Cherokees was ratified at Turkeytown, calling for the exchange of lands with the Cherokees. To encourage voluntary emigration from the Southeast, article 6 of the treaty stipulated:

> The United States do also bind themselves to give to all the poor warriors who may remove to the western side of the Mississippi river, one rifle gun and ammunition, one blanket, and one brass kettle, or, in lieu of the brass kettle, a beaver trap, which is to be considered as a full compensation for the improvements which they may leave; which articles are to be delivered at such point as the President of the United States may direct: and to aid in the removal of the emigrants, they further agree to furnish flat bottomed boats and provisions sufficient for that purpose: and to those emigrants whose improvements add real value to their lands, the United States agree to pay a full valuation for the same, which is to be ascertained by a commissioner appointed by the President of the United States for that purpose, and paid for as soon after the ratification of this treaty as practicable. The boats and provisions promised to the emigrants are to be furnished by the agent on the Tennessee river, at such time and place as the emigrants may notify him of; and it shall be his duty to furnish the same. (Kappler 1904–79, 2:143; see also Institute for the Development of Indian Law, n.d.b:23)

Immediately after the treaty was signed, over 700 Cherokees enrolled for removal (Royce [1887] 1975:89–90), and 1,102 actually emigrated. Although some have asserted a total of over 6,000 Cherokees in the West by 1819, this is an exaggeration; other reports placed the total at 5,000 (see New American State Papers [1789–1860] 1972,

2:679), and still others at 3,500 (see Royce [1887] 1975:90; Mooney [1900] 1982:106).

In 1819 the naturalist Thomas Nuttall ascended the Arkansas River. He described various Cherokee settlements along it, in the general vicinity of present-day Dardenelle, Arkansas. One, in the Galley hills, he described as consisting "of about a dozen families, who, in the construction and furniture of the houses, and in the management of their farms, imitate the whites, and appeared to be progressing towards civilization, were it not for their baneful attachment to whiskey." Elsewhere, Nuttall indicated that "along either bank the lands are generally elevated and fertile, and pretty thickly scattered with the cabins and farms of the Cherokee" (Thwaites 1905, 13:174).

Article 3 of the 1817 treaty specified a census of all the Cherokees, in order to distribute an annuity payment:

> A census shall be taken of the whole Cherokee nation, during the month of June, in the year of our Lord one thousand eight hundred and eighteen, in the following manner, viz: That the census of those on the east side of the Mississippi river, who declare their intention of remaining, shall be taken by a commissioner appointed by the President of the United States, and a commissioner appointed by the Cherokees on the Arkansas river, and those remaining there, and who, at that time, declare their intention of remaining there, shall be taken by a commissioner appointed by the President of the United States, and one appointed by the Cherokees east of the Mississippi river. (Kappler 1904–79, 2:142; see also Institute for the Development of Indian Law, n.d.b:24)

The census of the Western Cherokees was never conducted; it was dispensed with in a treaty of 1819 between the Eastern Cherokees and the United States government. At that time it was decided, and eventually agreed to by the Western Cherokees, that a census was not necessary for distributing an annuity payment. Rather, it was agreed "that the annuity payment to the Cherokee nation shall be paid, two-thirds to the Cherokees east of the Mississippi, and one-third to the Cherokees west of that river, as it is estimated that those who have emigrated, and who have enrolled for emigration, constitute one-third of the whole nation" (Kappler 1904–79, 2:179; see also Institute for the Development of Indian Law, n.d.b:29).

After this time other emigrations also occurred (see Baker 1977).

By then—that is, by 1818—the Western Cherokees had acquired former Osage lands, called the "Lovely purchase" after Major Lovely. The boundaries of the area were as follows: "Beginning at the Arkansaw river, at where the present Osage boundary line strikes the river at Frog Bayou; then up the Arkansaw and Verdigris, to the falls of Verdigris river; thence, eastwardly, to the said Osage boundary line, at a point twenty leagues north from the Arkansaw river; and, with that line, to the place of beginning" (Kappler 1904–79, 2:167; see also Institute for the Development of Indian Law, n.d.a:43). Shortly thereafter there was another emigration, not from the East but of Cherokees in the West. In 1819–20 the Bowl and sixty families of his followers moved to Texas, forsaking their village south of the Arkansas River, between Shoal and Petit Jean creeks. According to Starr ([1922] 1967:40), they moved because their village was outside the territory ceded to the Cherokees by the treaty of 1817 and because they wanted to live in Spanish territory. In 1822 they reportedly numbered 300: 100 "warriors" and 200 women and children (see Washburn 1910:145–64).

In 1824 the Western Cherokee lands were divided into four districts, and two representatives from each were chosen to constitute a national committee (Wardell [1938] 1977:6–7). Their national capital was at Piney, on Piney Creek, north of the Arkansas River in what is now Arkansas (Starr [1922] 1967:39). As Wardell wrote, this "began their national existence with written laws and it was not long after their establishing a government that the United States sent them a subagent" ([1938] 1977:7). At this time they may be called the Cherokee Nation West rather than Arkansas Cherokees or Western Cherokees.

This western land was given up later in a treaty of 1828, and as a result of increasing white settlement in the area, the Western Cherokees moved farther west to more-or-less permanent lands. The Cherokee Nation West established a new capital at Tahlonteeskee on the Illinois River, near the present town of Gore, Oklahoma (Starr [1922] 1967:40). It was named after Chief Tahlonteeskee, who in the early 1800s had led a band of some 300 Cherokee emigrants from the East. Six years later, on November 4, 1834, perhaps in preparation for increased immigrations from the East, they elected a keeper of public records: "Resolved by the National Committee and Council, in General Council Convened, That William Thornton, be, and he is hereby appointed and authorized to take charge of the National papers and documents of the Cherokee Nation, and the clerk of the Chiefs, and the clerk of the National Committee and Council shall be, and are hereby required to render to said person all the public papers and documents (Chief's papers excepted) which may be, now or hereafter, in their possession—Tah-lon-tee-skee, Nov. 4th, 1834, approved—John Jolly" (Washburn 1910:123).

After the treaty of 1828 other emigrations occurred, in large part because of conflicts between the Cherokee Nation and the state of Georgia, though Cherokees from other areas emigrated as well. For example, there was reported in 1828 "the emigration of four hundred and thirty-one Indians and seventy-nine slaves, comparatively few of whom were from Georgia. Nine months later three hundred and forty-six persons had emigrated from within the limits of that State" (Royce [1887] 1975:130). Georgia, of course, was eager for the Cherokees to leave. As a result of pressure from that state, the United States government inserted an inducement for emigration in the treaty of 1828, similar to the one in the treaty of 1817: "To each Head of a Cherokee family now residing within the chartered limits of Georgia, or of either of the States, East of the Mississippi, who may desire to remove West, shall be given, on enrolling himself for emigration, a good Rifle, a Blanket, and Kettle, and five pounds of Tobacco: (and to each member of his family one Blanket,) also, a just compensation for the property he may abandon, to be assessed by persons to be appointed by the President of the United States" (Kappler 1904–79, 2:290; see also Institute for the Development of Indian Law, n.d.b:33). Reportedly this "had but little effect in producing emigration" (*New American State Papers* [1789–1860] 1972, 12:267). Grant Foreman (1932:231, 244) noted, however, that 500 Cherokees emigrated in 1830 and 626 left in the spring of 1831, in addition to those listed above.

Events after 1835

After the treaty of 1835—the Treaty of New Echota —the Cherokees were divided into three more-or-less distinct large groups: two still in the East, one in the West. In the West were the "old settlers," those who had emigrated across the Mississippi River and formed their own formal government—the Cherokee Nation West or Western Cherokees; in the East was the Cherokee Nation, divided into the "treaty party," the small group who had signed and approved the Treaty of New Echota, and the "Ross party," or "antitreaty party," who opposed the Treaty of New Echota and removal west and were by far the largest of the three groups and in control of the formal Cherokee Nation—except, of course, for signing treaties with the United States government. (There were also numbers of Cherokees in Texas and in North Carolina, but not members of the Cherokee Nation.) In accordance with the Treaty of New Echota, the two eastern Cherokee Nation groups were to be removed within two years. This did not happen, at least for the large majority of the Eastern Cherokees, those of the "Ross party." Instead, most Cherokees in the East remained in their homeland, still not believing they could be forced to relocate. As James Mooney noted ([1900] 1982:129), only some 2,000 Cherokees departed for the West—mainly members of the "treaty party."[5]

Most of these traveled under United States government supervision. For example, one party of 466, half of them children, left Ross's Landing (at present-day Chattanooga, Tennessee) on March 1, 1837:

> They descended the Tennessee River to Decatur, Alabama, from whence an early railroad carried them to Tuscumbia, thereby avoiding the dangerous and all but impassable Muscle Shoals. There they again embarked on the Tennessee River on the steamboat *Newark* and two sixty ton keel boats in town.
>
> They descended the Tennessee, Ohio, and Mississippi rivers and ascended the Arkansas River as far as Little Rock; there the diminished depth of the water necessitated the exchange of the *Newark* for the steamboat *Revenue* which continued up the river with their keel boats. As soon as they had crossed the line into Indian Territory the emigrants were put ashore in the Cherokee Nation on the north bank of the river along which they located themselves and established new homes. (Lillybridge 1931:232–33)

Another group of 365 Cherokees departed on October 14, 1837, under the direction of Major B. B. Cannon. Fifteen of the emigrants died before reaching Indian Territory, perhaps mainly from diarrhea, malaria, and dysentery (Foreman 1932:280–83). Some Cherokees emigrated at this time using their own resources, perhaps believing that choosing routes according to the climate and the game available, and traveling in small parties, would be safer than the government-sponsored migrations (Howard 1970:76). This still left almost 15,000 Cherokees in the Southeast. In 1838 General Winfield Scott was sent to oversee their removal. On May 10, 1838, Scott wrote to the Cherokees stating his intentions:

Chiefs, head-men, warriors! Will you then, by resistance, compel us to resort to arms? God forbid! Or will you, by flight, seek to hide yourselves in mountains and forests, and thus oblige us to hunt you down? Remember that, in pursuit, it may be impossible to avoid conflicts. The blood of the white man or the blood of the red man may be spilt and, if spilt, however accidentally, it may be impossible for the discreet and humane among you, or among us, to prevent a general war and carnage. Think of this my Cherokee brethren! I am an old warrior, and I have been present at many a scene of slaughter; but spare me, I beseech you, the horror of wit-nessing the destruction of the Cherokees. (*New American State Papers* [1789–1860] 1972, 10:126)

What happened next has been described by James Mooney:

Under Scott's orders the troops were disposed at various points throughout the Cherokee country, where stockade forts were erected for gathering in and holding the Indians preparatory to re-moval. From these, squads of troops were sent to search out with rifle and bayonet every small cabin hidden away in the coves or by the sides of mountain streams, to seize and bring in as prisoners all the occupants, however or wherever they might be found. Fami-lies at dinner were startled by the sudden gleam of bayonets in the doorway and rose up to be driven with blows and oaths along the weary miles of trail that led to the stockade. Men were seized in their fields or going along the road, women were taken from their wheels and children from their play. In many cases, on turning for one last look as they crossed the ridge, they saw their homes in flames, fired by the lawless rabble that followed on the heels of the soldiers to loot and pillage. So keen were these outlaws on the scent that in some instances they were driving off the cattle and other stock of the Indians almost before the soldiers had fairly started their owners in the other direction. Systematic hunts were made by the same men for Indian graves, to rob them of the silver pendants and other valuables deposited with the dead. (Mooney [1900] 1982:130)

John G. Burnett, a soldier who participated in the removal, described other incidents:

Men working in the fields were arrested and driven to the stock-ades. Women were dragged from their homes by soldiers whose language they could not understand. Children were often sepa-

rated from their parents and driven into the stockades with the
sky for a blanket and the earth for a pillow. And often the old
and infirm were prodded with bayonets to hasten them to the
stockades.

In one home death had come during the night, a little sad faced
child had died and was lying on a bear skin couch and some women
were preparing the little body for burial. All were arrested and
driven out leaving the child in the cabin. I don't know who buried
the body.

In another home was a frail Mother, apparently a widow and
three small children, one just a baby. When told that she must go
the Mother gathered the children at her feet, prayed an humble
prayer in her native tongue, patted the old family dog on the head,
told the faithful creature good-bye, with a baby strapped on her
back and leading a child with each hand started on her exile. But
the task was too great for that frail Mother. A stroke of heart fail-
ure relieved her sufferings. She sunk and died with her baby on her
back, and her other two children clinging to her hands. (Burnett
1978:183)

A report in *Niles' National Register* (1838) stated: "The captors sometimes drove the people with whooping and bellowing, like cattle
through rivers, allowing them no time even to take off their shoes
and stockings. Many, when arrested, were not so much as permitted
to gather up their clothes."

According to Scott, 2,500 Cherokees had been made prisoner in
Georgia by May 30 (*New American State Papers* [1769–1860] 1972,
10:127), some 4,000 by June 4, and all were likely to be captured
in another week, "with the exception of a few families and refugees
in the mountains, whom we may not be able to collect in a week
or two more," said Scott (*New American State Papers* [1769–1860]
1972, 10:130). Scott also reported that by June 12 some 1,500 to 2,000
Cherokees from the states of North Carolina, Tennessee, and Alabama would have "presented themselves for voluntary emigration"
(*New American State Papers* [1769–1860] 1972, 10:130). On June 18
Scott wrote: "I . . . am happy to say that the militia of Georgia are
now assembling for discharge, the Indians having been removed from
that State. In the other three States, the collections by the troops
for emigration are rapidly advancing, and must be completed in a
few weeks, if not in eight or ten days" (*New American State Papers*
[1769–1860] 1972, 10:140).

Initially the Cherokees were put in stockades constructed on their land. James Mooney listed the following "stockade forts":

In North Carolina, Fort Lindsay, on the south side of the Tennessee River at the junction of Nantahala, in Swain county; Fort Scott, at Aquone, farther up Nantahala river, in Macon county; Fort Montgomery, at Robbinsville, in Graham county; Fort Hembrie, at Hayesville, in Clay county; Fort Delaney, at Valleytown, in Cherokee county; Fort Butler, at Murphy, in the same county. In Georgia, Fort Scudder, on Frogtown creek, north of Dahlonega, in Lumpkin county; Fort Gilmer, near Ellijay, in Gilmer county; Fort Coosawatee, in Murray county; Fort Talking-rock, near Jasper, in Pickens county; Fort Buffington, near Canton, in Cherokee county. In Tennessee, Fort Cass, at Calhoun, on Hiwassee river, in McMinn county. In Alabama, Fort Turkeytown, on Coosa river, at Center, in Cherokee county. (Mooney [1891] 1982:221)

The smaller groups of captured Cherokees were eventually aggregated at three locations: Old Agency, on the Hiwassee River, near present Calhoun, Tennessee; Ross's Landing, at present Chattanooga, Tennessee; and Gunter's Landing, at present Guntersville, Alabama. According to the *Niles' National Register* (1838), "the scenes of distress exhibited at Ross's Landing defy all description. On the arrival there of the Indians, the horses brought by some of them were demanded by the commissioners of Indian property, to be given up for the purpose of being sold. The owners refusing to give them up,— men, women, children *and horses* were driven promiscuously into one large pen, and the horses taken out by force, and cried off to the highest bidder, *and sold for almost nothing.*"

The Cherokees suffered greatly from disease as well during their stay: there was "general sickness" and "serious mortality" from measles, whooping cough, pleurisy, and "bilious fevers." At one stockade there were "upwards of 4,000 collected," but only three physicians (Howard 1970:77).

According to Mooney ([1900] 1982:131), the number initially totaled about 5,000. By the end of June, most of the Cherokees had been rounded up for removal;[6] some say about 1,000 managed to avoid capture (and eventual removal) by hiding in the almost inaccessible mountains. John R. Finger concluded:

Approximately eleven hundred North Carolina Cherokees avoided removal by hiding out in the mountains or taking advantage of a treaty provision allowing certain Indians to stay in their home states if they wished to become citizens. Mostly full-bloods, they resided in several scattered settlements in the western part of the state—on land owned by friendly whites, on unsurveyed state lands, and, in a few cases, on their own property. Some seven hundred lived around Quallatown, near present-day Cherokee, with smaller concentrations along the Cheoah, Valley, and Hiwassee rivers. An additional three hundred or so Cherokees lived in nearby areas of Georgia, Tennessee, and Alabama, including a number of mixed-bloods and whites who were Cherokees only by marriage. In general they were more acculturated than their North Carolina brethren, often owning their own land and sometimes a few slaves. (Finger 1980:17)

The 1835 residences of most of those escaping removal are listed in table 7.

Many of the first captured were taken by steamer down the Tennessee and Ohio rivers to the far side of the Mississippi, then continued overland to Indian Territory (Mooney [1900] 1982:131). On August 18, 1838, the *Niles' National Register* reported: "Then came the shipping off to the west. The agent endeavored to induce the people to go into the boats voluntarily; but none would agree to go. The agent then struck a line through the camp;—the soldiers rushed in and drove the devoted victims into the boats, regardless of the cries and agonies of the poor helpless sufferers. In this cruel work, the most painful separations of families occurred.—Children were sent off and parents left, and so of other relations."

The Cherokees so removed suffered greatly. One party of approximately 875, which left on June 12, had 73 or 74 deaths, 56 or 57 reportedly occurring on a 161-mile stretch of the journey lasting some twenty-four days. A doctor on the journey most frequently attributed the deaths to "flux"—diarrhea or dysentery—severe diarrhea with blood and mucus. The doctor also blamed the weather and the practice of frequently bathing in cold water and eating green fruit, but two scholars cite contaminated water and lack of precautions against the spread of bacterial infections (Howard and Allen 1975:352, 354).

The removal, in the heat of the summer, was so arduous that the Cherokee national council asked General Scott to let the Cherokee conduct their own emigration "in the fall, after the sickly season had ended" (Mooney [1900] 1982:131–32). One group—from the "darker

Table 7. 1835 Residences of Cherokees Who
Avoided Removal

Residence	Families	Individuals
Alabama	1	4
Alarka	10	36
Aquona	14	60
Beaver Dam	4	16
Brasstown	3	9
Buffalo (Snowbird)	12	48
Cheoih	19	78
Cherokee City	1	3
Ducktown, Tennessee	2	6
Fighting Creek	3	13
Hanging Dog	16	63
Hiwassee River	6	20
Little High Tower, Georgia	1	6
Little Hiwassee, Georgia	4	17
Nantahala	18	71
Nottala	6	34
Peachtree	2	11
Princess Creek	2	4
Qualla	54	229
Qualla Deep Creek	3	19
Shooting Creek	8	30
Stekoih	7	27
Talula (Cheioh Tulula)	5	23
Turtletown, Tennessee	2	6
Tusquitta	4	17
Union City, Georgia	3	9
Valley River	24	94
Vengeance Creek	3	14
Residence not listed	6	18
Total	247	999

Source: 1835 residences . . . (1979:240).

Figure 1. *The Trail of Tears*, by Robert Lindneux. Courtesy of Woolaroc Museum, Bartlesville, Oklahoma.

Table 8. Detachments of Cherokees during Trail of Tears Removal

Detachment	Departed	Number	Arrived	Number
Hair Conrad	August 23, 1838	729	January 17, 1839	654
Elijah Hicks	September 1, 1838	858	January 4, 1839	744
Jesse Bushyhead	September 3, 1838	950	February 27, 1839	898
John Benge	September 28, 1838	1,200	January 17, 1839	1,132
Situwakee	September 7, 1838	1,250	February 2, 1839	1,033
Old Field	September 24, 1838	983	February 23, 1839	921
Moses Daniel	September 30, 1838	1,035	March 2, 1839	924
Choowalooka	September 14, 1838	1,150	March 1839	970
James Brown	September 10, 1838	850	March 5, 1839	717
George Hicks	September 7, 1838	1,118	March 14, 1839	1,039
Richard Taylor	September 20, 1838	1,029	March 24, 1839	942
Peter Hildebrand	October 23, 1838	1,766	March 24, 1839	1,311
John Drew	December 5, 1838	231	March 18, 1839	219

Source: Emigration detachments (1978:186–87).

part of the nation," as they expressed it—made a personal request to General Scott: "We are Indians. Our wives and children are Indians, and some people do not pity Indians. But if we are Indians we have hearts that feel. We do not want to see our wives and children die. We do not want to die ourselves and leave them widows and orphans. We are in trouble sir our hearts are very heavy. The darkness of night is before us" (quoted in Young 1975:125–26).

The request was eventually granted, but not before more than 2,000 additional Cherokees had been removed, with 219 of them reportedly dying in the process (Young 1975:126). Nevertheless, "in this way the remainder, enrolled at about 13,000 (including negro slaves), started on the long march overland late in the fall," although "a very few went by the river route" (Mooney [1900] 1982:132). (See fig. 1.) The Cherokee emigrants journeyed in thirteen recorded groups averaging about 1,000 each, although the exact number in each group was a matter of some dispute. (See table 8.) Most traveled north and west across Tennessee and Kentucky, across southern Illinois and Missouri, and then into northeastern Indian Territory. (See map 3.)

Deaths were frequent during the journeys, from starvation, cold, hardship, deliberate killings, and accidents. According to Grant Foreman, many Cherokees also died from measles, cholera, dysentery,

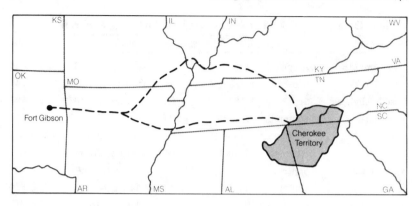

3. The Trail of Tears. After Morris, Goins, and McReynolds ([1965] 1986:20).

and whooping cough; other diseases included colds, influenza, diarrhea, fevers, and gonorrhea. Young children and the aged suffered particularly (Foreman 1932:262–63, 283): "A very small percentage of the old and infirm, and the very young survived the hardships of that ghastly undertaking" (Foreman 1934:282).

Deaths did not cease when the Cherokees arrived at new lands in Indian Territory; to the contrary, they likely intensified. Apparently most migrants did reach their new homelands, but a series of epidemic diseases struck and a great number died,[7] since they had no doctors or medicine (Doran 1975–76:497; see also Young 1979:135–37, n. 13).[8] Seemingly one of the diseases was smallpox: on December 14, 1838, T. Hartley Crawford, head of the Office of Indian Affairs, wrote to J. R. Poinsett, the secretary of war, about an epidemic of smallpox among the Cherokees and other Indians in Indian Territory:

A recently received letter states that the small-pox still prevails among the Choctaws, Chickasaws, Cherokees, Creeks, and Seminoles, and that its ravages, at the latest dates, were not arrested on the upper Missouri. The measures taken heretofore have, no doubt, saved many lives, and been useful in limiting the spread of this dreadful disease. The apathy which is manifested by the Indians, and their peculiar circumstances, lead to the apprehension that it will only cease to destroy them when there remain no subjects for its operation. Humanity calls upon us to interpose such relief as we can extend to them. The only beneficial step in our power is to order the use of vaccine matter by physicians paid for the purpose by the United States. The best plan that suggests itself to me is, to make the amount of compensation depend on the number vaccinated; to pay so much, say six cents, or less, or more, as may be deemed best, for each individual; the account to be settled on a roll of the names returned to the nearest agent, who will have the best means of knowing its correctness, and certify it to the Department. The sum heretofore appropriated for this object is exhausted. There is no fund for paying the expenses of such measures, and I respectfully recommend that an appropriation of $5,000 be asked of Congress, to defray them. (*New American State Papers* [1789–1860] 1972, 3:126–27)

Five years earlier, $200 had been appropriated to vaccinate the Cherokees, but apparently few, if any, were vaccinated (see, for example, *New American State Papers* [1789–1860] 1972, 3:21). Major General Ethan Allen Hitchcock (1930:89), traveling through the area in the early 1840s, heard that many Cherokees died in 1839 "for want of provisions."

Population Losses

How many Cherokees died as a result of the Trail of Tears? We do not know. William H. Thomas, an attorney for the Eastern Cherokees, asserted 2,000 had died by 1838. In his words, "At the time the emigration closed, in 1838, it was ascertained that at the places the Cherokee were collected for emigration, and when on their journey to the west, about 2,000 died, and thereby diminishing the number, embraced in the census, from 16,737 to 14,737" (*New American State Papers* [1789–1860] 1972, 11:778). This, of course, takes no account of those who died after the removal, say, during the initial year of their relocation in Indian Territory. James Mooney attempted to assess total mortality:

It is difficult to arrive at any accurate statement of the number of Cherokee who died as a result of the Removal. According to the official figures those who removed under the direction of Ross lost over 1,600 on the journey. The proportionate mortality among these previously removed under military supervision was probably greater, as it was their suffering that led to the proposition of the Cherokee national officers to take charge of the emigration.

Hundreds died in the stockades and the waiting camps, chiefly by reason of the rations furnished, which were of flour and other provisions to which they were unaccustomed and which they did not know how to prepare properly. Hundreds of others died soon after their arrival in Indian Territory, from sickness and exposure on the journey. Altogether it is asserted, probably with reason, that over 4,000 Cherokee died as the direct result of the removal. (Mooney [1900] 1982:133)

The figure of 4,000 deaths *directly related to removal* is generally accepted by more recent scholars, though some consider it too high. Englund (1974:81, 88–89) concluded that only about 2,000 Cherokees died. However, Foreman (1932:312) asserted that "all told, 4,000 died during the course of capture and detention in temporary stockades and the removal itself"; according to Howard and Allen (1975:354), "more than 4,000 Eastern Cherokees died during the removal or within a year of their arrival in the West"; and Knight (1954–55:425) indicated that "by the time the transplantation was completed in 1839, approximately four thousand Cherokees had died." Mary Young (1975:126) even concluded: "More than a quarter of those collected in May and June perished in the camps, on the steamboats, along the trail and in their period of adjustment to an area whose garrison at Fort Gibson was called the 'charnel house of the army.'"

A similar figure is given when scholars place mortality in the context of Cherokee population size at the time, either the approximately 16,000 removed or the total tribal number of over 20,000, which includes early westward emigrants as well as those who escaped removal. Thus Blue (1974:v) wrote, "It is commonly noted that 16,000 Cherokees were removed, 4,000 of whom died on what is called the Trail of Tears." And Swanton ([1946] 1979:113) asserted that Cherokee removal caused "intense suffering on the part of the Indians and the loss of nearly one-fourth of their numbers." The number lost here would be about 4,000 or 5,000, depending on whether he was referring to the 16,000 removed or the total of 20,000.

The source of Mooney's figure of 4,000 is not known. I have seen two mentions of the figure earlier than Mooney's report. One is in a letter written in 1890 by a soldier who, as a young man, participated in the removal. He wrote (Burnett 1978:182) that there were "four-thousand silent graves reaching from the foothills of the

Smoky Mountains to what is known as Indian Territory in the West."
An earlier mention, perhaps the original, dates from 1839, as cited
in Wilkins (1970:315; see also Young 1979:135–37, n. 13; Wilkins
1986:328): "No one knew exactly how many Cherokees had perished in the ordeal. The trail was especially hard on babies, children,
and the aged. Four thousand, nearly one-fifth of the entire Cherokee
population, is the estimate usually cited, one made by Dr. Butler the
Missionary."[9]

> Doctor Elizur Butler served as a physician to an emigrant party
> and wrote on October 10th, 1838, from McMinnville, Tennessee.
> He estimated that "two thousand or more, out of 15,000, had died
> since they were taken from their homes to the camps in June last;
> that is one eighth of the whole number, in less than four months."
> After burying 40 members of his own detachment by the journey's
> end on January 25, 1839, Doctor Butler revised his estimate of the
> total to 4,000 dead. By March, more parties had arrived west and
> Butler returned to Red Clay, Tennessee, to close the mission sta-
> tion and bring his wife west. In the belief that nearly one half had
> died during the winter from the estimated 1,000 hiding out in the
> mountains, Butler again raised his estimate to 4,600 Cherokees
> dead. (Howard 1970:79)

Given the speculative nature of the 4,000 Cherokee deaths during the Trail of Tears, I attempted a new estimate of their mortality,
based in part on a new perspective (Thornton 1984). I argued that
another way of looking at the demographic effects of Trail of Tears
is to compare Cherokee population size after the Trail of Tears with
what it would have been had removal not occurred. I used the year
1840 for the end of the Trail of Tears period, since population losses
were thought to have been heavy during the first year after all groups
of emigrants arrived in Indian Territory. Thus the removal period was
from 1835 to 1840. For example, Howard states:

> All residents in the western Cherokee Nation encountered many
> problems, but health matters assumed major importance. Cholera
> epidemics struck Fort Gibson and the surrounding area on several
> occasions before 1837. Many of the early mission families also
> were decimated by illnesses resembling typhoid fever. A smallpox
> epidemic afflicted the nearby Chickasaws and Choctaws in 1838.
> The western superintendent, William Armstrong, considered the

northern part of the Cherokee Nation more salubrious than other
areas of the Indian Territory. The Reverend Samuel Worcester, it
should be noted, however, moved soon after his arrival in 1835
from the post on the bottom land near the forks of the Illinois River
to higher ground at Park Hill three miles away, because he wished
to escape the prevailing ague and fevers. The western superintendent's official report for 1838 emphasized the usual process of
acclimation as reason for the high rate of illness among the new
Cherokee migrants during their first years. (Howard 1970:80)

At issue in my analysis was a lack of population data on the Cherokees for the year 1840, after the Trail of Tears had ended. Therefore
I had to make a projection forward in time from population sizes at
earlier dates. (I did so using the formula for a logarithmic curve: log
$y = a + bx$; where y is population size, a is y-intercept, b is slope,
and x is date.) Based on this projection, the Cherokee population in
1840 would have been 23,170 had the Trail of Tears not occurred.
In other words, the Cherokees would likely have had an increase
for the five-year period of 1,628 from the 1835 Cherokee population
of an estimated 21,542 (16,542 Cherokees in the Southeast plus an
estimated 5,000 in the West) (see Thornton 1984:295, table 1, 297,
table 2). According to another population projection (also based on a
logarithmic curve), this one backward in time from later nineteenth-
century population, the total Cherokee population in 1840 was only
13,032 (Thornton 1984:297, table 2).[10]

These two population projections are shown in figure 2. Subtract-
ing one from the other, 10,138 more Cherokees would have been
alive in 1840, according to my two projections, had removal not occurred. Of course some of these potential Cherokee lives represent
nonbirths, and some probably represent emigrants out of the population. Nevertheless, mortality from the Trail of Tears, including the
first year in Indian Territory particularly, seems even more severe
than heretofore realized. Our knowledge at the moment makes it
impossible to state the mortality of the Trail of Tears with any precision, and it is consequently not possible to state accurately the size
of the Cherokee population in 1840. As I indicated above, it may be
estimated at 13,032.

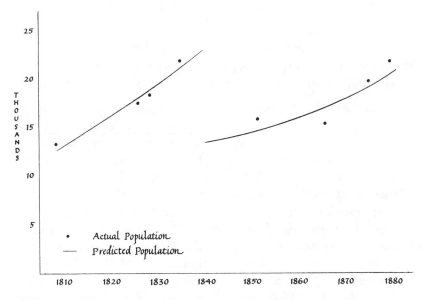

Figure 2. Possible population losses during the Trail of Tears. Source: Thornton (1984:296, fig. 1).

POLITICAL TURMOIL

After the removal of almost all the Cherokees to new lands in Indian Territory, a period of severe political turmoil occurred. In 1939 the Cherokee Nation West capital was moved for a short time to Takatoka (or Double Springs) on what was known as Fourteen Mile Creek (Starr [1922] 1967:40). On June 3, 1839, a council was called there to bring the two groups of Cherokees in the West together: the Cherokee Nation West, the "old settlers," who had now incorporated the early emigrants after 1835 (those of the "treaty party"); and the Ross party, who emigrated after 1835. By June 10 some 6,000 Cherokees had assembled at the meeting grounds. Various proposals were made to join the two governments, and "on June 15, the chief of the western Cherokee, together with William Thornton, Clerk of the National Council, wrote Agent Stokes asking for annuities, as well as any other money due them." However, John Ross and his party refused to accept the proposals of the Cherokee Nation West, and the national council was dismissed (Wardell [1938] 1977:15).

Revenge

John Ross and his party stayed at the council grounds until June 21, then the meeting was dissolved. The next day, June 22, Elias Boudinot, Major Ridge, and his son John Ridge were killed:

Before daylight on the morning of Saturday, June 22, 1839 the home of John Ridge, near the northwest corner of Arkansas, was surrounded, entered and he was dragged into the yard where two men held his arms while others of their party stabbed him repeatedly and then severed his jugular vein. A few hours later during the same morning while his father, Major Ridge, was traveling southward along the Cherokee Nation–Arkansas line road, he was fired on by an ambush party and killed. This was some twenty-five or thirty miles from the scene of the meurder [sic] of the son. At about the same time as the killing of Major Ridge, Elias Boudinot was shingling a new house near his residence and withing [sic] two miles of the residence of Chief John Ross. Three Cherokees appeared and requested medicine of a sick child of one of the party. Mr. Boudinot had studied medicine so that he could give gratuitous services and medicines to the needy. He started with them to get the required treatment when one of the three stepping behind stuck him in the spine with a bowie knife and his groan was the signal for the others to dispatch him with tomahawks. The place of his death was about thirty miles from the murder of Major Ridge and fifty miles from the assassination of John Ridge. (Starr [1922] 1967:113; see also Foreman, ed., 1934)

Boudinot and the Ridges were killed for having signed the Treaty of New Echota of 1835, and "in accordance with the law of the Nation —three times formulated, and still in existence—which made it treason, punishable with death, to cede away lands except by act of the general council of the Nation" (Mooney [1900] 1982:134). According to one report, others were also marked for death: Stand Watie, James Starr, John A. Bell, and George W. Adair (see Wardell [1938] 1977:17). It is said that members of John Ross's party drew lots to determine who would kill the men, but that John Ross was not to know anything about it.

An Act of Union

After the deaths of Boudinot and the Ridges, another convention was eventually held at Fort Gibson, under the leadership of John Ross and the newly emigrated Cherokees. On July 12, 1839, an act of union was signed by the presidents and chiefs of the separate groups of Cherokees: " 'George Lowry, President of the Eastern Cherokees' and 'George Guess (Sequoyah), President of the Western Cherokees,' as well as other headmen of both groups. Among these were 'John Ross, Principal Chief of Eastern Cherokees' and 'John Looney, Acting Principal Chief of the Western Cherokees'" (Wardell [1938] 1977:28). The act stated: "We, the people comprising the Eastern and Western Cherokee Nation, in National Convention assembled, by virtue of our original and unalienable rights, do hereby solemnly and mutually agree to form ourselves into one body politic, under the style and title of the Cherokee Nation" (*Constitution and Laws of the Cherokee Nation, 1839–51* 1852:16). Shortly thereafter a constitutional convention met at Tahlequah, and on September 6, 1839, a new constitution of the Cherokee Nation was completed and adopted, similar to the one of 1827. Further conflicts between the various groups continued, however, and on June 26, 1840 a new act of union was signed by both "old settlers" and the later emigrants: "The Old Settlers were to be allowed their just proportion of officers and representation in the government of the Nation for the first constitutional term. . . . After the first authorized term the Old Settlers were to take their chance at elections." Nevertheless, "civil war" among the Western Cherokees continued until 1846, when the conflicts were more or less settled through a treaty between the United States government and the various Cherokee factions (Wardell [1938] 1977:33, 41, 47–75).

Formation of Political Subdistricts

The Cherokees in Indian Territory did not settle primarily in towns or villages; instead the people were scattered, and each family generally built a separate log house with an enclosed area for raising corn and such (Hitchcock 1930:239).

Provided in the constitution was the division of "the Cherokee Nation into eight Districts; and if subsequently it should be deemed expedient, one or two may be added thereto." Representation to the

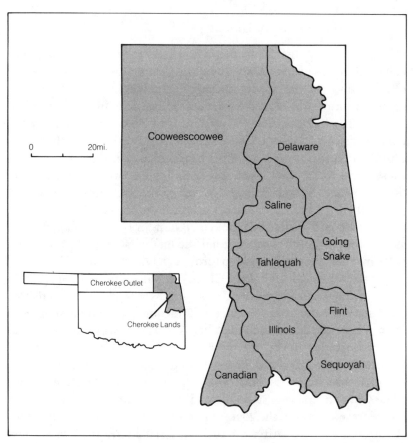

4. Cherokee Nation political subdivisions. After Morris, Goins, and McReynolds ([1965] 1986:22, 35).

central government was to be based on these districts, and precincts for voting were to be established. The nation was thus divided into the following eight districts on November 4, 1840: Skin Bayou district; Illinois district; Canadian district; Flint district; Going Snake district; Tahlequah district; Delaware district; and Saline district. Alterations in the boundaries were subsequently made, and on November 4, 1851, the name of Skin Bayou district was changed to Sequoyah (*Constitution and Laws of the Cherokee Nation, 1839–51* 1852:6, 39–42, 227. In 1856 Cooweescoowee district was organized out of Western Cherokee lands (Starr [1922] 1967:80). (See map 4.)

These nine districts remained as long as the Cherokee Nation in Indian Territory continued to exist, but this proved to be only about fifty more years.

CHAPTER 4

Decline, Recovery, and the United States Civil War: 1840 to 1865

The effects of removal and the first years in Indian Territory left the Cherokees demographically devastated, though just how devastated is not known. Further population decline followed, then came a period of recovery. Growth was short-lived, however, since the United States Civil War swept the Cherokee Nation in Indian Territory, bringing new devastation. The demographic effects of the Civil War may have been almost as severe as any the Cherokees had ever known. In contrast, the Cherokees in the East experienced a slow, steady population growth, interrupted only somewhat by the Civil War.

POPULATION DECLINE AND RECOVERY IN THE WEST

Since we do not know precisely the number of Cherokees about 1840, we cannot state with any precision the magnitude of either population decline or recovery before the Civil War. Indications are that the population may have continued to decline for several years after removal; data indicate that thereafter it showed significant growth up to the beginning of the Civil War.

Population Decline

William H. Thomas, attorney for the Cherokees remaining in the East, wrote to the commissioner of Indian affairs in the mid-1840s concerning the population decline of the Cherokees in Indian Territory. He stated that, after removal, "the portion of the tribe west have diminished in numbers so rapidly that unless the causes can be removed they must become extinct in a few generations" (*New American State Papers* [1769–1860] 1972, 11:778). The extent of any Cherokee decline is hard to ascertain because we lack information about population losses from removal.

Population Size, 1841 to 1852

The 1841 Cherokee population in Indian Territory was estimated at 18,000 (*New American State Papers* [1769–1860] 1972, 11:35). This seems far too high. The 1850 population was estimated at only 14,098 (Royce [1887] 1975:190), though conceivably this is an understatement. There were a reported 16,231 Cherokees, both Eastern and Western, in 1851, and a population of 17,530 in the Cherokee Nation (west of Arkansas) was reported in 1852 (*New American State Papers* [1769–1860] 1972:309, 463); however, the 1852 Drennen Roll placed the Cherokee Nation population (in Indian Territory) at 14,094 (Mooney [1900] 1987:9), some 13,821 of whom were "valid recipients" of an annuity payment, according to Doran (1975–76:500). In Doran's opinion, the Drennen Roll of the western Cherokee Nation may be considered fairly accurate:

> The most important fragment of ante-bellum statistical data that provides information on the pattern of occupance developed by any of the Five Civilized Tribes is the Drennen Payroll of 1852. Per capita annuity payments were made to each of the tribes for a number of years, but only this record remains intact. This payroll described the number of Cherokees receiving payments in 1852, and was helpfully noted in terms of the nation's eight political districts. As the Indians convened without fail to accept this money, the 13,821 citizens accepted as valid recipients give us a reasonably accurate idea of the size of the Cherokee citizenry at that date. (Doran 1975–76:500)

Despite Doran's arguments, the 14,094 figure for total Cherokee Nation population seems low; just how low is impossible to state. It was at this point, though, that the Western Cherokees suffered substantial population losses. Grant Foreman (1934:410), citing a letter from Agent Butler of September 13, 1853, noted: "There was a good deal of sickness caused by a wet spring and summer; during the preceding winter the Nation had been ravaged by smallpox that carried off many people. There were numbers of deaths from pneumonia, and chill and fever took their toll of strength and energy." Nevertheless, the 1855 Annual Report of the Commissioner of Indian Affairs continued to list the Cherokee population "west of Arkansas" as 17,530. (The report [U.S. Department of the Interior 1856:125, 255] also noted some 500 intermarried white men and women and an unspecified number of blacks, both "free and slave.")

The Texas Cherokees

Not all of the Cherokee population west of the Mississippi River was in Indian Territory. The group of Cherokees under the leadership of Chief Bowl had settled in 1817 in east Texas, then a part of Mexico. In 1820 they were living south and west of the Sabine River, along the Neches, the Angelina, and (possibly) the Trinity rivers. The area the Cherokees occupied had formerly been more heavily populated by groups of Caddoan Indians (Bolton 1987:26–27), but by this time the Caddoans had been depopulated by disease and the effects of the Spanish Catholic missions established there in the 1600s and 1700s. When the Cherokees arrived only vestiges of Caddoans remained. They were joined by other bands of Cherokees in subsequent years. By late 1822 they numbered perhaps 80 to 100 families, with a total population of 300 to 400. They lived in at least three villages and perhaps as many as seven (Everett 1985:177, 183, 230).

Members of other tribes had also migrated to the same area, as did the Cherokees, to escape Americans to the north. Some Kickapoos, for example, had moved there by shortly after 1800 (Callender, Pope, and Pope 1978:657); some Shawnees arrived about 1817 (Callender 1978:623, fig. 1, 632); and some Delawares had migrated there by 1827, having been in the Red River area in Arkansas since about 1817 (Goddard 1978:224). A census of 1816 listed 300 Choctaw "warriors" and 1,200 "souls" living on the "waters of Sabine and Nechez River" (Trimble, n.d.). (The same census listed a small group of Chickasaws living on the "Nacogdoches waters of Angelina." Reportedly they comprised thirty "warriors" and seventy "souls" [Trimble, n.d.].)

The Cherokees joined with these and other refugee Indians from the United States and formed a "loose confederacy" known, according to Mooney, as " 'the Cherokee and their associated bands,' consisting of Cherokee, Shawano, Delaware, Kickapoo, Quapaw, Choctaw,

Biloxi, 'Iawanie' (Heyowani, Yowani), 'Unataqua' (Nada'ko or Ana-
darko, another Caddo subtribe), 'Tahookatookie,' Alabama (a Creek
subtribe), and 'Cooshatta' (Koasa'ti, another Creek subtribe)." According to Mooney also, "the Cherokee being the largest and most
important band, their chief, Bowl—known to the whites as Colonel
Bowles—was regarded as the chief and principal man of them all"
(Mooney [1900] 1982:143; see also Everett 1985).

Jean Louis Berlandier traveled to their area in 1828 as a biologist
for the Mexican Comisión de Limites. He reported the Cherokees
numbered "scarcely 600," in approximately 90 to 100 families. He
said of them: "They have built their homes to the west of the Sabine
on the lands of the Thoen Colony, and they hope that Mexico will
cede them the land permanently. They have good houses surrounded
by fences. They are well armed and fond of war, at which they are
highly skilled. They are friendly with their neighbors. The Cherokees bring their agricultural produce in abundance to Nacogdoches,
where they also come to sell their livestock" (Berlandier 1969:111,
113).

Berlandier (1969:104, 105, 106, 109, 124, 125, 127, 135, 138, 142)
also gave population figures for other Texas groups affiliated, according to Mooney, with the Cherokees: the Alabamas, 600 (60 to 100
families); the Biloxis, 100 (25 families); the Choctaws, 10 to 15 "scattered families"; the Koasatis, 400 (50 to 60 families); the Delawares,
150 families; the Kickapoos, 110 families (probably too low a number); the Quapaws, 150 families; the Nadacos, 150 (30 families); the
Shawnees, 300 families; and the Yowanis(?), 150 to 200 (40 to 50
families). (He also gave a figure for the Caddos of 300 families. This
probably referred to only some of the Caddos.)

Six years later, in 1834, the Department of Nacogdoches was established, encompassing most of the area east of the Trinity River. One
report for this same year gave 800 Cherokees in all of Texas. The Department of Nacogdoches reported at about this time that the Indian
population in its area totaled 4,500, including 500 Cherokees, 500
Choctaws, 600 Creeks, 400 Shawnees, 800 Kickapoos, 100 Tejas, 300
Nacogdoches, 500 Coushattas, and 500 Caddos (Everett 1985:231,
255–56). (The department also reported that the non-Indian population was 9,000. This was probably too high.)

On February 23, 1836, a contract was signed with the new Texas
Republic giving a reservation to the Cherokees and a dozen affiliated
groups of Indians (Everett 1985:262). The agreed-upon lands were

somewhat more restricted than those the Cherokees had claimed a few years earlier, the difference being the land between the Neches and the Trinity rivers. The area of Cherokee occupancy in Texas now coincided, more or less, with present-day Cherokee and Smith counties. Others of the groups above also occupied the area. For example: "The Shawnee Indians occupied what is now Rusk county, their principal village being near where the town of Henderson is now situated. The Delaware Indians then lived in the eastern part of what is now Henderson county" (Reagan 1897:38).

The Kickapoos had lived in the northeast part of present-day Anderson County (Reagan 1897:38). They had had many conflicts with settlers in the area by 1837. At this time, "Chief Bowles, fearing reprisal from the Texans, . . . declared the Kickapoos to be renegades, and no longer recognized them as members of the Indian confederacy." The following year, on October 15, 1838, the main Kickapoo town was attacked by Colonel Thomas J. Rusk. Many Kickapoos moved north into Indian Territory at this time, while others remained there (Latorre and Latorre 1976:10, 11; Callender, Pope, and Pope 1978:663).

The Kickapoos were not the only ones to fight the Texans. Conflicts between the Cherokees (and their allies) and local whites had occurred for some time. (The Texas Cherokees even consulted John Ross about the possibility of both groups' joining together and resettling in California [Reagan 1897:41].) In 1839 the government of Texas accused all Indians living near Nacogdoches of conspiring with Mexican agents (Latorre and Latorre 1976:11). Consequently the Cherokees were forced to give up their land. A large battle resulted—the Cherokees, the Shawnees, the Delawares, and their allies against two regiments of Texas volunteers under Colonels Landrum and Rusk and a regiment of regular soldiers under Colonel Burleson. All three regiments united under the command of General Kelsey H. Douglas. Battles ensued on July 15 and 16, 1839, the major one on the second day. A participant described the death of Chief Bowl during the battle:

When at last the Indians retreated, Chief Bowles was the last one to attempt to leave the battlefield. His horse had been wounded many times, and he shot through the thigh. His horse was disabled and could go no further, and he dismounted and started to walk off. He was shot in the back by Henry Conner [sic], afterwards Major

Connor; walked forward a little and fell, and then rose to a sitting position facing us, and immediately in front of the company to which I belonged. I had witnessed his dignity and manliness in council, his devotion to his tribe in sustaining their decision for war against his judgment, and his courage in battle, and, wishing to save his life, ran towards him, and, as I approached him from one direction, my captain, Robert Smith, approached him from another, with his pistol drawn. As we got to him, I said, "Captain, don't shoot him," but as I spoke he fired, shooting the chief in the head, which caused instant death. (Reagan 1897:45–46)

Thus died Chief Bowl during the Texas War of Independence.

Some of Bowl's followers, under his son John Bowles, were driven from their homes. Although John Bowles was killed along the way, the group fled to Coahuila, Mexico, and eventually established a village near present-day Zaragoza, formerly San Fernando de las Rosas (Pulte and Altom 1984:35). Other reports indicated that at least some of the Cherokees fled to Indian Territory at this time (see Berlandier 1969, 113n.149). They perhaps settled with the Choctaws, outside Cherokee lands. Their population was estimated as high as 1,500 in 1842 (Hitchcock 1930:256). (This seems an exaggeration.) A participant in the 1839 battle wrote: "The Indians dispersed, some going to the cross timbers, some to the north of Red river, and some to Mexico. A year or more later—I do not remember the precise date—the wives and some of the children of Chief Bowles came to the Rio Grande at Laredo, and asked permission to pass through Texas on the way to the Cherokees north of Red river, and President Lamar granted their request, furnished them an escort, and transportation and rations, on their way through Texas. I saw them on the San Antonio road east of the Neches" (Reagan 1897:46).

In the early 1840s the famous Sequoyah journeyed to find the Mexican Cherokee village, but he died during the trip in 1843 (Mooney [1900] 1982:147–48). Possibly the village was attacked shortly thereafter by "Mexican bandits." Some 30 Cherokees may have fled to Texas, then to Indian Territory. In 1848 there reportedly were 100 Cherokees in Texas (Latorre and Latorre 1976:11); in 1849 there reportedly were only 25, "only five of whom were warriors" (Berlandier 1969, 113n. 149). Apparently some remaining Cherokees found refuge with Kickapoos who had a village in Coahuila: "These Cherokees maintained their identity while living among the Kicka-

poo for some fifty years, until an epidemic resulted in the deaths of
most members of the group late in the nineteenth century"[1] (Pulte
and Altom 1984:35). The surviving Cherokees then left the Kickapoo village, moving westward to Sonora with some Kickapoos and
losing contact with the village.

Population Recovery

Whatever the Cherokee population in the West about
1852, it seems to have increased somewhat in the ensuing few years
up to the time of the United States Civil War. Generally this may
be accounted for by "healthy conditions" in Indian Territory. For
example, Thomas S. Drew, superintendent of Indian affairs at Fort
Smith, Arkansas, reported in 1854: "The health of the Indian population in the southern superintendency has been good during the
past year" (U.S. Department of the Interior 1855:113). Similarly,
the Cherokee agent George Butler reported the following year: "The
health of the Cherokee people has been remarkably good during the
past year, notwithstanding the many hardships they have had to en-
dure and the many difficulties they have had to contend with. What
diseases were among them were those common throughout the western country, and attended by very little mortality" (U.S. Department
of the Interior 1856:124). According to Butler, the Cherokee Nation
in Indian Territory numbered 21,000 in 1859, exclusive of 1,000
whites and 4,000 slaves (Foreman 1934:418; Englund 1974:91), and
the *Report of the Commissioner of Indian Affairs for 1861* (U.S. Department of the Interior 1861:215) gave the total of 22,000 Cherokees
"in" Cherokee Agency in 1860.

The totals above for whites and slaves may not be accurate.
Through a mistake in the instructions to enumerators in the 1860
United States census, slaves—held by both whites and Indians—
and whites in the Cherokee Nation were counted in this United
States census. As compiled by Michael F. Doran (1978:337, 347,
table 3), the census returns indicated 716 whites and 2,511 slaves
(1,226 males and 1,285 females) in the Cherokee Nation in 1860. As
in earlier years, most of the slaves of the Cherokees were "owned"
by the mixed-bloods. However, not all the slaves were owned by the
Cherokees: Doran reported that 55 of the 716 alien residents were
slave owners (1978:348, table 4). (He also reported that 330 Chero-

kees owned slaves.) Moreover, he indicated, "The slaves of the Indian Territory were bound to localities according to the settlement preferences of their owners. As the dominant tendency of the mixed bloods was to locate in the fertile alluvial lowlands, where bases for both extensive farming and cattle ranching were better placed, the great mass of the slaves was also found there." For the Cherokees this meant that slave populations were on the Arkansas River, near the Arkansas border, and also somewhat north of the Arkansas River—here again, close to the Arkansas border. Another large concentration of slaves was on the Grand River, north of where the Grand joined the Arkansas, where there were various salt springs and the Cherokees carried on active salt production and trade (Doran 1978:341, 342, 343, fig. 2).[2]

GROWTH IN THE EAST

The demographic situation seemed somewhat better for those Cherokees remaining in the East than for their tribesmen to the west. Their attorney, William H. Thomas, reported in 1846 that since the time of removal the Cherokees "remaining east, under wholesome laws and regulations, have increased in about the same ratio as the white population." He noted:

The Cherokees in North Carolina, at the time a census was taken, in 1840, numbered 1,069. Since then no census has been taken of the Cherokees east, except one town by the name of Qualla, situated on the lands granted by the act of 1783. At the time the former census was taken, in 1840, the total number was 669. Four years afterwards, when the census was again taken, it showed an increase of 113, making the total number 782. . . . Supposing the balance of the North Carolina Indians to have increased in the same proportion, and that the increase has continued to the present time, it would give in that State, including scattering individuals that have removed there from the State of Georgia, 1,489. (*New American State Papers* [1769–1860] 1972, 11:778)

The Cherokee attorney may have slightly underestimated the Cherokee population in the East. As Mooney wrote: "A census taken by their agent, Colonel Thomas, in 1841, gave the number of East Cherokee (possibly only those in North Carolina intended) as 1,220."

According to Charles Lanman, who visited the Eastern Cherokees in 1848, "Qualla town" was populated by about 800 Cherokees and 100 Catawbas, with over 200 more Indians in the western part of North Carolina (cited in Mooney [1900] 1982:166, 168).[3]

A census was taken of the North Carolina Cherokees in 1848–49 by J. C. Mullay (see Blankenship 1978:27–36; Finger 1984:48–50) under an act of Congress, in order to distribute benefits provided in the treaty of 1835, even though these Cherokees had not been removed. Mullay was instructed to ascertain "the number and names of such individuals and families, including each member of every family of the Cherokee tribe of Indians that remained in the state of North Carolina at the time of the ratification of the treaty of New Echota, May 23, 1836, and who have not removed west of the Mississippi or received the commutation for removal and subsistence." He was not to include children born after May 23, 1836, "as children born since the ratification of the treaty are excluded by the act." Moreover, "No white person unless intermarried with a Cherokee prior to the date mentioned, and, if a male, elected or adopted by a formal act of the tribe as a member thereof, will be included" (quoted in Litton 1940:207). According to Charles Royce ([1887] 1975:191), "The number found to be entitled to the benefits of the appropriation was 1,517, which by additions was increased to 2,133." This was in 1851, using a census by David W. Siler (Siler [1851] 1972; also Litton 1940:210–12; Blankenship 1978:37–48). The total number of names on the census was 2,343; however, my reading of the census is that 363 were whites and "disallowed" individuals (and one person was skipped in the numbering): the total then becomes 1,981. This census was subsequently "corrected" by Alfred Chapman in 1852, to 2,133 individuals (see Litton 1940:212–14; Blankenship 1978:49–64; Royce [1887] 1975:192; Mooney [1900] 1982:167–68). A report of the secretary of the interior in 1855 (*New American State Papers* [1769–1860] 1972, 2:463) listed the 1851 Eastern Cherokee population as 2,200. According to Finger (1980:21), the 1860 population of Quallatown alone was "1,063 Indians living in 256 separate dwellings, an average of a little more than four members per household." The total Eastern Cherokee population at that date is not known.

THE UNITED STATES CIVIL WAR

The United States Civil War proved destructive to both Eastern and Western Cherokees, but particularly to those in the West.

War in Indian Territory

The Cherokee Nation resisted being thrust into the Civil War as long as possible, though one faction, headed by Stand Watie, early and openly declared support for the Confederacy. John Ross, principal chief of the Cherokee Nation, wrote in mid-1861: "We do not wish our soil to become the battleground between the States, and our homes to be rendered desolate and miserable by the horrors of a civil war" (U.S. Department of the Interior 1864:232). After much pressure the majority of the Cherokee Nation, under John Ross, finally declared for the Confederacy, long after the Chickasaws, the Choctaws, the Creeks, the Seminoles, the Osages, and the Comanches had done so. Formal siding with the South came on October 7, 1861, under a treaty at Tahlequah (near Park Hill), the capital of the Cherokee Nation, signed with Commissioner Albert Pike (Mooney [1900] 1982:148). Some 1,400 Cherokees were reportedly "in arms" for the Confederacy at this time (U.S. Department of the Interior 1861:48). Other Cherokees, however, remained "loyal" to the Union, perhaps 300 of which—mainly women and children—sought early refuge in Kansas (U.S. Department of the Interior 1864:23).

Two regiments of Cherokees soon entered the Civil War on the side of the Confederacy: one under Stand Watie, one under Colonel John Drew. Some additional Cherokees also served under General Albert Pike. It was reported that a total of 3,000 Cherokee men joined the Confederate forces during the war (U.S. Bureau of the Census 1894b:293) and that about 8,500 Cherokees were supporters of the Confederacy and left Cherokee lands. Some of the others who remained—reportedly about 13,500 in all—were also said to support the Confederacy (U.S. Congress 1867:441).

In the summer of 1862 Drew's regiment deserted the Confederacy in favor of the Union, shortly after the Battle of Pea Ridge (Arkansas). Chief John Ross then left Indian Territory, more or less as a "prisoner of war." He spent the rest of the war in Washington, D.C., and

Philadelphia. Soon, according to Mooney ([1900] 1982:149), "Indian Territory was ravaged alternately by contending factions and armed bands, and thousands of loyal fugitives were obliged to take refuge in Kansas, where they were cared for by the government." It was reported that by early fall 1862 "from fifteen hundred to two thousand others, also in the main women and children, and claiming . . . protection, made their way to a point on the Cherokee neutral lands, about twelve miles south of Fort Scott, Kansas" (U.S. Department of the Interior 1864:23). Mooney ([1900] 1982:149) asserted that there were 2,000 refugee Cherokees in Kansas by the end of 1862. At about this time the condition of the Cherokee Nation was described thus: "There was little to subsist upon and the few Indians lingering there were in a deplorable state of deprivation, little food, little clothing and it was wintertime" (Abel 1919:217).

Many of those who emigrated to Kansas were sent back to Indian Territory the following spring. There they encountered Stand Watie and the remaining Confederate Cherokees. According to Mooney ([1900] 1982:149), "Stand Watie and his men, with the Confederate Creeks and others, scoured the country at will, destroying or carrying off everything belonging to the loyal Cherokee, who had now, to the number of nearly seven thousand, taken refuge at Fort Gibson." Another report stated, similarly:

> In the Cherokee nation, the rebel Indians were let loose on the loyal Cherokees by the rebel army, and protected by them, in murdering, robbing, and capturing the loyal Cherokees, and stealing their horses, cattle, wagons, hogs, farming utensils, beds, bedding and clothing, and burning their houses, barns and fencing, and everything else which they could find, and could not carry away. Some fled into the mountains, abandoning everything they had, glad to escape with their lives. And these remained for months in the winter season, exposed, in their destitute condition, to all the inclemencies of the season, and many died of exposure. In the spring of 1863 the small-pox broke out among them. No amount of persuasion could induce a large majority of them to be vaccinated. They took it in the natural way, and great numbers died. (U.S. Congress 1867:442)

In this regard Abel noted: "Malnutrition, overcrowding and bad hygienic conditions generally offered fertile soil for disease. Small-pox alone carried the refugees off by the hundreds." At this time J. T. Cox,

Table 9. Census of the Cherokee Nation, 1863

	Sex		
Group	Males	Females	Total
Men			2,291
Under sixty years of age	200		
Over sixty years of age, and infirm under sixty years of age	291		
Boys over fifteen years of age	300		
Soldiers in two Cherokee regiments	1,500		
Women			2,912
Widows		977	
Married		1,100	
Single		835	
Children			4,077
Orphans	564	455	(1,019)
Fatherless, mother living	671	580	(1,251)
Parents living	1,022	785	(1,807)
Residents not enrolled			800
At Sac and Fox agency			300
Total			10,380

Source: Abel (1925:51).

special agent for the Cherokees in Indian Territory, pleaded for medical aid as "indispensably necessary," but it was not provided (Abel 1925:50).

By 1863 it was reported that "the balance of the nation are loyal" (U.S. Department of the Interior 1864:214). During this year the "Northern Cherokees" met at Cowskin Prairie in Indian Territory, abrogated the treaty with the Confederacy, and abolished slavery. Thomas Pegg became acting chief in the absence of John Ross. From then until the end of the war there were more or less two Cherokee "nations" in Indian Territory: the "Southern" and the "Northern" Cherokees.

During 1863 the people of the Cherokee Nation continued in a terrible condition and suffered severe population losses. Men died in battle or from sickness and exposure; women and children surely fared worse, since they were more exposed to sickness and death than the men (U.S. Department of the Interior 1864:214). In 1863 the condition of the Cherokees was described by the United States

Indian agent at Leavenworth, Kansas: "Their condition is the most pitiable imaginable. They were, only a few years ago, the most powerful, wealthy and intelligent Indians in the United States, and were pleased of their power, wealth and intelligence. They are now reduced to a third-rate power among Indians, and their wealth all gone. They fully understand their position, and are humbled" (U.S. Department of the Interior 1864:215). This same year, Cox reported a census of the Cherokees in Indian Territory. As shown in table 9, he gave a total count of only 10,380.

Battles in the Cherokee Nation

Most of the Cherokee suffering from conflicts during the Civil War was not from regular battles, but from "the irregular fighting of partisan groups—raids, the flight and pursuit of civilian bands, the burning of homes and schools, and the readjustments to refugee camps." However, various formal battles did occur: at Caving Banks in 1861; at Cowskin Prairie, Fort Wayne, and Locust Grove in 1862; at Cabin Creek and Webbers Falls in 1863; and again at Cabin Creek in 1864 (Morris, Goins, and McReynolds 1986:28).

The Keetoowahs

At about the time of the United States Civil War—1859—an important Cherokee secret society, the Keetoowah Society,[4] was formed, or at least renewed, in the western Cherokee Nation: the name probably was derived from the ancient Cherokee settlement of Kituhwa, discussed earlier. Some say the society had been formed much earlier, as an effort to return to the old ways during the early 1800s when the Cherokees were accepting many Euro-American ways of life (see, for example, Hendrix 1983a:24–25). It may even be traced to an ancient Cherokee clan or "medicine society" known as the Ani-Kutani (Fogelson 1984). Nevertheless, the 1859 organization is the first one known from written records (Hendrix 1983a:24).[5]

Ostensibly the society was organized for the "purpose of cultivating a national feeling among the full-bloods, in opposition to the innovating tendencies of the mixed blood element" (Mooney [1900] 1982:225) and also to preserve traditional Cherokee rituals and ceremonies (McLoughlin 1984:468). However, according to scholars (see, for example, Royce [1887] 1975:201; Mooney ([1900] 1982:225;

McLoughlin 1984:467), it was really to counteract the influence of other secret secessionist organizations such as the "Blue Lodge" and the Knights of the Golden Circle, formed by the slaveholding Cherokees, particularly the mixed-bloods. After the Civil War the Keetoowahs were opposed "to every scheme looking to the curtailment or destruction of Cherokee national self-government" (Mooney [1900] 1982:226). As we shall see, they have played an important role in the history of the Cherokees, an influence that continues today.

The End of the War

At the end of the United States Civil War, the Cherokees in Indian Territory were devastated: "Raided and sacked alternatively, not only by the Confederate and Union forces, but by the vindictive ferocity and hate of their own factional divisions, their country became a blackened and desolate waste. . . . [T]hat entire portion of their country which had been occupied by their settlements was distinguishable from the virgin prairie only by the scorced [sic] and blackened chimneys and the plowed but now neglected fields" (Royce [1887] 1975:254). Mooney ([1900] 1982:150) summarized the experience simply: "After five years of desolation the Cherokee emerged from the war with their numbers reduced from 21,000 to 14,000, and their whole country in ashes." Thus the Cherokees reportedly numbered only 14,000 after the Civil War (U.S. Department of the Interior 1865:589), and a census taken in 1867 (the Tompkins Roll) enumerated only 13,566 (Royce [1887] 1975:229). Englund, however, considered this figure too low, since it did not account for "refugees who had not yet returned and for people who were absent for other reasons" (Englund 1974:115). A more accurate population figure would be over 17,000. Englund's figure (1974, table 7) includes, however, all Cherokee citizens—that is, Cherokees, freedmen, white Shawnees, and Delawares. Considering only Cherokees by blood lowers the figure considerably. They probably numbered not more than 15,000, if that many. Thus on August 1, 1865, Cherokee agent Justin Harlan reported that the number of Cherokees "had decreased in three years, of those who remained in the nation, not much (if any) less than two thousand five hundred, over the natural increase by birth."

Agent Harlan additionally reported that the most common diseases then were "bilious fever and fever and ague", and that venereal disease was decreasing their population and enfeebling their offspring. He noted of venereal disease among the Cherokees: "A frequent recurrence of such diseases with both sexes causes impotence, and prevents natural increase, undermines their constitutions, and shortens their lives. When the disease has not occurred with such malignity, or has not reoccurred so often as to cause impotence, it greatly enfeebles the powers of procreation. This enfeebled constitution is inherited by their children, and their lives are shortened. From all of this I infer their numbers are diminished, their increase is prevented, and their offspring enfeebled; but to what extent I cannot say" (U.S. Congress, 1867:442–43).

A Family's Plight

Recorded testimony of a Cherokee man, Wallace Thornton, in 1937 indicates the plight of one Cherokee family during the Civil War in Indian Territory.

I was born December 3, 1853, two miles west of where Vian, Oklahoma, now stands in the Cherokee Nation.

My mother, Betsey Ratcliff [Lifter], a full-blood Cherokee Indian, was born in Georgia and came to the Cherokee Nation with her parents in the year of 1838 when the Indians were removed from that state. She was a very small child at that time but I do not know just how old she was.

My father, Walter (better known as Watt) Thornton, was also a Cherokee Indian. He was known as an old settler, having come to the Territory before the removal.

In the year of 1861, the Civil War broke out. I was only eight years old at the time and my two brothers were younger than I. At the very beginning of the war, all the settlers of the country were forced to leave and seek safety for themselves and families. Some went north seeking protection from the northern armies and others fled to the south.

My father was neutral and did not want to go away; he did not believe in fighting. Also, he did not believe in slavery and long before the war he freed the one negro slave whom he had inherited from his father's estate.

In 1861, a company of Southern soldiers, led by Captain Charley Holt, came to our place. Captain Holt called to father and said, "Get ready, Watt and let's go, you will have to fight." Consequently, father was forced into the Southern army.

At the time they took father away, there were no other families left in the country. We had three horses and mother got on
one of them and took my youngest brother (who was only about
three years old) and my other brother took our feather bed and
quilts on another pony. I was on the third one, loaded with all the
pots, pans, and cooking utensils I could carry. We started out and
for several days we just scouted around, up and down the Canadian River, trying to stay as near to father as we could. We could
get plenty to eat anywhere. Everyone had gone, leaving chickens,
cattle and everything to run wild, and there was lots of corn in
the little fields; but in a short time the war became so fierce that
mother realized that we must get out of the country or be killed so
we headed south and kept going until we reached the Red River.
We were not able to cross the river and upon scouting around, we
found that this was Choctaw Country and that the Choctaws were
not being molested by the war so we decided to stay here, and did
stay for the duration of the war.

Father continued in the service of the Southern army, serving
under General Stan Watie until 1865, when he died of sickness[6]
right at the close of the war. He was buried at a little place that
was called Jackson in an Indian cemetery.

As soon as the war was over, we came home. The Arkansas River
was a line between the north and the south and those who had
gone north were afraid to cross to the south side of the river and
those who had gone south were afraid to cross to the north side.
When we returned to our old home, we found one chair which was
made of hickory by the famous Sequoyah, writer of the Cherokee
alphabet, in the potato cellar under the house. I still have the old
chair. We also found our old black mottled face milch cow who
had escaped being eaten by the soldiers. She was almost wild but
soon grew gentle again. That is all we had to start our home on
again. (W. Thornton 1937)

In the East

The Eastern Cherokees also suffered from the United
States Civil War. Though less information is available about their
plight and they suffered less than their kinsmen in Indian Territory,
the Civil War became for them "a most momentous period in their
history" (Mooney [1900] 1982:168).

In 1862 Washington Morgan was sent as an emissary to the Eastern Cherokees, to enlist their aid for the Confederacy. He apparently was very successful, for "by appealing to old-time memories so aroused the war spirit among them that a large number declared themselves ready to follow wherever he led." They soon joined the war effort under the leadership of their agent, Colonel William H. Thomas. Thomas had in total some 2,800 men under his command, almost 400 of whom were Cherokees, reportedly "about every able-bodied man in the tribe" (Mooney [1900] 1982:169). They fought in various battles in the Southeast but mostly were used as guards and scouts in eastern Tennessee and western North Carolina (Finger 1980:23). As with their relatives to the west, some of the Eastern Cherokees switched sides. A small group—perhaps about 30 (Finger 1980:25)— was captured by the Union army and, "having become dissatisfied with their experience in the Confederate service, they were easily persuaded to go over to the Union side." At the end of the war "they returned to their homes to find their tribesmen so bitterly incensed against them that for some time their lives were in danger" (Mooney [1900] 1982:171).

Unlike the case of the Cherokees in Indian Territory, we have no solid idea of Eastern Cherokee population losses during the Civil War. Undoubtedly, though, they were nowhere as extensive as among the western Cherokee Nation. It was likely, moreover, that the most serious losses "from the war" came neither as a direct result of it nor during the actual war years. Rather, they resulted from disease brought to the Eastern Cherokees in 1866 by a returning Cherokee who had joined the Union forces. This "Union Cherokee" may have contracted smallpox from a camp near Knoxville, Tennessee; he died soon after returning to his people. Other Cherokees were infected: "As the characteristic pustules had not appeared, . . . the nature of his sickness was not at first suspected . . . and his funeral was largely attended. A week later a number of those who had been present became sick, and the disease was recognized . . . as smallpox in all its virulence" (Mooney [1900] 1982:171–72). The smallpox spread quickly throughout the tribe in the early spring of 1866. Colonel Thomas sought aid for the stricken Eastern Cherokees, but the vaccine brought by a doctor proved ineffective: "The Cherokees became so disillusioned with white medicine that some resorted to more traditional remedies, including plunge baths in the icy rivers and the 'cold-water douche.' These practices almost always proved fatal for those infected" (Finger 1980:25). Reports on how many died are varied, ranging from over a hundred to several hundred (Mooney [1900] 1982:72). John Finger estimated that about 125 died during the epidemic and noted that "many of the most prominent perished, contributing to the lack of postwar leadership." He also noted that most of the survivors were destitute (Finger 1984:101, 1980:25). Mooney ([1900] 1982:172) concluded: "Thus did the war bring its harvest of death, misery and civil feud to the East Cherokee."

CHAPTER 5

Population Growth: 1865 to 1900

T he total Cherokee population grew following the devastation of the United States Civil War, with few periods of decline. But during the decades from the war to the end of the century the Cherokees started to become a very different population as both the eastern and western Cherokee tribes incorporated increasing numbers of whites, blacks, and non-Cherokee Indians and intermarried with them.

THE CHEROKEE NATION TO 1890

As we have seen, the Cherokees in Indian Territory officially numbered only about 14,000 near the end of the United States Civil War (U.S. Department of the Interior 1866:372, 1868: 396). Similarly, the census taken by Colonel H. Tompkins of Tennessee in July 1867, authorized under the treaty of 1866, discussed below, listed a mere 13,566 at that time (Royce [1887] 1975:229).[1] As I indicated in chapter 4, these figures do not account for those who migrated out of Cherokee territory during the Civil War and had not yet returned. Five years later in 1872, therefore, a "census" by their agent estimated them at 18,000, and a report in 1873 gave their population as 17,217: 8,817 males and 8,400 females (U.S. Department of the Interior 1874a:336). Presumably these reports included some 130 Eastern Cherokees who immigrated to Indian Territory in 1871, but a report in 1871 gave their population as only 14,682 (U.S. Department of the Interior 1872a:164–65, 1872b:33).

Delawares, Munsees, and Shawnees

At the end of the Civil War the Cherokee Nation signed a new treaty with the federal government on July 19, 1866. It voided the treaty of 1861 with the Confederate states and declared amnesty for all involved in the war. It also called for ceding lands to the United States in Kansas (the "Cherokee Strip"), lands formerly sold to the Cherokees under the treaty of 1835 (but this was not accomplished until the 1890s). Article 15 of the treaty stipulated the following: "The United States may settle any civilized Indians, friendly with the Cherokees and adjacent tribes, within the Cherokee country, on unoccupied lands east of 96°, on such terms as may be agreed upon by any such tribe and the Cherokees, subject to the approval of the President of the United States" (Kappler 1904–79, 2:946; see also Institute for the Development of Indian Law, n.d.b:63). Article 16 allowed the United States to settle "friendly" Indians on Cherokee country *west* of 96° (Kappler 1904–79, 2:947; see also Institute for the Development of Indian Law, n.d.b:64).

Under article 15 several tribes, then in Kansas, were eventually settled on Cherokee lands. (Some, e.g., the Sacs and the Foxes in Missouri, had sought relocation to Cherokee lands as early as 1857; see Abel 1915:36n.27). The first were the Delawares, including some Munsee-Delawares, about 1,000 of whom agreed to remove themselves to the new lands in 1867, having by then relocated to Kansas from the mid-Atlantic area. They sold their lands in Kansas to the Union Pacific Railroad Company (U.S. Bureau of the Census 1894a: 44), moved to Indian Territory in the winter of 1867–68, and lost some population during the removal (see Mooney 1911:339). (Later about 300 left seeking better conditions but returned after two years [Wardell [1938] 1977:218].) They bought lands from the Cherokees and made an agreement with them specifying that the Delawares would become members of the Cherokee Nation, "and the children hereafter born of such Delawares so incorporated into the Cherokee Nation, shall in all respects be regarded as native Cherokees" (Institute for the Development of Indian Law, n.d.b:69). (Apparently, after the Delawares came to the Cherokee country in 1867, the tribes fought for some years, and many were killed [U.S. Bureau of the Census 1894a:47].) Also in 1867 another small group of Munsees (sometimes called Christian Indians) affiliated with the Delawares, who had been living with a group of Chippewas in present-day Franklin

County, Kansas, considered removing to Indian Territory. They appealed to the Cherokees that "the condition of our people is such that they are not far enough advanced to live amongst the whites, and they would prosper better by being away from the whites." They made an agreement to move to the Cherokee Nation on December 6, 1897, but did not do so (Wardell [1938] 1977:219; Weslager 1974). The third group were the Shawnees, who numbered some 770 (Royce [1887] 1975:235–36). These Shawnees were descended from a group who had earlier been in Ohio but had moved to Kansas between 1832 and 1835 (Callender 1978:632). They were relocated in 1864–70 (see Institute for the Development of Indian Law, n.d.b:72–73; Callender 1978:632). Under article 16, several groups were settled to the west of the Cherokee Nation: the Osages, the Kaws, the Pawnees, the Poncas, the Otos and Missouris, and the Tonkowas; for a time a group of Nez Perces, under Chief Joseph, was also there (Mooney [1900] 1982:151).

Cherokee Freedmen

After most members of the Cherokee Nation shifted their allegiance from the Confederacy to the Union during the United States Civil War, the Cherokees formally abrogated their treaty with the Confederate states on February 19, 1863. This occurred at a specially convened meeting of the Cherokee national council at Cowskin Prairie. Included in the legislation enacted was the abolition of slavery in the Cherokee Nation (Mooney [1900] 1982:210); slaves were to become "freedmen." The legislation was to be effective on June 25, 1863. As Wardell stated, "Of all slave-holding communities the Cherokee Nation was the only one to abolish slavery during the Civil War." However, as he also noted, "Of course, those Cherokee loyal to the Union had little to lose in the act because the large slave-owners among the Cherokees were in the Confederate forces, who took no recognition of the law until after the fall of the Confederacy" ([1938] 1977:174).

Also by this time, many of the slaves with their "owners," as well as many other Cherokees loyal to the Confederacy, had fled the Cherokee Nation either to Kansas or to Texas. Soon after passage of the Cherokee "emancipation" act, numbers of slaves came back to Cherokee territory, following on the heels of Union troops moving from Kansas to Fort Gibson (Littlefield 1978:15–16). It was

reported that in February 1864 500 former slaves were destitute at
Fort Gibson alone (Abel 1925:272). At the end of the Civil War
others followed, since the treaty of 1866 also formally abolished
slavery (see Kappler 1904–79, 2:942–50; Institute for the Development of Indian Law, n.d.b:60–67). By 1867 the total number of freedmen in Cherokee territory was estimated at between 2,000 and 2,500,
most in Illinois district, because Fort Gibson was situated there
(Littlefield 1978:28). A census taken by agent John N. Craig in 1870
listed 1,545 Cherokees "of African descent," but these made up only
two-thirds of the former Cherokee slaves and free blacks and their descendants (Littlefield 1978:76). There were also more than 700 black
intruders on Cherokee lands. Despite this, the *Annual Report of the
Commissioner of Indian Affairs* for 1874 gave a figure of only 1,300
freedmen (U.S. Department of the Interior 1874b:68).

Whites in the Cherokee Nation

Even before the first Cherokees arrived in what
would become Indian Territory, numbers of whites had begun to
move into the area. This movement accelerated after the Battle of
New Orleans in 1815, which ended the war with Great Britain (Foreman 1930:160). With the establishment of Fort Smith in 1817, the
ceding of land from the Quapaws to the United States in 1818 (see
Kappler 1904–79, 2:160–61; Institute for the Development of Indian
Law, n.d.a:39–41), and the treaty of 1819 with Spain, whereby the
Red River was established as the boundary between the United States
and Spanish occupied lands, "the whites began adventuring in greater
numbers to . . . eastern Oklahoma; and finding the lands along the
streams rich and productive, many remained" (Foreman 1930:162–
63). Meanwhile, the county of Arkansas was established on December 31, 1813, by the General Assembly of Missouri, encompassing
much of what is now the state of Arkansas. Other counties were
soon established, including some in present-day Oklahoma. Parts of
this area even became densely settled with whites, but when the
country was appropriated for the emigrant Indians the usual formula
was reversed and the settlers were driven out. Most concentrations
of whites were to the south, along the Red River in what is now
southern Arkansas (Foreman 1930:160, 167–68, 328). This was below
Cherokee lands; however, numbers of whites were settled throughout Cherokee lands in Lovely's purchase of 1816.

    In 1828 Cherokee "Arkansas" land was exchanged for land farther to the west, "together with 'a perpetual outlet west' . . . , as far west as the sovereignty of the United States might extend." Five years later this was modified "so as to be practically equivalent to the present territory [in 1900] of the Cherokee Nation in Indian Territory, with the Cherokee strip recently ceded" (Mooney [1900] 1982:139).

Article 3 of the treaty of 1828 specified that the United States would remove all whites from the newly created Western Cherokee lands, "and also all others, should there be any there, who may be unacceptable to the Cherokees, so that no obstacles arising out of the presence of a white population, or a population of any other sort, shall exist to annoy the Cherokees" (Kappler 1904–79, 2:289; see also Institute for the Development of Indian Law, n.d.b:32). It also promised to keep such populations out in the future.

In 1856 some white settlers were removed from Cherokee lands under military force. Attempts were made to remove others in 1859, but they agreed to go voluntarily at a later date and were not then removed. The events of the Civil War and an error in surveying Cherokee lands apparently allowed them to remain (Royce [1887] 1975:200–202). As I noted in chapter 4, the 1860 census counted 716 whites in the Cherokee Nation.

The treaty of 1866 with the United States government also provided for protection against the intrusion of "all unauthorized citizens of the United States who may attempt to settle on their lands or reside in their territory" (Kappler 1904–79, 2:949; Institute for the Development of Indian Law, n.d.b:66). Even given these events, by the mid-1870s there were still many whites in Cherokee territory. Many of them had intermarried with Cherokees; others were there "on various pretexts," as Royce ([1887] 1975:245) put it. This became an important concern within the Cherokee Nation.

Population of the Cherokee Nation in the Mid-1870s

In 1871 the Cherokees in the Cherokee Nation were estimated at about 18,000 (U.S. Bureau of the Census 1894a:5). At about this time the total population of the Cherokee Nation consisted of the following groups, as detailed in the 1873 *Annual Report of the Commissioner of Indian Affairs*:

    1st. The full-blood Cherokees.
    2nd. The half-breed Cherokees.

3rd. The Delawares, both full-blood and half-breed.

4th. The Shawnees, both full-blood and half-breed.

5th. The white men and women who have intermarried with these.

6th. A few Creeks who broke away from their own tribe, and have been citizens of the Cherokee Nation for many years.

7th. A few Creeks who are not citizens.

8th. A few Natchez Indians who are citizens.

9th. The freedmen adopted under the treaty of 1866.

10th. Freedmen not adopted, but not removed as intruders, owing to an order from the Indian Department directing agent to remove them. (U.S. Department of the Interior 1874a:202)

In addition there were others in the Cherokee Nation—both whites and blacks—whom the nation was attempting to remove at this time (see Royce [1887] 1975:245–49).

In 1876 there were officially 18,672 Cherokees in Indian Territory: 9,379 males and 9,293 females; the sex ratio was 100.9. Of these, 10,010 were designated "full-bloods." It was reported that there were 1,500 whites "lawfully on the reservation." There were also some 1,300 Cherokee freedmen there about this time. In 1879 the Cherokee Nation population was estimated at 20,000 (U.S. Department of the Interior 1876:212, 1874b:68, 1879:234).

The Cherokee Nation in 1880

In 1880 the Cherokee Nation conducted its own census. Information in it provides a demographic picture of the Cherokee Nation population, by districts, at this time. The census enumerated 19,735 citizens of the Cherokee Nation; 15,150 of these were listed as "native," and 4,585 were listed as "adopted" (see table 10). Also reported were 351 orphans under sixteen years of age (Cherokee Nation 1881:14, table M). This total of 20,086 is very close to the estimate reported above of 20,000 Cherokees in Indian Territory; however, "by joint resolution in Council, 601 names were added to correct the Census, that number having been omitted, making a total population of 20,336" (Cherokee Nation 1881:14, table M). (The U.S. Department of the Interior [1880: map, 1881: map] reported the Cherokee population as 19,270 for both 1880 and 1881.) The 19,735 individuals shown in table 10 were enumerated in 4,262 families, making

Table 10. "Citizen" Population of the Cherokee Nation, 1880

District	Families	Males	Females	Native	Adopted	Total
Canadian	281	896	684	1,259	321	1,580
Cooweescoowee	790	1,733	1,725	1,797	1,661	3,458
Delaware	652	1,562	1,468	2,474	556	3,030
Flint	332	761	779	1,318	222	1,540
Going Snake	317	1,081	1,052	2,015	118	2,133
Illinois	536	1,139	1,202	1,556	785	2,341
Saline	420	673	680	1,212	141	1,353
Sequoyah	304	734	678	1,221	191	1,412
Tahlequah	630	1,432	1,456	2,298	590	2,888
Total	4,262	10,011	9,724	15,150	4,585	19,735

Source: Cherokee Nation (1881:6, table A).

Table 11. Population of the Cherokee Nation by Race and District, 1880

District	Cherokees	White	Black	Delaware	Shawnee	Creek	Miscellaneous	Total
Canadian	1,372	128	70	0	0	8	2	1,580
Cooweescoowee	1,797	220	546	600	290	1	4	3,458
Delaware	2,371	274	101	72	209	0	3	3,030
Flint	1,469	49	12	0	0	10	0	1,540
Going Snake	2,015	108	5	0	0	5	0	2,133
Illinois	1,556	87	539	0	4	155	0	2,341
Saline	1,212	19	122	0	0	0	0	1,353
Sequoyah	1,217	54	125	0	0	12	4	1,412
Tahlequah	2,298	93	456	0	0	41	0	2,888
Total	15,307	1,032	1,976	672	503	232	13	19,735

Source: Cherokee Nation (1881:7, table B).

an average family size of 4.63. There were 10,011 males and 9,724 females; the sex ratio was therefore 103.[2]

Table 11 shows the enumeration of the so-called citizen population by race and district: 15,307 were enumerated as Cherokee, 1,032 as white, and 1,976 as black, and there were 1,420 American Indians of other tribes.

In addition, there were enumerated 5,352 noncitizens of the Cherokee Nation: 521 of these had been rejected for citizenship; 265 had claims pending; 2,745 were individuals permitted in the Cherokee Nation; and 1,821 were classified as intruders (Cherokee Nation 1881:12, table J, 13, table K, 14, table M). This last group were the "boomers." The total population residing in the Cherokee Nation in 1880 was therefore 25,438 as enumerated, or 26,039 with the added 601 names.

The Cherokee Nation to 1890

By 1882 the Cherokee population in Indian Territory was listed as 20,336, the same as given in the adjusted 1880 Cherokee census. However, the figure included some recent immigrants from the East: 161 Eastern Cherokees emigrated to Indian Territory in 1881 (U.S. Department of the Interior 1882:334,lxx). Included among the immigrants to Indian Territory was John Ross, a chief of the Eastern Cherokees. (This was not the John Ross who was chief during the removal period and thereafter, who died in 1866.) By 1883 the Cherokees in Indian Territory were estimated at 22,000, based on the same 1880 census (U.S. Department of the Interior 1883:87).

In 1884 the total Cherokee population was given as 23,000. It was noted in the 1884 *Annual Report of the Commissioner of Indian Affairs*: "The number of full-blood Indians is decreasing, while the increased number of mixed-bloods, and the adopted white and colored citizens make the population about the same from year to year." It was also noted that the number of whites was increasing (U.S. Department of the Interior 1884:98).[3] The official estimate of the 1885 Cherokee population was about 22,000, however (U.S. Department of the Interior 1885:103, 342). Referring to the Cherokee Nation, the 1885 *Annual Report of the Commissioner of Indian Affairs* stated:

> Her citizens are full-blood Cherokees; half-blood Cherokees to one sixty-fourth Cherokee and ——— white stock; Cherokee crossed on Creek, on Choctaw, on Chickasaw, &c., and on the African stock; adopted citizens of the Cherokee Nation—full-blood Shawnees, full-blood Delawares, full-blood Creeks, full-blood white men, full-blood Africans, and the same stock variously blended with Cherokees and with other races, including Creeks, Choctaws, Osages, Chickasaws. The much larger part of the nation is of the Cherokee blood, about 8,000 full-blood and 8,000 mixed-blood, and about 5,000 of the other races mentioned.[4] (U.S. Department of the Interior 1885:105–6)

By 1886 the population had apparently increased again to an estimated 23,000 Cherokees, adopted whites, Delawares, Shawnees, and "freedmen."[5] This same figure was given for 1887 by the commissioner of Indian affairs (U.S. Department of the Interior 1886:147, 1887:100, 354). It was also noted in 1887 that there were 10,200 mixed-bloods and that the adopted citizens totaled 4,815: 1,100 whites, 550 Shawnees, 765 Delawares, and 2,400 blacks. In 1888 it was reported that the population had increased by 300: from 23,000 to 23,300. In 1889 the population was given as 24,400 (U.S. Department of the Interior 1887:113, 354, 1888:416, 1889:202, 502). The Wallace Roll of freedmen taken at this time listed 3,524 freedman claimants (Mooney [1900] 1987:14; also Wardell [1938] 1977:236). Rolls of Delawares and Shawnees taken at the same time listed 759 Delawares and 624 Shawnees (subsequently revised to 737) (Wardell [1938] 1977:37).

The Cherokee Nation in 1890

The Cherokees in Indian Territory were included in the regular United States decennial census for the first time in 1890, in the Eleventh Census, as were all American Indians in the United States. (American Indians not on reservations were included in earlier censuses, and sometimes reservation Indians were counted under special enumerations.) This was pursuant to the Census Act of March 1, 1889: "The Superintendent of Census may employ special agents or other means to make an enumeration of all Indians living within the jurisdiction of the United States, with such information as to their condition as may be obtainable, classifying them as to Indians taxed and Indians not taxed" (U.S. Bureau of the Census 1894b:24).

According to the 1890 census, there were 22,015 American Indians in the Cherokee Nation plus 34,294 individuals of other races: 5,127 blacks, 29,166 whites, and 1 Chinese; the total population on Cherokee land in Indian Territory was thus 56,309 (U.S. Bureau of the Census 1894a:4). The Census Bureau stated in this regard:

A serious difficulty was met in the answer to "Are you an Indian?" Under the laws of the Five Tribes or nations of the Indian Territory a person, white in color and features, is frequently an Indian, being so by remote degree of blood or by adoption. There are many whites now resident claiming to be Indians whose claims have not as yet been acted upon by the nations. Negroes are frequently

Table 12. "Citizen" Population of the
Cherokee Nation, 1890

District	Population
Canadian	2,302
Cooweescoowee	5,621
Delaware	3,893
Flint	1,881
Going Snake	2,675
Illinois	2,686
Saline	1,514
Sequoyah	1,440
Tahlequah	3,966
Total	25,978

Source: U.S. Bureau of the Census (1894a: 5).

met who speak nothing but Indian languages, and are Indians by tribal law and custom, and others are met who call themselves Indians, who have not yet been so acknowledged by the tribes. These circumstances necessarily produced some confusion as to the number of Indians separately designated. However, the total population as given is correct. (U.S. Bureau of the Census 1894a: 3)

Be this as it may, of the 22,015 American Indians counted, 20,624 were Cherokees—11,531 were full-bloods—and 1,391 were other American Indians. There were 754 Delawares in the Cherokee Nation, "as part of it," about 175 of whom were full-bloods; these Delawares resided "in a compact body by themselves in 2 districts, known as Cooweescoowee and Delaware districts" and were "increasing in numbers." There were also 694 Shawnees in the Cherokee Nation in 1890; they generally lived "in close neighborhood" and were preserving their "language and customs" (U.S. Bureau of the Census 1894a: 44, 50). Of the 5,127 "blacks," 4,658 were designated as black, 421 as "mulatto," fourteen as "octoroon," 32 as "quadroon," 1 as "negro Choctaw," and 1 as "negro Cherokee" (U.S. Bureau of the Census 1894a: 5). Of the total 56,309 counted in the 1890 United States census, 25,978 were citizens of the Cherokee Nation as determined in the 1890 Cherokee national census and as shown in table 12. To this total could be added Cherokees elsewhere in Indian Territory; for example: 149 Cherokees, 1 Pottawatomie-Cherokee, 56 "white Cherokees," and 4 "black Cherokees" in the Chickasaw Nation; 87

Cherokees, 1 "Cherokee octoroon," and 1 "one-sixteenth Cherokee" in the Choctaw Nation; and 426 Cherokees in the Creek Nation (U.S. Bureau of the Census 1894a: 5, 6).

THE EASTERN CHEROKEES TO 1890

In 1868, shortly after the Civil War, Congress ordered a census of the Cherokees in the East in order to distribute future payments to individuals due under the treaty of 1835. The census was "to include only those persons whose names had appeared on the Mullay roll of 1848 and their legal heirs and representatives" (Mooney [1900] 1982:172). This census was conducted by Silas H. Swetland in 1868–69. Swetland was instructed: "It will be your duty therefore to make a new roll based upon that reported by Mr. Mullay, of all Cherokees whose names are embraced wherein who are living at the present time; and also, of the heirs and legal representatives of all those who were enrolled by Mr. Mullay and entitled to be paid under the act of July 29, 1848, and who have since deceased. These and no other persons will be included in the roll" (quoted in Litton 1940:214–15). The census brought many complaints and even litigation (Royce [1887] 1975:192) and thus seems of little use. Swetland did find 800 Cherokee full-bloods at the Qualla settlement; almost 400 Cherokees, "mostly fullblood," at Cheoah; about 500 Cherokees around Murphy, "many of whom are partly or largely of white blood," only a part of whom were listed on his roll; and a few Cherokees at Sand Town (Litton 1940:216).

Population to 1880

In 1872 there were officially 1,700 Cherokees in North Carolina, Tennessee, and Georgia; about 130 had removed to Indian Territory in 1871. In 1874 there were reported to be 2,000 Cherokees in North Carolina and adjacent states. In 1876 they were reported as numbering 1,600 in North Carolina—805 males and 795 females—of whom 750 were full-bloods. The Cherokee population of Georgia, South Carolina, and Tennessee was given as 800 (U.S. Department of the Interior 1872:25, 1874b:64, 1876:216). In 1878 the commissioner of Indian affairs listed the Cherokee population of North Carolina, Georgia, South Carolina, and Tennessee as 2,200:

1,105 males and 1,095 females (U.S. Department of the Interior 1878: 292). (The numbers were from his report of a year earlier.)

By this time the Cherokees in the East had developed a new tribal government, adopted a new tribal constitution, and regained lands in North Carolina consisting of the Qualla Boundary and several individual tracts outside it (Mooney [1900] 1982:173), particularly an adjacent 3,200-acre tract. (See map 5.) They had now formally established the Eastern Band of Cherokees though they as yet had not achieved state or federal recognition. Nevertheless an agency was reestablished among the Eastern Band of Cherokees, and Joseph G. Hester was appointed to take a census of all Cherokees east of the Mississippi River (Mooney [1900] 1982:176). (The Hester census was not completed until June 1884.)

Population in the 1880s

In 1883, while preparations were being made for this census, it was estimated that the Eastern Band of Cherokees totaled 3,000 (U.S. Department of the Interior 1883:276); the population of the Eastern Cherokees in North Carolina was listed at 2,000: "One thousand members of this tribe live within the Qualla boundary situated in the counties of Swain and Jackson, North Carolina; these are mainly of full blood. In the counties of Graham and Cherokee about 600 reside, half of whom are full blood, and the other half being more or less mixed. In the counties of Buncombe, Yancy, Madison, and Clay, are near 400, none of whom are full blood. . . . The physical condition of this people may be regarded as at a standstill, and the increase, especially among the full bloods, is very slight" (U.S. Department of the Interior 1883:125–26).

A year later the Department of the Interior estimated the population at 3,100 and noted: "There has been some sickness and a few deaths among this people during the last year, but no serious epidemic has prevailed among them" (U.S. Department of the Interior 1884:294, 140). This same year the Hester census enumerated 2,956 individuals: 1,881 in North Carolina, 758 in Georgia, 213 in Tennessee, 71 in Alabama, 11 in Kentucky, 8 in New Jersey, 5 in Virginia, 3 each in Kansas and South Carolina, and 1 each in California, Colorado, and Illinois (U.S. Bureau of the Census 1894b:501; also Litton 1940:220–21; Blankenship 1978:65–86). According to Mooney, writing in 1900, "Although this census received the approval and certifi-

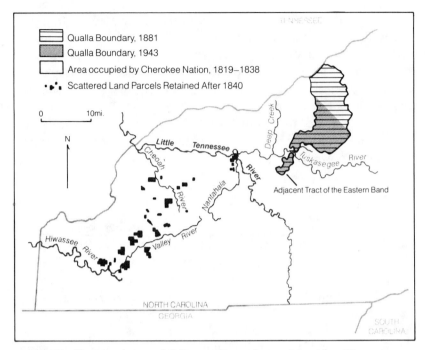

5. The Qualla Boundary and Adjacent Tract about 1880. After Finger
(1984:123, map 3) and Gilbert (1943: fig. 38).

cate [*sic*] of the East Cherokee council, a large portion of the band still
refuse to recognize it as authoritative, claiming that a large number of
persons therein enrolled have no Cherokee blood" ([1900] 1982:176).

For the following five years the *Annual Report of the Commissioner of Indian Affairs* listed the population at 3,000 (see U.S. Department of the Interior 1885:348, 1886:404, 1887:358, 1888:422,
1889:508). In 1886 it was noted that there were 1,000 mixed-bloods,
1,400 males and 1,600 females, and 600 children between the ages
of six and sixteen; in 1887 it was reported that there were thirty-
six births and eighteen deaths and in 1888, eight births and seven
deaths.

Mooney's Concern

James Mooney visited the Eastern Band of Cherokees for the second time in July 1888. His biographer noted that he spent most of the
month studying the 1882 census of the Eastern Cherokees (Moses

1984:32). Dr. Washington Matthews of the Army Medical Museum asked Mooney to compile statistics on disease and mortality among certain tribes, and Mooney discovered that the death rate of the Eastern Cherokees far outpaced the birthrate (Moses 1984:33), despite the official figures above. Poor sanitation, tuberculosis, and alcoholism were serious health problems (Finger 1984:155). This information was communicated to the Bureau of Indian Affairs via Matthews, and the bureau sent a medical team to treat the Cherokees and begin a program of preventive medicine (Moses 1984:33).

The Eastern Cherokees in 1890

On March 11, 1889, the Eastern Cherokees in North Carolina were incorporated by the general assembly of the state of North Carolina, becoming the Eastern Band of Cherokee Indians (U.S. Bureau of the Census 1892:7). There were then two groups of Eastern Cherokees: this band and all those Cherokees elsewhere in the East, though both were often considered Eastern Cherokees. As enumerated in the 1890 United States census, the population of the Eastern Band of Cherokee Indians was 1,520, many of whom were full-blood Cherokees: 774 males and 746 females; the sex ratio was 103.8 (U.S. Bureau of the Census, 1892:7–8).[6] (Fourteen of the males had served in the Union army in the Civil War, all but one in Company A, Third Regiment, North Carolina mounted infantry; fifty had served in the Confederate army [U.S. Bureau of the Census 1894:508].) Eastern Cherokees elsewhere were enumerated at 1,365: 936 in Georgia, 318 in Tennessee, and 111 in Alabama. The census noted that "the few living in Kentucky, Virginia, and other states had been incorporated into the white population (U.S. Bureau of the Census 1892:7). The total population was thus 2,885.

THE CHEROKEE NATION AND THE EASTERN CHEROKEES TO 1900

From 1890 to 1900 the two Cherokee populations, East and West, had somewhat different patterns. Characteristic of the Cherokees in Indian Territory, even during this single decade, was a marked tendency to incorporate non-Cherokees into their population.

The Cherokee Nation

The western Cherokee Nation population of 1892 was reported as 26,256. In 1895 it was reported as only 25,388: 21,232 Cherokees "by blood," 2,052 "freedmen," and 2,011 intermarried whites plus 82 Creeks and 11 Choctaws: this same year it was ruled that 759 Delawares, 737 Shawnees, and no additional freedmen were "entitled" to citizenship (U.S. Department of the Interior 1892:786, 1896:162, 82). In 1898 the population was reported as 34,461: 26,500 Cherokees by blood, 4,000 freedmen, 2,300 intermarried whites, 871 Delawares, and 790 Shawnees (U.S. Department of the Interior 1898:159, 600). According to these figures, then, the Cherokee population increased by 9,073 from 1895 to 1898. Of this increase only 5,268, or 58 percent, was in Cherokees "by blood"; the remainder was in freedmen, 1,948, or 21.5 percent; intermarried whites, 289, or 3.2 percent; and Delaware and Shawnee Indians, 1,568, or 17.3 percent. As given in the 1900 United States census but obtained from reports of the commissioner of Indian affairs, there were 31,000 Cherokees in Indian Territory, apparently exclusive of intermarried whites and freedmen (U.S. Bureau of the Census 1915:83).

The Ceding of the Cherokee Outlet

Although specified in the treaty of 1866, the ceding of the western strip of land known as the Cherokee Outlet by the Cherokee Nation did not occur until the 1890s. In 1891 Cherokee Nation representatives agreed to cede the Outlet for a consideration of over $9,000,000 (Wardell [1938] 1977:237). Provision was made for payments to freedmen, Delawares, and Shawnees. The "Wallace roll" was to be the basis of distribution to the freedmen, but the Cherokees objected that it was inaccurate (Wardell [1938] 1977:237). Instead they wanted the 1880 Cherokee census to be used, supplemented by a special commission: the Wallace roll specified 3,524 freedman claimants; the 1880 census listed 1,976 blacks (plus others with "claims" to citizenship).

Turmoil followed, but eventually the Cherokee Nation ceded the Outlet. Congress approved the purchase of the Outlet on March 3, 1893, and the sale was ratified by the Cherokee Nation on May 17, 1893. One participant in the decision for the Cherokee Nation, Wallace Thornton, recalls the vote and the circumstances surrounding it:

I was a member of the Cherokee Council and voted to open up the Cherokee Strip in 1893. Joel B. Mayes was Chief of the Cherokee Nation. The day that we were to vote on the bill, every citizen in the whole country came to Tahlequah and would gang up at the windows and try to hear and see how we were voting.

The north, what is now republicans, were opposed to the bill and the south or democrats favored it. Senator George Clark made a speech before the Council that day. In his speech he said, "I am going to vote for the bill because the people want it, but when that is done, the next thing will be the allotting of the land and every Indian will only be allowed so much land." And his prophecy came to pass in a very short time. But the next thing to take place was the Cherokee Payment. Every one was interested then and no one opposed that bill. This payment was made at Fort Gibson. Everyone had to go there to get their money. The payment was made in currency, no checks. This, of course, was very slow work and the Indians gathered there by the thousands and camped. Some of them for weeks, waiting their turn to get their money. There was much drinking and gambling going on there and many fights. Some Indians would get their money and lose much of it before they would leave. Others made money swapping horses and so on.

The election of officers among the Indians were very different to our elections now. Instead of having a primary like we have now to nominate candidates for the various offices, the council would have a meeting somewhere and anyone who wanted to attend could do so. They would all sit around in a circle and the men would get up and nominate the person they wanted for a certain office and someone else would nominate a different person. A clerk would make a list of the names and what office he was nominated for.

When election day came, there were many full-bloods who could not read and write so they were let into a room, one at a time as their turn came and they would tell a clerk who they wanted to vote for and he would write their names down and drop them into the box to be counted. (W. Thornton 1937)

On September 16, 1893, at high noon, the former Cherokee Outlet was opened for settlement. It resulted in perhaps the greatest land rush in the history of the United States. Many invaded the Outlet before the designated time to stake claims to the land—they became known as "sooners."

The Eastern Cherokees

The population of the Eastern Cherokees in 1895 was given as 2,893 by the commissioner of Indian affairs: 1,479 in North Carolina within the Qualla Boundary and in Graham and Cherokee counties and 1,414 elsewhere (U.S. Department of the Interior 1896:572).[7] Mooney noted, regarding the North Carolina Cherokees, that in 1896 "an epidemic of grippe spread through the band, with the result that the census of 1897 shows but 1,312. . . . In the next year the population had recovered to 1,351" (Mooney [1900] 1982:179). Officially in 1900, Eastern Cherokees in North Carolina numbered 1,376 (U.S. Bureau of the Census 1915:83), 1,100 of whom were on the Qualla reservation, "the rest living farther to the west, on Nantahala, Cheowa and Hiwassee rivers. This does not include mixed-bloods in adjoining states and some hundreds of unrecognized claimants" (Mooney [1900] 1982:180).

CHAPTER 6

New Cherokees:
1900 to 1980

On February 8, 1887, the Dawes Act was approved by the United States Congress to provide for the possible allotment of American Indian tribal lands in severalty—that is, to individual tribal members.[1] It did not extend to the Cherokee Nation of Indian Territory, to the other Five Civilized Tribes, or to certain additional American Indian tribes (see Prucha 1975:171–74; Washburn 1975). The Commission to the Five Civilized Tribes (Dawes Commission) and the Curtis Act were in the same vein as the Dawes Act. The Commission to the Five Civilized Tribes was created on March 3, 1893, to negotiate with the Cherokee Nation and the others of the Five Tribes "for the purpose of the extinguishment of the national or tribal title to any lands within that Territory now held by any and all of such nations or tribes" (Prucha 1975:189). The Curtis Act was passed on June 28, 1898, to establish tribal rolls and allot lands to individual members based on the rolls (see Prucha 1975:197–98). A subsequent agreement was made with the Cherokee Nation in 1900 for the allotment of their tribal lands (Kappler 1904–79, 2:715–29; see also Institute for the Development of American Indian Law, n.d.b.:77–88). In 1902 the Act to Allot the Lands of the Cherokee Nation was formally approved (Kappler 1904–79, 2:787–98; see also Institute for the Development of American Indian Law, n.d.b.:89–98). A final tribal roll was to be established for the purpose of this allotment; the tribal government of the Cherokee Nation was not to continue past March 4, 1906. The total Cherokee Nation population in Indian Territory at that time was estimated at 35,000 (U.S. Department of the Interior 1903:172). The total population *residing* in the Cherokee Nation in 1900 was 101,754 (U.S. Bureau of the Census 1907:8, table 2); the difference, of course, was primarily composed of nontribal whites and blacks.

As one might expect, the situation resulted in considerable conflict in the Cherokee Nation. Full-bloods resisted being placed on the tribal rolls, since they did not want to allot the Cherokee lands, particularly to mixed-bloods and intermarried whites. Many managed to avoid enrollment for a considerable time. (It has been reported that about this time mixed-bloods outnumbered full-bloods by about three to one [see Littlefield 1971:405].) Many full-bloods subsequently became affiliated with the Keetoowah Society, which was incorporated in 1905 under a United States court order (Wright 1951:74–75). Given the turmoil, the Keetoowah Society soon became factionalized, and one leader, Redbird Smith, strongly opposed to allotment, withdrew, taking his followers with him, and formed the organization known as the Nighthawk Keetoowahs (Hendrix 1983b:80), with Smith as chairman. In 1906 Smith's title was changed from chairman to chief. Hendrix maintains that this was the Nighthawks' way of making a political statement, since the Cherokees now had no principal chief (1983b:81). The Nighthawks continued to avoid allotment, and they and other full-bloods envisioned forming their own "utopian" society, perhaps in Mexico (see, for example, Littlefield 1971). The 1906 *Annual Report of the Department of the Interior* stated in this regard: "The opposing element has been more noticable in the Cherokee Nation than in the other tribes. Here most of the full bloods continue to dream of a land inhabited only by Indians and wild animals. The greater number of these Indians are known as 'Ketoowahs,' or 'Night-Hawks'" (U.S. Department of the Interior 1907a:623).

Eventually Cherokee lands were allotted to individual tribal members, full-bloods included, as established by a tribal roll, pursuant to the acts of 1898 and 1902 and subsequent acts of Congress:

> The actual work in the preparation of the rolls of Cherokee citizens under the act of June 28, 1898, was begun in May, 1900, . . . the act of July 1, 1902 (32 stat. L., 716), which was ratified by the citizens of the Cherokee Nation August 7, 1902, fixt September 1 of that year as the date for the closing of the rolls and October 31, 1902 as the limit within which applications for enrollment as Cherokee citizens could be received. The limitation for the reception of original applications for enrollment as Cherokee citizens was

later extended by the act of April 26, 1906 to December 1, 1905. (U.S. Department of the Interior 1907a:622)

The date of extension for the enrollment of minor children was even later, to July 26, 1906. The rolls were to be closed on March 4, 1907 (U.S. Department of the Interior, 1907a:624–55; 1907b:290, 292).

Individual applicants for the tribal roll were interviewed and an Indian blood quantum was determined, but many were enrolled at a lower blood quantum than they actually possessed. This is shown in the testimony and subsequent enrollment of Wallace Thornton, who as a boy had fled the destruction of the Cherokee Nation during the Civil War:

What is your name? Wallace Thornton.
What is your age Mr Thornton? Forty four.
What is your Postoffice? Vian.
Your district: Illinois.
For whom do you apply for enrollment? Myself and family.
That means your wife? Yes sir.
And how many children? Four.
You apply then for yourself, wife and four children? Yes sir.
Do you apply for yourself as a Cherokee by blood? Yes sir.
Do you apply for your wife as a Cherokee by blood? Yes sir.
What proportion of Cherokee blood do you claim? About three-fourths.
(W. Thornton 1937)

Wallace Thornton was enrolled as only one-half Cherokee. As shown in figure 3, however, which is the enrollment certificate of his son Walter (named after his grandfather, Walter or Watt), Wallace Thornton's full brother Smith was enrolled as three-fourths Cherokee.

Subsequently enrolled members of the Cherokee Nation were then eligible for an allotment of land and also a homestead, since nonallotted land was to be opened for homesteading by anyone. For example, Walter Thornton received both an allotment and a homestead. (See figs. 4 and 5.)

To sell their newly acquired individual parcels of land within five years (homesteads within twenty-one years), Cherokee "citizens by blood" had to receive approval from the United States government. (See fig. 6.) Intermarried whites and "freedmen," except children, could sell their land, except homesteads, without approval. By June 30, 1905, 577 Cherokee petitions had been filed for removal of

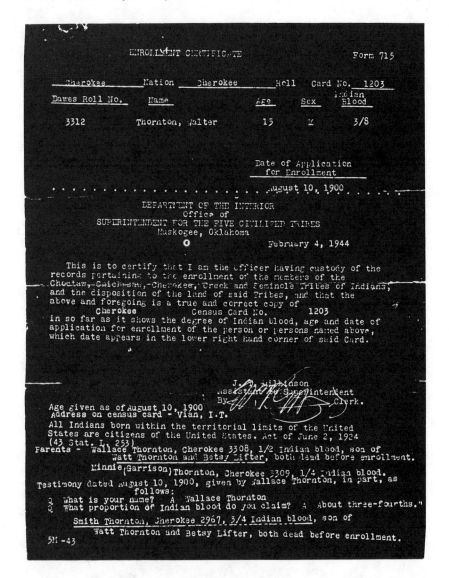

Figure 3. Enrollment certificate of Walter Thornton.

restrictions; 138 had been approved (U.S. Department of the Interior 1906:216–17).

By the end of fiscal year 1906, there had been 51,167 applications for enrollment; 35,949 citizens of the Cherokee Nation had been enrolled: 31,839 Cherokees by blood and 4,110 freedmen. There were

ALLOTMENT DEED. 10178 (77)   Cherokee Citizen   ROLL. No. 3312

THE CHEROKEE NATION,
INDIAN TERRITORY.

To All To Whom These Presents Shall Come, Greeting:

WHEREAS, By the Act of Congress approved July 1, 1902 (32 Stat., 716), ratified by the Cherokee Nation August 7, 1902, it is provided that there shall be allotted by the Commission to the Five Civilized Tribes, to each citizen of the Cherokee Tribe, land equal in value to one hundred and ten acres of the average allottable lands of the Cherokee Nation, and,

WHEREAS, It was provided by said Act of Congress that each citizen shall designate or have designated and selected for him, at the time of his selection of allotment, out of his allotment, as a homestead, land equal in value to forty acres of the average allottable lands of the Cherokee Nation, as nearly as may be, for which he shall receive a separate certificate, and,

WHEREAS, The said Commission to the Five Civilized Tribes has certified that the land

hereinafter described has been selected by or on behalf of

_____Walter Thornton_____, a citizen of said tribe, as an allotment, exclusive of land equal in value to forty acres of the average allottable lands of the Cherokee Nation, selected as a homestead as aforesaid,

NOW, THEREFORE, I, the undersigned Principal Chief of the Cherokee Nation, by virtue of the power and authority vested in me by aforesaid Act of the Congress of the United States, have granted and conveyed, and by these presents do grant and convey unto the said

Walter Thornton

all right, title and interest of the Cherokee Nation, and of all other citizens of said Nation, in and to the following described land, viz: The South East Quarter of the North East Quarter of the South West Quarter and the South West Quarter of the North West Quarter of the South East Quarter and the South West Quarter of the South East Quarter of Section Thirty-five (35), Township Twelve (12) North and Range Twenty-one (21) East, and the North West Nine and 86/100 (9.86) Acres of Lot Two (2) of Section Two (2), Township Eleven (11) North and Range Twenty-one (21) East, and the North West Quarter of the North West Quarter of the North West Quarter of Section Twenty-one (21), Township Twelve (12) North and Range Twenty-two (22) East

of the Indian Base and Meridian in Indian Territory, containing

_____Seventy-nine and 86/100 (79.86)_____ acres, more or less, as the case may be, according to the United States survey thereof, subject, however, to all the provisions of said Act of Congress.

IN WITNESS WHEREOF, I, the Principal Chief of the Cherokee Nation, have hereunto set my hand and caused the Great Seal of said Nation to be affixed this _____ day of _____ A. D. 190 .

Principal Chief of the Cherokee Nation.

Department of the Interior,

Approved

_____ Secretary.

By _____ Clerk.

Figure 4. Allotment certificate of Walter Thornton.

HOMESTEAD DEED. 10178 (80)   Cherokee Citizen   ROLL, NO. 3312

THE CHEROKEE NATION,

INDIAN TERRITORY.

To All To Whom These Presents Shall Come, Greeting:

WHEREAS, By the Act of Congress approved July 1, 1902, (32 Stat., 716), ratified by the Cherokee Nation August 7, 1902, it was provided that there should be allotted, by the Commission to the Five Civilized Tribes, to each citizen of the Cherokee Nation, land equal in value to one hundred and ten acres of the average allottable lands of the Cherokee Nation, and,

WHEREAS, It was provided by said Act of Congress that each member of said tribe shall, at the time of the selection of his allotment, designate, or have selected and designated for him, from his allotment, land equal in value to forty acres of the average allottable lands of the Cherokee Nation, as nearly as may be, as a homestead, for which separate certificate shall issue; and,

WHEREAS, The said Commission to the Five Civilized Tribes has certified that the land hereinafter described has been selected by or on behalf of

Walter Thornton , a citizen of said tribe, as a homestead,

Now, THEREFORE, I, the undersigned, the Principal Chief of the Cherokee Nation, by virtue of the power and authority vested in me by the aforesaid Act of the Congress of the United States, have granted and conveyed, and by these presents do grant and convey unto the said

Walter Thornton

all right, title and interest of the Cherokee Nation, and of all other citizens of said Nation, in and to the following described land, viz.: The South East Quarter of the South West

Quarter of Section Thirty-five (35), Township Twelve (12) North and

Range Twenty-one (21) East

of the Indian Base and Meridian, in Indian Territory, containing

Forty (40)

acres, more or less, as the case may be, according to the United States survey thereof, subject, however, to the conditions provided by said Act of Congress pertaining to allotted homesteads.

IN WITNESS WHEREOF, I, the Principal Chief of the Cherokee Nation, have hereunto

set my hand and caused the Great Seal of said Nation to be affixed this _____ day

of ____ May ____ A. D., 190 .

Principal Chief of the Cherokee Nation.

Department of the Interior,

Approved ____ 1906 , 190 .

Thomas Ryan
Secretary.

By _Oliver A. Phelps_
Clerk.

Figure 5. Homestead certificate of Walter Thornton.

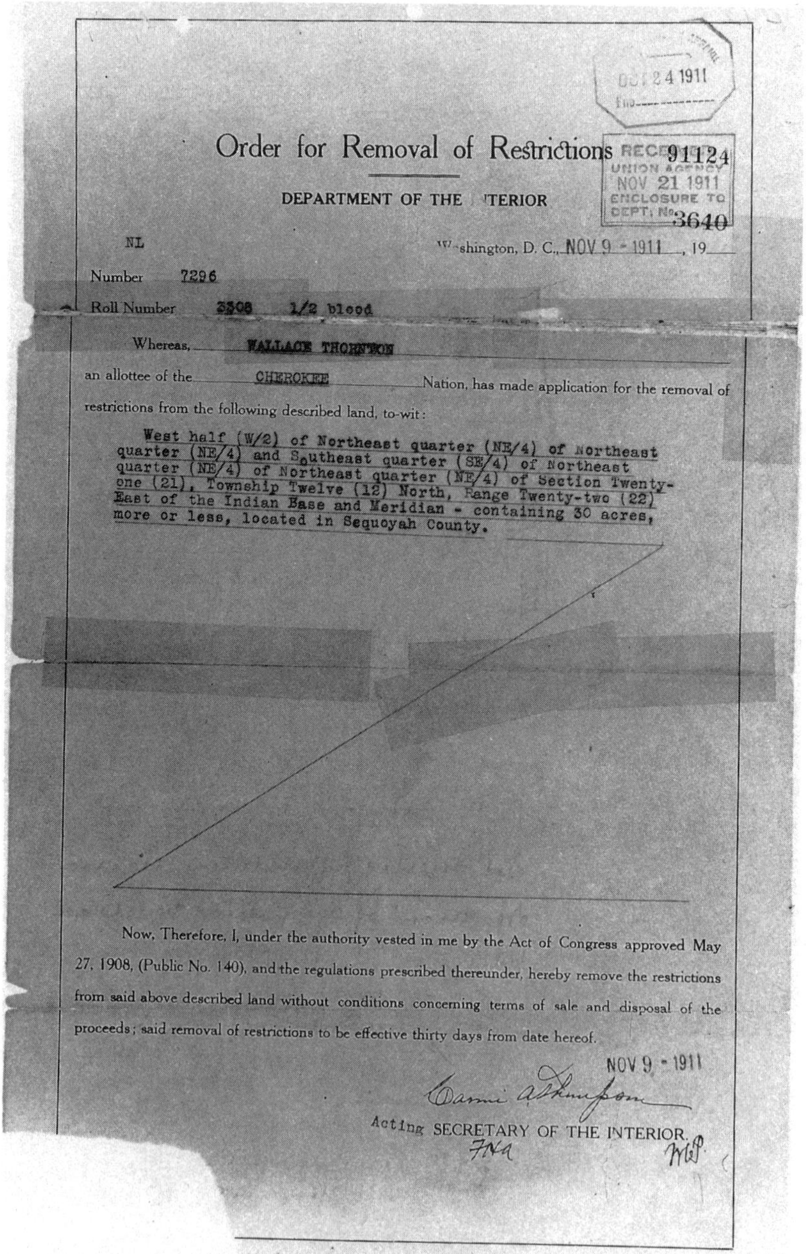

OCT 24 1911

Order for Removal of Restrictions

91124

RECEIVED UNION AGENCY NOV 21 1911 ENCLOSURE TO DEPT. No. 3640

DEPARTMENT OF THE INTERIOR

NL

Washington, D. C., NOV 9 - 1911, 19

Number 7296

Roll Number 3308 1/2 blood

Whereas, WALLACE THORNTON

an allottee of the CHEROKEE Nation, has made application for the removal of restrictions from the following described land, to-wit:

West half (W/2) of Northeast quarter (NE/4) of Northeast quarter (NE/4) and Southeast quarter (SE/4) of Northeast quarter (NE/4) of Northeast quarter (NE/4) of Section Twenty-one (21), Township Twelve (12) North, Range Twenty-two (22) East of the Indian Base and Meridian - containing 30 acres, more or less, located in Sequoyah County.

Now, Therefore, I, under the authority vested in me by the Act of Congress approved May 27, 1908, (Public No. 140), and the regulations prescribed thereunder, hereby remove the restrictions from said above described land without conditions concerning terms of sale and disposal of the proceeds; said removal of restrictions to be effective thirty days from date hereof.

NOV 9 - 1911

Carmi A. Thompson

Acting SECRETARY OF THE INTERIOR.

Figure 6. Order for removal of restrictions of Wallace Thornton.

also 196 registered Cherokee-Delawares (Delawares born since the register of 1867 [U.S. Department of the Interior 1904:117]); the situation of 1,143 intermarried whites was still pending (U.S. Department of the Interior 1907a:145, 622, 626).

On July 1, 1907, the final and complete roll of the Cherokee Nation was closed. It contained the names of 41,798 citizens: 31,400 Cherokees by blood, including 8,698 full-bloods and over 1,000 Delawares and some Shawnees; 197 registered Delaware-Cherokees; 4,991 Cherokee minors; 286 intermarried whites; 4,305 freedmen; and 619 freedmen minors (U.S. Department of the Interior 1907b:292; also Wardell [1938] 1977:332–33). Thus only 27.7 percent of the Cherokees by blood were full-bloods. There had been a total of 53,724 applicants: 42,253 Cherokees by blood, Delawares, and Shawnees; 7,844 Cherokee freedmen; and 3,627 intermarried whites (U.S. Department of the Interior 1907b:292). At that time, 1907, given the large influx of whites and others into the Cherokee Nation, the total population in the geographic area that was formerly the Cherokee Nation was 140,415 (U.S. Bureau of the Census 1907:8, table 2).

That same year the Cherokee Nation and Indian Territory became part of the then-created state of Oklahoma. Although in 1906 the government of the Cherokee Nation was to have ended, it was continued —in a restructured form—until June 30, 1914, by an act of Congress. (Actually, the principal chief at the time, William C. Rogers, continued to serve until 1917 in order to sign deeds to Cherokee lands.)

THE CHEROKEES IN 1910

The 1910 United States census enumerated 265,683 American Indians (plus 25,331 Native Americans in Alaska): 31,489 were Cherokees (which compares closely with the 31,400 Cherokees by blood on the final roll of the Cherokee Nation in 1907). There were 16,105 males and 15,384 females, making a sex ratio of 104.7 (U.S. Bureau of the Census 1915:132, table 51). (The sex ratio for all American Indians was 103.5 [U.S. Bureau of the Census 1915:44, table 24].) The Cherokees were the largest American Indian group in the United States at that time and were enumerated in twenty-five states, but only Oklahoma and North Carolina had more than 1,000: Oklahoma with 29,610, and North Carolina with 1,406 (U.S. Bureau of the Census 1915:10, table 1, 14, 15, table 8, 17, table 9).

Full-Bloods and Mixed-Bloods

The United States census was not an enumeration of Cherokee "citizens," as frequently reported above; rather, it was of Cherokees "by blood." The 1910 Census Bureau report pointed out: "It should be noted that all persons of mixed white and Indian blood who have an appreciable amount of Indian blood are counted as Indians, even though the proportion of white blood may exceed that of Indian blood." Only 6,900, or 21.9 percent, of the Cherokees were enumerated as full-blood (U.S. Bureau of the Census 1915:10, 33, table 14). (The blood quantum of 260 Cherokees, or 0.8 percent, was not reported.) This 21.9 percent compared with 56.5 percent of the total American Indian population enumerated as full-blood (U.S. Bureau of the Census 1915:31, table 12). (The blood quantum of 8.4 percent of the total American Indian population was not reported.) It also compared with the 27.7 percent of full-bloods among Cherokees by blood on the final roll of 1907.

Percentage of Cherokee full-bloods varied greatly from Oklahoma to North Carolina: 5,919, or 20.0 percent, of Oklahoma Cherokees were reported as full-blood; 934, or 65.4 percent, of North Carolina Cherokees were reported as full-blood (see table 13). Of those Cherokees enumerated as full-blood Indians, the overwhelming majority—98.3 percent—were enumerated as full-blood Cherokees, as shown in table 14, rather than as Cherokee and other tribal blood or even full-blood with exclusive non-Cherokee ancestry. This was greater than the 92.8 percent of the full-tribal blood in the total United States American Indian population. Thus full-blood Cherokees had intermarried with full-blood members of other tribes to a

Table 13. American Indian and United States, Oklahoma, and North Carolina Cherokee Population by Blood, 1910

	Full-Blood		Mixed-Blood		Blood Not Reported		
	N	%	N	%	N	%	Total
American Indian	150,053	56.5	93,423	35.2	22,207	8.4	265,683
Cherokee							
United States	6,900	21.9	24,329	77.3	260	0.8	31,489
Oklahoma	5,919	20.0	23,440	79.2	251	0.8	29,610
North Carolina	934	66.4	469	33.4	3	0.2	1,406

Source: U.S. Bureau of the Census (1915:31, table 12, 33, table 14).

Table 14. American Indian and United States, Oklahoma, and North Carolina Cherokee Full-Bloods, 1910

	Full Tribal		Mixed Tribal		Unknown Tribal		Total
	N	%	N	%	N	%	
American Indian	139,289	92.8	10,251	6.8	513	0.3	150,053
Cherokee							
United States	6,785	98.3	95	1.4	20	0.3	6,900
Oklahoma	5,827	98.4	72	1.2	20	0.3	5,919
North Carolina	920	98.5	14	1.5	0	0.0	934

Source: U.S. Bureau of the Census (1915:38, table 19, 41, table 22).

Table 15. American Indian and United States, Oklahoma, and North Carolina Cherokee Mixed-Bloods, 1910

	White/Indian		Black/Indian		Black/White/Indian		Unknown[a]		Total
	N	%	N	%	N	%	N	%	
American Indian	88,030	94.2	2,255	2.4	1,793	1.9	1,345	1.4	93,423
Cherokee									
United States	23,510	96.6	299	1.2	165	0.7	355	1.5	24,329
Oklahoma	22,722	96.9	278	1.2	86	0.4	354	1.5	23,440
North Carolina	429	91.5	2	4.3	38	8.1	0	0.0	469

Source: U.S. Bureau of the Census (1915:31, table 12, 132, table 51).
[a] Includes other mixtures.

lesser extent than had other American Indians, had relatively fewer full-bloods from other tribes in their population, or both. (Note: There were about 800 Shawnees among the Cherokees at this time [Wright 1951:241]. They may or may not have been enumerated as Cherokees in the census, though probably most if not all were not so enumerated.)

Of the 24,329 Cherokees enumerated as mixed-blood, by far the most were of solely white and American Indian mixture: 96.6 percent. This is somewhat greater than for the total United States American Indian population: 94.2 percent. Nevertheless, a significant percentage of North Carolina Cherokees reported a triracial black-white-American Indian mixture (see table 15). With the notable exception of the North Carolina Cherokees, most of the solely white-mixed Cherokee were over 50 percent of white blood, as shown in table 16. Fewer than half of the solely white-mixed North Caro-

Table 16. American Indian and United States, Oklahoma, and North
Carolina Cherokees of White Mixed Blood, 1910

	Below 50%		50%		Over 50%		Unknown		
	N	%	N	%	N	%	N	%	Total
American Indian	18,169	20.6	24,353	27.7	43,937	49.9	1,571	1.8	88,030
Cherokee									
United States	1,702	7.2	2,294	9.8	19,384	82.5	130	0.6	23,510
Oklahoma	1,429	6.3	2,172	9.6	18,997	83.6	124	0.5	22,722
North Carolina	192	44.8	39	9.1	198	46.2	0	0.0	429

Source: U.S. Bureau of the Census (1915:35, table 15, 36, table 17).

Table 17. American Indian and United States, Oklahoma, and North
Carolina Cherokees of Black Mixed Blood, 1910

	Below 50%		50%		Over 50%		Unknown		
	N	%	N	%	N	%	N	%	Total
American Indian	717	31.8	729	32.3	780	34.6	29	1.3	2,255
Cherokee									
United States	51	17.1	58	19.4	190	63.5	0	0.0	299
Oklahoma	49	17.6	53	19.1	176	63.0	0	0.0	278
North Carolina	1	50.0	1	50.0	0	0.0	0	0.0	2

Source: U.S. Bureau of the Census (1915:38, table 18, 132, table 51).

lina Cherokees were over 50 percent white. About 50 percent of
the white-mixed-blood American Indians in the total United States
population were over 50 percent white. As shown in table 17, most
of the solely black-mixed Cherokees were over 50 percent black,
although the percentage is less dramatic than with the solely white-
mixed Cherokees—overall, 63.5 percent compared with 82.5 percent.
This also is far greater than for the total American Indian population of the United States: only 34.6 percent of solely black-mixed
American Indians were over 50 percent black.

Sterility, Fertility, Fecundity

In reporting the 1910 census enumeration of Ameri-
can Indians, the Bureau of the Census reported data on the sterility
(inability to have children), fecundity (potential to have children), and
fertility (actual childbearing) of American Indian women "who were
between 15 and 44 years of age, who had been married for at least

one year, and who were neither widowed nor divorced nor married a second or subsequent time" (U.S. Bureau of the Census 1915:157).[2] The Census Bureau also reported data on the vitality (ability to survive) of these women's children. The data show a significant, general pattern of lower reproductive behavior of full-blood marriages than for other types. For example, 10.4 percent of these marriages among full-bloods (of the same tribe) had produced no children, compared with only 6.9 percent of marriages of mixed-bloods (white only); the average number of children born of these full-blood marriages for those married ten to twenty years was 4.5, but an average of 5.3 were born of similar-length mixed-blood marriages; and finally, all full-blood marriages had 70.0 of their children surviving, whereas all mixed-blood marriages had 77.8 of their children surviving (see table 18).

The Bureau of the Census concluded in this regard, "The increase of the mixed-blood Indians is much greater than that of the full-blood Indians, and that unless the tendencies now at work undergo a decided change the full-bloods are destined to form a decreasing proportion of the total Indian population and ultimately disappear altogether" (U.S. Bureau of the Census 1915:159).

Some few data were reported for specific American Indian tribes, including the Cherokees in Oklahoma (table 18). The data show that

Table 18. Fecundity, Fertility, and Vitality of Full-Blood and Mixed-Blood American Indian and Oklahoma Cherokee Marriages, 1910

	Children		
	Percentage None	Average Born	Percentage Surviving
Total American Indian marriages[a]	8.6	4.8	74.7
Full-blood marriages[b]	10.4	4.5	70.0
Mixed-blood marriages[c]	6.9	5.3	77.8
Oklahoma Cherokee marriages[a]	—	—	—
Full-blood marriages[b]	7.3	3.7	71.8
Mixed-blood marriages[c]	6.4	3.5	82.0

Source: U.S. Bureau of the Census (1915:157, table 53, 158, tables 55 and 56, 160).
[a] Women between fifteen and forty-four years of age, married at least one year, and neither divorced, widowed, nor married more than once. Average number of children born refers to marriages of from ten to twenty years.
[b] Husband and wife of same tribe.
[c] Both husband and wife of white and Indian blood.

Table 19. American Indian and United States, Oklahoma, and North Carolina Cherokee Full-Bloods and Mixed-Bloods under Twenty Years of Age, 1910

	Full-Bloods			Mixed-Bloods		
		Under Twenty			Under Twenty	
	Total	N	%	Total	N	%
American Indian	150,053	67,129	44.7	93,423	58,553	62.7
Cherokee						
United States	6,900	3,075	44.6	24,329	15,810	65.0
Oklahoma	5,919	2,684	45.3	23,440	15,268	65.1
North Carolina	934	378	40.5	469	300	64.0

Source: U.S. Bureau of the Census (1915:58, table 39, 132, table 51).

7.3 percent of Oklahoma Cherokee full-blood marriages produced no children, but only 6.4 percent of Oklahoma Cherokee mixed-blood marriages produced none; the average number of children in Cherokee full-blood marriages of ten to twenty years was 3.7, somewhat higher than the average of 3.5 children in similar mixed-blood marriages; and Cherokee full-blood marriages had 71.8 percent of their children surviving, whereas 82.0 percent of the children were surviving in mixed-blood marriages. For the Cherokees this suggested, too, that the full-blood population was decreasing relative to the mixed-blood population simply because of differences in reproductive behavior and outcome, irrespective of any patterns of intermarriage between Cherokees and non-Indians.

Of course these changes in the proportion of full-bloods and mixed-bloods in the Cherokee population, as well as in the total American Indian population, were due to other factors besides reproductive behavior—for example, mortality differences and marriage patterns. No data were available on mortality differences, but the percentage of children surviving does address this issue. Similarly, marriage patterns were not directly addressed.[3]

Nevertheless, that change was occurring can also be seen in the data presented in table 19, reporting the percentage of the populations under twenty years of age. Only 44.7 percent of the total American Indian full-blood population was under twenty, compared with 62.7 percent of the mixed-blood population. The data for the Cherokees show a similar pattern. This suggests—in fact, indicates—that more of the children being born and surviving were mixed-blood than full-blood.

THE CHEROKEE POPULATION IN 1930

By 1930 the total American Indian population had grown to 332,397, plus 29,983 Native Americans in Alaska, as enumerated in the United States census of that year. The Cherokee population numbered 45,238—22,872 males and 22,366 females, with a sex ratio of 102.3 (U.S. Bureau of the Census 1937:2, table 1, 103, table 21). (The sex ratio for all American Indians was 105.1 [U.S. Bureau of the Census 1937:91, table 20].) The median age of the Cherokees was 17.7 years (17.6 years for males, 17.8 years for females); the median age for all American Indians was 19.6 years (20.0 years for males, 19.1 years for females) (U.S. Bureau of the Census 1937:89, table 18). Thus the Cherokee population was somewhat younger than the total American Indian population. Of the total Cherokee population, there were 40,904 Cherokees in Oklahoma and 1,963 in North Carolina; the rest were in forty-two other states, particularly Alabama, Virginia, and California. The Cherokees were still the largest American Indian people in the United States; they were also "geographically by far the most widely distributed" (U.S. Bureau of the Census, 1937:59–60, table 9, 43).

Enumeration procedures in this census differed slightly from those in 1910: "The enumerators in the Fifteenth Census were instructed to return as Indians, not only those of full Indian blood, but also those of mixed white and Indian blood, 'except where the percentage of Indian blood is very small,' or where the individual was 'regarded as a white person in the community where he lives.' . . . 'A person of mixed Indian and Negro blood should be returned as a Negro unless the Indian blood predominates and the status as an Indian is generally accepted in the community' "[4] (U.S. Bureau of the Census 1937:1).

Full-Bloods and Mixed-Bloods

As enumerated, there were large changes from 1910 to 1930 in the relative proportion of full-bloods and mixed-bloods in the total American Indian population, as can be seen by comparing table 13 above with table 20: The American Indian population changed from well over half full-blood to only about half full-blood during these two decades. The change for the total Cherokees was far less dramatic, as shown in the tables; yet the Cherokee population

Table 20. American Indian and United States, Oklahoma, and North
Carolina Cherokee Populations by Blood, 1930

	Full-Bloods		Mixed-Bloods		Blood Not Reported		
	N	%	N	%	N	%	Total
American Indian	153,933	46.3	141,101	42.5	37,363	11.2	332,397
Cherokee							
United States	8,047	17.8	36,844	81.4	347	0.8	45,238
Oklahoma	7,091	17.3	33,634	82.2	179	0.4	40,904
North Carolina	759	38.7	1,204	61.3	0	0.0	1,963

Source: U.S. Bureau of the Census (1937:75–79, table 13).

Table 21. American Indian and United States Cherokee Full-Bloods and
Mixed-Bloods under Twenty Years of Age, 1930

	Full-Bloods			Mixed-Bloods		
		Under Twenty			Under Twenty	
	Total	N	%	Total	N	%
American Indian	153,933	70,786	46.0	141,101	82,830	58.7
Cherokee, United States	8,047	3,383	42.0	36,844	21,669	58.8

Source: U.S. Bureau of the Census (1937:96, 103, table 21).

was already predominantly mixed-blood by 1910. The North Carolina Cherokee population did change greatly in this regard, however:
from 66.4 percent full-bloods in 1910 to 38.7 percent in 1930. Also,
in 1910 the North Carolina Cherokees had a *higher* proportion of
full-bloods than the total American Indian population, but in 1930
they had a *lower* proportion.

As in 1910, the mixed-blood segment of the American Indian
population in 1930 was younger than the full-blood segment: the
median age of full-bloods was 22.2 years; for mixed-bloods it was
16.5 years (U.S. Bureau of the Census 1937:89, table 18). Using data
comparable to those for 1910 reported above, 58.7 percent of the
mixed-bloods were under twenty years of age as opposed to 46.0 percent of the full-bloods (see table 21). Thus, there was a slight increase
in the proportion of full-bloods under twenty years of age from 1910
to 1930 but a slight decrease in this regard for the mixed-bloods (see
tables 19 and 21).

Regarding only the Cherokees, the median age for full-bloods in
1930 was 24.2 years (24.3 years for males, 24.1 years for females);

the median age for mixed-bloods was 16.5 years (16.4 for males, 16.6 for females) (U.S. Bureau of the Census 1937:89, table 18). However, from 1910 to 1930 the proportion of full-bloods under twenty years of age decreased slightly. The proportion of mixed-bloods under twenty also decreased, but the decrease was larger than for the full-bloods. (No separate data were available for Oklahoma and North Carolina Cherokees in 1930.)

Some of these differences are surely attributable to enumeration procedures and errors in the census; nevertheless, some probably reflect real changes in the populations over time. Both the total American Indian population and the Cherokees were becoming ever more populations of mixed-bloods.

Cherokees Elsewhere, 1910 to 1930

During the decades from 1910 to 1930 the Cherokees became even more geographically dispersed. In 1910 Cherokee were living in only twenty-three states other than Oklahoma and North Carolina, as shown in table 22. In 1930 they were living in over forty-two states besides Oklahoma and North Carolina (table 22). Moreover, no state other than Oklahoma or North Carolina had as many as 100 Cherokees in 1910 (and most had fewer than 20). In 1930 eight states besides Oklahoma and North Carolina had more than 100 Cherokees (and twenty-two states had over 20).

THE CHEROKEE POPULATION IN 1970

From 1930 to 1970, the Cherokee population grew to total 66,150. As indicated by the census and other data, different demographic processes operated in the separate segments of the Cherokee population during these four decades.

The Western Cherokees to 1970

By far the largest growth occurred in the Western Cherokee population of Oklahoma, but now growth was significant elsewhere in the United States. No census data for the Cherokees are available for the separate decades between 1930 and 1970, but other figures are. The Department of the Interior estimated the Oklahoma

Table 22. Cherokee Population of States,
1910 to 1930

State	Population	
	1910	1930
Alabama	9	287
Arizona	4	101
Arkansas	0	180
California	34	258
Colorado	12	76
Florida	0	5
Georgia	0	15
Idaho	8	36
Illinois	0	18
Indiana	0	10
Iowa	0	26
Kansas	71	191
Louisiana	1	12
Massachusetts	0	8
Michigan	3	96
Minnesota	2	5
Mississippi	0	6
Missouri	13	88
Montana	12	41
Nebraska	0	25
Nevada	0	9
New Jersey	0	7
New Mexico	1	61
New York	5	26
North Carolina	1,406	1,963
North Dakota	34?	4?
Ohio	15	29
Oklahoma	29,610	40,904
Oregon	19	126
Pennsylvania	50	18
South Carolina	87?	2?
South Dakota	7	13
Tennessee	45	38
Texas	0	117
Virginia	19	268

Table 22. Continued

State	Population	
	1910	1930
Washington	8	82
Wisconsin	14	0
Wyoming	0	13
Other states	0	11[a]
Total	31,489	45,238

Source: U.S. Bureau of the Census (1937:59–60, table 9).
[a] Cherokees were living in six "other states."

Cherokee population under its jurisdiction at 43,757 in 1941,[5] including enrolled members and their descendants (U.S. Department of
the Interior 1941:8, 13, table 3, n. 6). (The Department of the Interior
[1941:9, table 3] also listed 11 Cherokees—7 males and 4 females—
in Oregon, under the Grand Ronde-Siletz Agency.) In 1943 the department's estimate was 46,300 (plus 11 in Oregon),[6] and in 1945 it
was 46,850 (plus, here again, 11 in Oregon) (U.S. Department of the
Interior 1943: 10, 11, table 3; 1945:10, 11, table 11). Wright has estimated that there were about 1,100 Shawnees among these Cherokees
in the mid-1940s (1951:241). (Estimates for these years of Cherokees
in the East are discussed below.)

One estimate placed the number of Oklahoma Cherokees of at
least one-fourth blood quantum at more than 25,600 in about 1950
(Debo 1951:5); another estimate placed the number of people in Oklahoma with "a claim to being Cherokee" at 75,000 by about the mid-
1950s (Wahrhaftig 1968:510). Concerning the former estimate, Debo
asserted: "It is my considered judgment that practically all of these
are half-bloods or over" (1951:5). Wahrhaftig pointed out that most
of the 75,000 he cited should be considered only "white Americans
of Cherokee ancestry" (1968:510). This estimate was based on work
conducted by anthropologist Sol Tax (1960) and his associates at the
University of Chicago, who produced a map detailing the distribution of descendants of American Indians in self-identified American Indian "communities." (Tax [1960] also indicated there were
about 1,100 Shawnees and 1,250 Delawares among the Cherokees
at this time, plus small, unspecified numbers of Creeks, Natchez,
and Seminoles.) Furthermore, Wahrhaftig has estimated that only
about 9,500 Oklahoma Cherokees lived and functioned "in Cherokee
settlements" in 1963. These were in five eastern Oklahoma counties

formed from former Indian lands: Adair (3,012), Cherokee (2,058), Delaware (1,838), Mayes (1,197), and Sequoyah (1,191).[7] In addition, Wahrhaftig asserted that there were another 2,000 individuals who did not live in Cherokee settlements but functioned as part of them. He also noted that there were about 10,500 Oklahomans "reared in Cherokee settlements and resident in Cherokee Nation" and 16,000 or more individuals "reared in Cherokee settlements but not necessarily participants in Cherokee society, regardless of residence." He then argued that using the same criteria of Cherokees living in Cherokee settlements and functioning in traditional Cherokee institutions, there had been only about 8,000 "conservative" Cherokees in 1902. In these terms, then, the "real Cherokee" population had increased by only a few thousand since then, and roughly three-fourths of the natural increase in the Oklahoma Cherokee population since 1902 had become assimilated into general American society (Wahrhaftig 1968:512, table 1, 513, 518).[8]

The Eastern Cherokees to 1970

The Department of the Interior estimated the population of Cherokees "under its jurisdiction" in North Carolina in the early to mid-1940s as: 1941, 3,556; 1943, 3,665; and 1945, 3,795 (U.S. Department of the Interior 1941, 8, table 3; 1943, 9, table 11; 1945, 9, table 11). (See also table 23.)

The 1950 United States census reported 2,943 Cherokees in the "Indian agency area" of North Carolina, defined as Cherokee, Graham, Jackson, and Swain counties (U.S. Bureau of the Census 1953:6, 61, table 16). In the 1950s, similarly, the population of the Eastern Band of Cherokee Indians living on the Qualla Boundary and the adjacent 3,200-acre tract, which now constituted the Eastern Cherokee reservation (see map 5), was estimated at about 3,000, out of about 3,300 in the entire reservation area (Gulick 1960:7; see also Gilbert 1957). The work by Sol Tax (1960) mentioned above noted 4,266 "Cherokees" in the area in 1959. In 1960 the total population of the Eastern Band of Cherokees, living in the area or not, was 4,494 (Kupferer 1968:89). It was also estimated that almost 75 percent of this population was one-half or more full-blood, even though membership in the band could be extended to anyone at least one-thirty-second full-blood (Gulick 1960:17, table 1, 16). (See table 24.)

Table 23. Population of Eastern Cherokees by Sex and
Residence, 1941, 1943, and 1945

Population	Date		
	1941	1943	1945
Residing at jurisdiction where enrolled			
Male	1,257	1,157	1,222
Female	1,155	1,177	1,234
Total	2,412	2,334	2,456
Residing at another jurisdiction			
Male	17	16	16
Female	15	9	9
Total	32	25	25
Residing elsewhere			
Male	582	743	745
Female	530	563	569
Total	1,112	1,306	1,314
Total male	1,856	1,916	1,983
Total female	1,700	1,749	1,812
Total	3,556	3,665	3,795

Sources: U.S. Department of the Interior (1941:8, table 3; 1943:9, table 11;
1945:9, table 11).

Table 24. Percentage of "Indian Blood" in the
Eastern Band of Cherokees, 1924 and 1957

Blood Quantum	1924[a]	1957[b]
Four-fourths	20.1	22.9
Three-fourths	12.8	25.9
One-half	7.2	20.0
One-fourth	7.1	16.3
Less than one-fourth	52.2[c]	15.0

Sources: Gulick (1960:17, table 1), Kupferer (1968:90, table 1).
[a] From Baker roll.
[b] Estimated from school population.
[c] Some 24.1 percent were one-sixteenth, and 28.1 percent were
less than one-sixteenth.

Cherokees Elsewhere

Tax and his associates also identified several other "Cherokee" communities in the 1950s: 104 "Cherokees" in central Pennsylvania, 820 "Cherokees" (Cajuns) in extreme southwestern Alabama, and 300 Cherokees in north-central California (Tax 1960).

CHEROKEES EAST AND WEST IN THE 1970S

By 1970 both Cherokee populations had grown; as I indicated, the 1970 census enumerated 66,150 Cherokees. Only 5.5 percent of these, 3,629 individuals, lived on reservations, primarily the Eastern Cherokee reservation. The 1970 census also enumerated a total of 792,730 American Indians: 28.0 percent lived on identified reservations. Thus, the Cherokees made up 8.3 percent of all American Indians but were considerably less likely to live on a reservation than American Indians in general. They were the second largest American Indian group; the Navajos were the largest with 96,743 people, 61.9 percent of them living on reservations (U.S. Bureau of the Census 1973b:188, table 16, 4).

Social and Demographic Characteristics

Data from the 1970 census permit a more detailed social and demographic description of the Cherokees than has yet been possible, as well as a comparison of the total Cherokee population with the Eastern Cherokee reservation population, the total American Indian population, and the total United States population.

Selected social and demographic characteristics of these populations are presented in table 25. They encompass not only size, sex ratio, and median age, but also the percentage living in urban areas, the age/fertility ratio (number of children ever born to 1,000 married women aged fifteen to forty-four years), percentage married, median years of education, median income, and percentage unemployed.

As shown in the table, the total Cherokee population in 1970 was in almost all ways more similar to the total United States population than was the total American Indian population. Thus the Cherokee population, like the United States population, had relatively more

Table 25. Selected Social and Demographic Characteristics of United States, American Indian, Cherokee, and Eastern Cherokee Reservation Populations, 1970

Characteristic	United States	American Indian	Cherokee	Eastern Cherokee Reservation
Size	203,211,926	792,730	66,150	3,455
Sex ratio[a]	94.8	96.7	95.4	102.8
Median age	28.1	20.4	27.2	19.9
Males	26.8	19.9	26.4	19.5
Females	29.3	20.9	28.0	20.3
Percentage urban	73.5	44.6	55.8	0.0
Age/fertility ratio[b]	2,520	3,221	2,691	3,231
Percentage married[c]	63.4	61.0	60.9	59.0
Males	65.7	60.3	63.1	57.2
Females	61.2	61.7	58.9	60.9
Median years of education[d]	12.1	9.8	10.4	9.0
Median income[e]				
Males	6,444	3,509	4,047	2,372
Females	2,328	1,697	1,839	1,582
Percentage unemployed[f]	4.4	11.1	10.4	12.7
Males	3.9	11.6	7.1	8.3
Females	5.2	10.2	15.5	22.1

Sources: U.S. Bureau of the Census (1971:43, table 4; 1973a:591, table 189, 640 and 641, table 203, 627, table 199, 671, table 212, 679, table 215, 833, table 244; 1973b:xi, table II, 1, table 1, 2, table 2, 18, table 3, 36, table 5, 141 and 144, table 11, 151 and 154, table 12, 161 and 164, table 13, 171 and 174, table 14, 188, table 16).
[a] Males per 100 females.
[b] Children ever born per 1,000 ever married women aged fifteen to forty-four years.
[c] Aged fourteen years and over; includes separated and spouse absent.
[d] Aged twenty-five years and over.
[e] Aged sixteen years and over with income.
[f] Aged sixteen years and over in civilian labor force.

females, was older, was more likely to live in urban areas, and had fewer children, more education, higher incomes, and less unemployment than was the case for American Indians in general. The only exception was that American Indians in general, like the total United States population, were more likely to be married. This was due to the low percentage of married Cherokee females.

As is clearly indicated from this information, however, the Cherokees and the Eastern Cherokee reservation populations were distinct from one another. They were different in virtually all regards, but particularly noteworthy were differences in sex ratio, age, percentage urban (to be expected), fertility, marriage rates for males, education, income of males, and unemployment rates, especially for females. Thus the Eastern Cherokee reservation population in 1970 had relatively more males, was considerably younger, had more children born, was less likely to be married, was less well educated, had lower incomes, and was more likely to be unemployed than were Cherokees in general. And none of the Eastern Cherokee reservation population lived in urban areas, whereas 55.8 percent of the total Cherokee population did.

A Note on Intermarriage

In 1970, 63.3 percent of married American Indians aged fourteen years and over, with their spouses present, were married to other American Indians. Males were somewhat more likely to be married to other American Indians than were females: the percentages were 65.2 percent for men and 61.6 percent for women. Conversely, over one-third of all these American Indians were married to non-Indians. Only 41.0 percent of the Cherokees had Indian spouses, however. (The rates for males [41.1 percent] and females [40.9 percent] were virtually identical.) Hence, almost 60 percent of the Cherokees had non-Indian spouses. Moreover, Cherokees on the Eastern Cherokee reservation were over twice as likely to have Indian spouses as were Cherokees in general. Their overall rate of intermarriage was 88.3 percent: 85.3 percent for males and 91.4 percent for females (U.S. Bureau of the Census, 1973b:36, table 5, 151, 152, table 12).

TRIBAL MEMBERSHIP

As specified below, based on their membership requirements, not all of the Cherokees in the 1970 census were actual members of the various Cherokee tribes. Only about 12,000 were enrolled in the Cherokee Nation of Oklahoma in 1975 (*Cherokee Advocate*, January 1986:15A). Some 8,381 individuals were enrolled in the Eastern Band of Cherokee Indians in 1974: reportedly, 5,550 of these resided on tribal lands and 2,831 lived elsewhere (Blankenship 1978:6). However, the 1970 census enumerated only 3,455 residing on the Eastern Cherokee reservation (U.S. Bureau of the Census 1973b:190, table 17). Perhaps a few thousand Cherokees were also enrolled in the United Keetoowah Band of Cherokee Indians, Oklahoma, since the Keetoowahs were now a formal, federally recognized American Indian group. Hence only about 35 percent of those enumerated as Cherokees in the 1970 census were actually members of one of the three Cherokee tribes.

Membership Criteria

By the 1970s all three formally organized groups of Cherokees had established their own unique membership criteria, which constituted the basis for formal membership in each of the three separate tribal groups.

Background

Most of the slightly over three hundred American Indian tribes today are organized under the Indian Reorganization Act of 1934, subsequent decisions by the Indian Claims Commission, or state authority.[9] Most also operate according to written constitutions (and bylaws and corporation charters), typically containing specific criteria for formal membership in the tribe. Membership requirements may involve blood quantum, lineage, enrollment or allotment status, and residence, often in some complex combination. Considerable diversity from tribe to tribe is shown in virtually all membership requirements. Blood quantum is probably as diverse as any, however. Many tribes do not require a minimum blood quantum; when one is specified, the modal requirement is one-fourth, although some tribes require as much as one-half and several tribes—particularly in California and Oklahoma—require a minimum of one-eighth or one-sixteenth (see Thornton 1987b).

The Cherokee Nation of Oklahoma

After Cherokee land allotment and the "dissolving" of the Cherokee Nation as a republic in 1906, the president of the United States was granted power by Congress to appoint a "principal chief" of the Cherokees to conduct official tribal business. During ensuing decades, the "Cherokee Nation" continued to exist, though it lay

dormant in many respects. In the 1970s there was a rebirth of the
Cherokee Nation (as well as of many American Indian tribes throughout the United States). In large part this was a result of a new policy
by the federal government—under Presidents Lyndon B. Johnson and
Richard M. Nixon—whereby American Indian rights to "self-deter-
mination" were reaffirmed. In 1971 the Cherokee Nation of Oklahoma elected its principal chief for the first time since 1902. On
June 26, 1976, a new Cherokee constitution was approved, supplant-
ing the still-in-effect Cherokee Nation constitution of September 6,
1839.

Traditionally, tribal membership was determined by lineage: anyone born of a Cherokee mother was Cherokee. The old constitution did not provide specific qualifications for tribal membership. It
stated, in this regard, indicating the Cherokee departure from traditional ways by 1839: "The descendents of Cherokee men by all
free women except the African race, whose parents may have been
living together as man and wife, according to the customs and laws
of this Nation, shall be entitled to all the rights and privileges of this
Nation, as well as the posterity of Cherokee women by all free men"
(Constitution and Laws of the Cherokee Nation, 1839–51, 1852:7).
Subsequently, various acts were passed admitting certain Creek Indians (and their families) and certain white men to citizenship in the
Cherokee Nation (see, for example, Constitution and Laws of the
Cherokee Nation, 1839–52, 1852:91–92, 173, 200, 205). Of course,
the earlier discussed Agreement between the Delaware and Cherokee Tribes in 1867 and Agreement between the Shawnees and the
Cherokees in 1869 admitted certain Delawares and Shawnees into
the Cherokee Nation. Additionally, the final roll established in 1907
also admitted numerous "freedmen" and whites to "citizenship" in
the Cherokee Nation. The new constitution of the Cherokee Nation
provided a new, specific set of membership criteria. The new constitution stated in this regard: "All members of the Cherokee Nation
must be citizens as proven by reference to the Dawes Commission
Rolls, including the Delaware Cherokees of Article II of the Delaware Agreement dated the 8th day of May, 1867, and the Shawnee
Cherokees as of Article III of the Shawnee Agreement dated the 9th
day of June, 1869, and/or their descendants" (Constitution of the
Cherokee Nation of Oklahoma, 1976: sect. 1). Thus no minimum
blood quantum is specified for membership, and descendants of all
those appearing on the Dawes Commission rolls—including blacks

and whites—are eligible for membership in the Cherokee Nation of Oklahoma.

The Eastern Band of Cherokee Indians

Membership in the Eastern Band of Cherokee Indians is somewhat more complex. New tribal rolls for the Eastern Band of Cherokee Indians were established in 1924 and 1931. The so-called Baker roll of 1924 was in response to the federal government's assuming a trust responsibility for the band and specified a minimum of one-thirty-second Indian blood. The roll of 1931, basically a supplement to the Baker roll, added 31 individuals. Rolls and membership criteria were subsequently revised. Membership today consists of those on earlier rolls in addition to those meeting certain requirements. The requirements specify that those living on August 21, 1957, who applied for membership before August 14, 1963, must be one-thirty-second Eastern Cherokee, and those applying for membership on August 14, 1963, or later must be one-sixteenth Eastern Cherokee (Blankenship, 1978:103, 128).

United Keetoowah Band of Cherokee Indians in Oklahoma

On October 3, 1950, the Keetoowahs became a formally organized and federally recognized band of American Indians under the Indian Reorganization Act of June 18, 1934, and the Oklahoma Indian Welfare Act of June 26, 1936. Membership in the band was specified as "all persons whose name appears on the list of members identified by a resolution dated April 19, 1949, and certified by the Superintendent of the Five Civilized Tribes Agency on November 6, 1949; Provided, that within five (5) years after the approval of this Constitution and Bylaws, such roll may be corrected by the Council of the United Keetoowah Band of Cherokees, subject to the approval of the Secretary of the Interior." In addition, it was specified: "The governing body of the Band shall have power to prescribe rules and regulations giving future membership" (*Constitution and By-laws of the United Keetoowah Band of Cherokee Indians, Oklahoma* 1950: secs. 1 and 2).

Implications

In the 1970s Ronald Trosper examined tribal membership and definition on the Flathead Indian reservation in northwestern Montana, where he sought to answer two basic questions: "(1) Why did the Confederated Salish and Kootenai Tribes of the Flathead Indian Reservation exist as a legally defined group in 1970? (2) Why did the confederated Salish and Kootenai Tribes have 5,500 enrolled tribal members in 1970?" (Trosper 1976:256).

The first question was important, Trosper argued, because the tribes had been disappearing as recently as fifty years ago, and in 1954 a bill had been prepared in Congress to terminate the tribes, abolish the reservation, and end the Confederated Salish and Kootenais' status as a federally recognized tribe. The second question was important, according to Trosper, because the tribes were composed mainly of mixed-bloods:

> Thirty percent have less than one-fourth Indian blood, 40% are between one-fourth and one-half, and the remaining 30% have more than one-half Indian blood. Only 3% of the tribal membership is full-blood. . . . The requirements to enroll children have tightened since 1935. If all those with Indian blood had been included, in 1970 the tribal population would have been 7,100 rather than the enrolled 5,500. The rule since 1960 has been that only those born with a quarter or more Indian blood can become tribal members. (Trosper 1976:256)

To answer both questions, Trosper studied the inhabitants of the Flathead reservation from 1860 to 1970. He concluded: "Tribal leaders adopted the policy of entrenchment in order to protect the existence of the reservation. This policy involved adopting a definition of Indian which led to a membership of 5,500" (1976:256). The new definition of Indian for tribal membership emphasized blood quantum rather than community, which had previously been stressed. Thus the Confederated Salish and Kootenai Tribes became more exclusive in determining membership in order to protect the tribes as entities. If they had not done so, they probably would not have survived as tribes, according to Trosper.[10]

In contrast to the survival of the Confederated Salish and Kootenai Tribes are the histories of the three Cherokee tribes today. Whereas the Confederated Salish and Kootenai Tribes attained tribal survival through development of a new policy of exclusiveness, the Cherokees in Oklahoma have more or less maintained a policy of inclusiveness. This inclusiveness has seemingly operated to ensure tribal survival. As the Cherokees in Oklahoma lost their land, they came in increasing contact with whites and blacks, mixed with them, and became a population of predominantly mixed-bloods. They were dispersed throughout Oklahoma and the United States. This large, dispersed mixed-blood population enabled them to achieve "political power" as a tribe and to protect a "core" of more full-blood, more traditional Cherokee, as Wahrhaftig argued. Perhaps without a contemporary reservation land base the Cherokees in Oklahoma—both the Cherokee Nation of Oklahoma and the United Keetoowah Band of Cherokee Indians in Oklahoma—had to adopt an inclusive policy for tribal membership. Without one, perhaps many more mixed-blood Cherokees, and even full-blood Cherokees, would have become "lost" in the total Oklahoma and United States populations and the tribe would have ceased to exist. Indeed, it almost did cease for many decades. In contrast, the Eastern Band of Cherokee Indians, with their reservation land base, have become more exclusive in recent decades, though they continue to have a fairly generous policy for tribal membership. (Interesting in this regard is the far greater percentage of members with one-half or more blood quantum in the late 1950s than in the mid-1920s [table 24]. The data for the two time periods are not directly comparable, however.)

Many American Indian tribes having no minimum blood quantum requirements for membership are found in Oklahoma, a state with only one reservation, that of the Osages. And the thirty-five tribes in Oklahoma with known blood quantum requirements differ greatly from the total of American Indian tribes in minimum blood quantum requirements for membership: 51.4 percent of Oklahoma tribes require no minimum, compared with 22.7 percent nationally; 45.7 percent require between one-sixteenth and one-fourth, compared with 68.4 percent nationally; and only 2.9 percent require as much as one-third, compared with 8.8 percent nationally (Thornton 1987b).

THE NEW CHEROKEES

During the twentieth century different Cherokee populations grew out of racial mixture and geographical dispersion, but the roots of the new populations go back centuries. They may be traced ultimately to the first child of a Cherokee and white or black union and to emigration of Cherokees out of the Southeast to avoid, if not escape, the intrusion of non-Indians on their land. These roots were nourished by events of the nineteenth century in particular: the forced exodus of Cherokees to Indian Territory and their contact with growing populations of non-Indians in the area. The allotment of tribal land and the dissolving of the Cherokee Nation early in the present century in soon-to-be Oklahoma fostered growth of the new populations, as Cherokees mixed further with non-Indians and began to spread throughout the United States. During these decades, the Cherokees became an overwhelmingly mixed American Indian population and widely dispersed geographically, not only between North Carolina and Oklahoma, but within Oklahoma and through-out the United States. Many mixed and dispersed Cherokees lost their identity as Cherokees, at least for a time.

The growth of the Cherokee population between 1960 and 1970, as measured by new census enumeration procedures established in 1960 using self-identification to determine race, indicated that many Cherokees not previously identified by the Census Bureau or even self-identified in the 1960 census changed their identification to Cherokee in the 1970 census. (See Appendix.) (This same trend was characteristic of American Indians in general, as Jeffrey S. Passel [1976; see also Passel and Berman 1985] has shown.) Thus there was a circulation of Cherokees out of and then back into the Cherokee population enumerated in censuses during this century. This, I think, explains the similarity between the Cherokee population and the total United States population in 1970 in terms of the social and demographic characteristics presented.

During this time also the Cherokees became a predominantly nontribal population: most individuals identified or self-identified as Cherokees were not actually members of one of the three Cherokee tribes by 1970, despite the tribes' generally generous blood quan-tum requirements for membership. They were really only "census Cherokees."

CHAPTER 7

Cherokees Today

The United States census of 1980 enumerated 1,366,676 American Indians (Swagerty and Thornton 1982; U.S. Bureau of the Census 1983:2, table A).[1] The basis of this enumeration was self-identification; individuals responding to the census questionnaire were asked to identify the racial group to which they belonged.[2] Those listing themselves as American Indian also were asked to specify an American Indian tribe they identified with: 232,344 (17 percent) of the 1,366,676 self-identified American Indians identified themselves as Cherokees. (See Appendix for further discussion of census enumeration procedures.) The Cherokees were by far the largest American Indian group in the United States in 1980. The second largest self-identified group was the Navajo tribe, which numbered 158,633 (11.6 percent of all American Indians; U.S. Bureau of the Census, 1985: B-18, and unpublished 1980 census data). At least as measured in census enumerations, the Cherokees experienced phenomenal growth from 1970 to 1980, and in this period they more than doubled the percentage of the total American Indian population they represented. In this final chapter, we describe these 232,344 self-identified Cherokees.

1980 GEOGRAPHIC DISTRIBUTION

By 1980, again as measured in the census, Cherokees had become widely distributed geographically, far more so than in 1970. As shown in tables 26 and 27, large numbers of Cherokees now lived in all regions and divisions of the United States. Nevertheless, Cherokees were concentrated in the South (47.2 percent) and

Nancy Breen and C. Matthew Snipp are coauthors with me of chapter 7.

Table 26. American Indian and Cherokee Populations by
Region of the United States, 1980

| | Population | | | | Percentage Cherokee of American Indians |
| | American Indian | | Cherokee | | |
Region	N	%	N	%	
Northeast	77,430	5.7	11,951	5.1	15.4
Midwest	246,365	18.0	35,442	15.3	14.4
South	370,198	27.1	109,568	47.2	29.6
West	672,683	49.2	75,383	32.4	11.2
Total	1,366,676	100.0	232,344	100.0	17.0

Source: Unpublished data, U.S. Bureau of the Census, 1987.

Table 27. American Indian and Cherokee Populations by Division of the
United States, 1980

| | Population | | | | Percentage Cherokee of American Indians |
| | American Indian | | Cherokee | | |
Division	N	%	N	%	
New England[a]	21,108	1.5	2,503	1.1	11.9
Middle Atlantic[a]	56,322	4.1	9,448	4.1	16.8
East North Central[b]	104,567	7.7	22,081	9.5	21.1
West North Central[b]	141,798	10.4	13,361	5.8	9.4
South Atlantic[c]	117,669	8.6	21,467	9.2	18.2
East South Central[c]	22,164	1.6	6,855	3.0	30.9
West South Central[c]	230,365	16.9	81,246	35.0	35.3
Mountain[d]	365,107	26.7	12,526	5.4	3.4
Pacific[d]	307,516	22.5	62,857	27.1	20.4
Total	1,366,676	100.0	232,344	100.2	17.0

Source: U.S. Bureau of the Census (1984, 14, table 1); unpublished data, U.S. Bureau of the Census,
1987.
[a] Northeast region.
[b] Midwest region (formerly North Central region).
[c] South region.
[d] West region.

the West (32.4 percent), and in the West South Central division (35.0
percent) of the South and the Pacific (27.1 percent) division of the
West.

Thirty-two states had over 1,000 Cherokees residing in them:
Oklahoma had the largest number (59,308) and Vermont the smallest
(77) (see table 28). The large recent growth of the Cherokee population in California, now the state with the second largest number of

Table 28. American Indian and Cherokee Populations of State, 1980

State	American Indian N	American Indian %	Cherokee N	Cherokee %	Percentage Cherokee of American Indians
Alabama	7,502	0.5	2,033	0.9	27.1
Alaska	21,869	1.6	707	0.3	3.2
Arizona	152,498	11.2	2,704	1.2	1.8
Arkansas	9,364	0.7	6,385	2.7	68.2
California	198,275	14.5	51,394	22.1	25.9
Colorado	17,734	1.3	3,780	1.6	21.3
Connecticut	4,431	0.3	699	0.3	15.8
Delaware	1,307	0.1	215	0.1	16.4
District of Columbia	996	0.1	221	0.1	22.2
Florida	19,134	1.4	5,042	2.2	26.4
Georgia	7,442	0.5	2,855	1.2	38.4
Hawaii	2,655	0.2	691	0.3	26.0
Idaho	10,418	0.8	1,088	0.5	10.4
Illinois	15,846	1.2	4,182	1.8	26.4
Indiana	7,682	0.6	3,265	1.4	42.5
Iowa	5,369	0.4	1,015	0.4	18.9
Kansas	15,256	1.1	4,760	2.0	31.2
Kentucky	3,518	2.6	1,801	0.8	51.2
Louisiana	11,969	0.9	1,631	0.7	13.6
Maine	4,057	0.3	201	0.1	5.0
Maryland	7,823	0.6	1,852	0.8	23.7
Massachusetts	7,483	0.5	1,105	0.5	14.8
Michigan	39,734	2.9	8,027	3.5	20.2
Minnesota	34,831	2.5	842	0.4	2.4
Mississippi	6,131	0.4	703	0.3	11.5
Missouri	12,129	0.9	5,857	2.5	48.3
Montana	37,598	2.8	851	0.4	2.3
Nebraska	9,145	0.7	475	0.2	5.2
Nevada	13,306	1.0	1,309	0.6	9.8
New Hampshire	1,297	0.1	112	0.0	8.6
New Jersey	8,176	0.6	2,053	0.9	25.1
New Mexico	107,338	7.9	1,200	0.5	1.1
New York	38,967	2.9	4,587	2.0	11.8
North Carolina	64,536	4.7	7,775	3.3	12.0
North Dakota	20,120	1.4	175	0.1	0.9

Table 28. Continued

State	Population				Percentage Cherokee of American Indians
	American Indian		Cherokee		
	N	%	N	%	
Ohio	11,985	0.9	5,667	2.4	47.3
Oklahoma	169,292	12.4	59,308	25.5	35.0
Oregon	26,591	1.9	4,864	2.1	18.3
Pennsylvania	9,179	0.7	2,808	1.2	30.6
Rhode Island	2,872	0.2	309	0.1	10.8
South Carolina	5,665	0.4	1,092	0.5	19.3
South Dakota	44,948	3.3	237	0.1	0.5
Tennessee	5,013	0.4	2,318	1.0	46.2
Texas	39,740	2.9	13,922	6.0	35.0
Utah	19,158	1.4	955	0.4	5.0
Vermont	968	0.1	77	0.0	8.0
Virginia	9,211	0.7	1,836	0.8	19.9
Washington	58,186	4.3	5,201	2.2	8.9
West Virginia	1,555	0.1	579	0.2	37.2
Wisconsin	29,320	2.1	940	0.4	3.2
Wyoming	7,057	0.5	639	0.3	9.1
Total	1,366,676	101.6	232,344	100.0	17.0

Source: U.S. Bureau of the Census (1984:14, table 1); unpublished data, U.S. Bureau of the Census, 1987.

Cherokees, is remarkable. There were 51,394 Cherokees in California in 1980, whereas only 258 lived there in 1930.

Much of this growth in the California Cherokee population likely came from the immigration of Cherokees into California from Oklahoma and other states. Heizer and Elsasser (1980:225) indicated that half of the almost 200,000 American Indians in California in 1980 were migrants to the state or descendants of migrants. This immigration of Cherokees probably came during the 1930s, 1940s, and early 1950s. John Price (1968:169), for example, noted that this was the first wave of American Indian immigrants to the state and that they came primarily from Oklahoma (in the 1930s) and scattered nonreservation areas in other states (in the 1940s and early 1950s). (By contrast, the second and more massive wave of immigrants came around 1955, most from reservation areas in Arizona, New Mexico, North and South Dakota, and Montana.)

Two other reasons also account for the massive growth in the California Cherokee population. First, and quite simply, there was a natural increase in California Cherokees—there were more births than deaths, and thus the population grew. Second, perhaps much or even most of this growth surely came from changing self-identification of individuals in census enumerations between 1960, 1970, and 1980: As we shall see below, California Cherokees have the least "Indian ancestry" of any of the Cherokee populations we identify.

Also shown in table 28 is the percentage of each state's American Indian population that was Cherokee in 1980. The states with the largest percentage of Cherokees among their American Indians were those with moderate Cherokee populations: Arkansas, Kentucky, Missouri, Ohio, and Tennessee. A sizable portion of the American Indian populations of Oklahoma and California was Cherokee—35.0 percent and 25.9 percent, respectively—but only a small portion of North Carolina's American Indian population was Cherokee: 12.0 percent.[3]

Shown in table 29 are the ten United States cities with the largest Cherokee populations in 1980. Tulsa had the largest number, being a large city at the edge of the traditional Cherokee lands in northeastern Oklahoma. Other Oklahoma cities among cities with the ten largest Cherokee populations were Oklahoma City, Muskogee, and Tahlequah. Muskogee is adjacent to the former Cherokee Nation; Tahlequah is within it and is the site of the former Cherokee national

Table 29. United States Cities with the Ten
Largest Cherokee Populations, 1980

City	Population
Tulsa, Oklahoma	5,883
Los Angeles, California	3,474
New York, New York	2,432
Oklahoma City, Oklahoma	2,264
Muskogee, Oklahoma	1,588
Tahlequah, Oklahoma	1,481
San Jose, California	1,346
Houston, Texas	1,100
San Diego, California	1,051
Detroit, Michigan	1,020

Source: Unpublished data, U.S. Bureau of the Census, 1987.

capital and present-day Cherokee tribal headquarters. Oklahoma City, though not near former Cherokee lands, is the largest city in the state. It is noteworthy that California had three of the top ten cities, while North Carolina, with its now relatively small Cherokee population, had none.

SOME SOCIAL AND DEMOGRAPHIC CHARACTERISTICS

From data collected in the 1980 census, we computed basic social and demographic characteristics of the Cherokees, as was done for the Cherokees in the 1970 census. These were sex ratio, median age, percentage of population living in metropolitan areas (earlier, urban areas were used),[4] age/fertility ratio (number of children ever born per 1,000 women aged fifteen to forty-four years [earlier, only *married* women]), percentage of the population (over the age of fifteen years) that is married, median years of education (for those aged twenty-five years and over), percentage unemployed in the civilian labor force (for those aged sixteen and over), and median income (for those aged sixteen and over with income). These characteristics are then compared with those of the total United States population and the total population of American Indians. They are also used to make comparisons between different Cherokee populations and to compare these Cherokee populations with related non-Cherokee populations of the United States.

Total Populations

Table 30 presents these basic social and demographic characteristics of the 1980 Cherokees, along with those for the total 1980 United States population and the total 1980 United States American Indian population.

In terms of median age, percentage living in metropolitan areas, age/fertility ratio, median years of education, unemployment, and income, the Cherokee population was midway between the total United States population and the American Indian population. The Cherokee population had a lower median age, education, and income, a lower percentage living in metropolitan areas, and a higher age/fertility ratio and percentage unemployed than the total United

Table 30. Social and Demographic Characteristics of United
States, American Indian, and Cherokee Populations, 1980

Characteristic	Population		
	United States	American Indian	Cherokee
Size	226,545,805	1,366,676	232,344
Sex ratio[a]	94.5	97.5	92.4
Median age	30.0	22.9	27.1
Males	28.8	22.3	25.8
Females	31.2	23.5	28.3
Percentage metropolitan	74.8	49.8	67.4
Males	74.6	49.8	66.7
Females	75.0	49.8	68.0
Age/fertility ratio[b]	1,302	1,687	1,666
Percentage married[c]	59.6	52.6	60.4
Males	62.0	53.0	62.6
Females	57.4	52.1	58.6
Median years of education[d]	12.5	12.2	12.4
Males	12.6	—	12.4
Females	12.4	—	12.3
Median income (dollars)[e]	11,232	—	9,005
Males	15,124	8,077	10,300
Females	6,928	4,263	6,505
Percentage unemployed[f]	6.5	13.2	11.2
Males	6.5	13.2	11.2
Females	6.5	11.9	11.3

Sources: Thornton (1987a:160, 168, 169); U.S. Bureau of the Census (1983a:19, table
37, 20, table 38, 44, table 46, 50, table 47; 1983b:21 and 23, table 83, 26, table 86,
55 and 59, table 95, 98, table 123, 100, table 124, 111–12, table 128; 1984, 14, table
1); unpublished data, U.S. Bureau of the Census, 1987.
[a] Males per 100 females.
[b] Children ever born per 1,000 women aged fifteen to forty-four years.
[c] Aged fifteen years and over; includes separated.
[d] Aged twenty-five years and over.
[e] Aged fifteen years and over with income.
[f] Aged sixteen years and over in civilian labor force.

States population, but they were above other American Indians. In
terms of the sex ratio and percentage married, however, the Cherokee population "surpassed" both the United States population and
the American Indian population. Cherokees therefore tended to be
older and to have fewer children, were better educated, more often
were employed and had more income, and were more likely to live in

metropolitan areas than American Indians in general. But the Cherokees tended to be younger and to have more children, were less well
educated, were more likely to be unemployed and had less income,
and less often lived in metropolitan areas than was the case for the
total United States population. Conversely, the total Cherokee population had relatively more females than males and a higher percentage of married males and females than either the total United States
population or the total American Indian population.

State Populations and the Red-Black Cherokees

As has been shown in previous chapters, the total
Cherokee population is not homogeneous. Instead, there are various
Cherokee populations, each produced by events in Cherokee history.
These events in turn initially produced two distinct geographical
population centers—Eastern (primarily North Carolina) and Western (primarily Oklahoma) Cherokees. Recent growth in California
has produced yet another population center. Historical events also
introduced racial diversity into the Cherokee population. Through
contact with whites, the Cherokees became predominantly a population of mixed-bloods; through contact with blacks and by adopting
blacks into the tribe, Red-Black Cherokees were created.

In this section we describe the characteristics of the Cherokee
populations in North Carolina, Oklahoma, and California, as well
as those of the Red-Black Cherokees. These populations are then
compared with relevant state populations or, in the case of the Red-
Black Cherokees, with the United States black population. This is
because differences among these Cherokee populations, and between
the total populations presented in table 28, may partly reflect differences in state populations or, in the case of Red-Black Cherokees, the
social and demographic uniqueness of blacks in the United States.

Table 31 presents characteristics for Cherokee populations of the
three different states and the Red-Black Cherokee population. Also
included in table 31 are characteristics of the total populations of
North Carolina, Oklahoma, and California, as well as those of blacks
in the United States. Several differences in these populations are
noteworthy, representing the distinctiveness of each population.

North Carolina Cherokees

Most striking in table 31 is that the North Carolina Cherokees were an extremely nonmetropolitan population in 1980; only 30.1 percent lived in metropolitan areas (and Cherokee males in the state were even less likely to do so than Cherokee females). This is less than half the number—67.4 percent—of Cherokees nationwide who lived in metropolitan areas. North Carolina in general has a relatively low proportion of its population living in metropolitan areas: only 52.7 percent of the entire state population lived in metropolitan areas in 1980, compared with 74.8 percent of the population nationwide. Nevertheless, North Carolina Cherokees—particularly males—were only half as likely to be found in metropolitan areas of the state as were North Carolinians in general. Undoubtedly this is because many of the state's Cherokees live on the rural Eastern Cherokee reservation, the only Cherokee reservation that now exists.

North Carolina Cherokees were also considerably younger than the total North Carolina population. Overall they were about six years younger, and the difference is virtually the same for males and females. The median age of the North Carolina Cherokees was, however, about the same as the median age of the total United States American Indian population (see tables 30 and 31). North Carolina Cherokees were also less likely to be married than were individuals in either the total Cherokee population, the total United States population, or the total North Carolina population. Yet they were more likely to be married than American Indians in general. North Carolina Cherokees also tended to have more children than did North Carolinians as a whole: the Cherokee age/fertility ratio—the number of children ever born per 1,000 women aged fifteen to forty-four years—was 1,724, compared with 1,317 for the total North Carolina population. This was the highest of any of the populations identified in either table 30 or 31. Also striking were the extremely high unemployment rates for North Carolina Cherokees, their exceptionally low levels of education for both males and females, and income for males. Low male income may account for the exceptionally low rates of family formation as measured by the marriage variable.

Table 31. Social and Demographic Characteristics of Selected States and State Cherokee Populations, and United States Red-Black Cherokees and United States Blacks, 1980

	North Carolina		Oklahoma		California		United States	
	Total	Cherokee	Total	Cherokee	Total	Cherokee	Blacks	Red-Black Cherokee
Size	5,881,766	7,775	3,025,290	59,308	23,667,902	51,394	26,495,025	4,588
Sex ratio[a]	94.3	94.5	95.3	91.2	97.2	89.7	89.6	88.2
Median age	29.6	23.6	30.1	25.6	29.9	28.5	24.9	25.4
Males	28.1	22.6	28.6	23.5	28.9	27.4	23.5	23.6
Females	31.1	24.5	31.6	27.6	30.9	29.4	26.1	29.0
Percentage metropolitan	52.7	30.1	58.5	46.0	94.9	90.4	81.1	87.0
Males	52.9	28.0	58.6	44.8	94.8	90.2	80.8	84.9
Females	52.5	32.1	58.4	47.1	95.0	90.6	81.3	88.8
Age/fertility ratio[b]	1,317	1,724	1,410	1,603	1,231	1,590	1,576	1,604
Percentage married[c]	62.3	58.5	64.0	58.9	56.9	57.1	42.9	44.4
Males	64.8	58.5	66.5	61.6	58.2	57.2	48.4	44.2
Females	60.1	58.5	61.6	56.6	55.6	56.9	38.3	44.7

Median years of education[d]	12.2	10.9	12.5	12.0	12.7	12.6	12.0	12.6
Males	—	10.6	—	12.0	—	12.6	12.0	12.7
Females	—	11.2	—	12.0	—	12.4	12.0	12.6
Median income (dollars)[e]	—	6,255	—	8,005	—	9,995	7,905	8,845
Males	9,586	7,360	11,246	9,995	12,885	12,005	7,827	8,525
Females	5,191	5,005	4,679	5,765	6,056	8,005	4,674	9,605
Percentage unemployed[f]	5.7	14.6	4.1	8.2	6.5	10.6	11.8	15.9
Males	5.4	14.7	3.9	8.9	6.5	10.6	12.3	15.0
Females	6.3	14.4	4.4	7.4	6.5	10.7	11.3	16.9

Sources: U.S. Bureau of the Census (1982a:43, table 19, 44, table 19, 109, table 66, 110, table 67, 114, table 71; 1982b:28, table 19, 29, table 19, 61, table 66, 62, table 67, 66, table 48, 46, table 129, table 161, 146, table 65, 160, table 67, 176, table 67; 1982c:29, table 19, 25, table 19, 47, table 66, 48, table 67, 52, table 71; 1983a:20, table 38, 46, table 129, table 161, 146, table 65, 160, table 67, 176, table 67; 1983b:23, table 83, 24, table 84, 26, table 86, 59, table 95, 300–301, table 237, 302, table 237); unpublished data, U.S. Bureau of the Census, 1987.

[a] Males per 100 females.
[b] Children ever born per 1,000 women aged fifteen to forty-four years.
[c] Aged fifteen years and over; includes separated.
[d] Aged twenty-five years and over.
[e] Aged fifteen years and over with income.
[f] Aged sixteen years and over in civilian labor force.

Oklahoma Cherokees

The Oklahoma Cherokee population had relatively more females per male than any of the three total populations presented in table 30 or the total Oklahoma population. The median age of 25.6 years for Oklahoma Cherokees was considerably lower than that of 30.1 years for Oklahomans in general. However, Oklahoma Cherokees were somewhat older than American Indians in general.

Most Oklahoma Cherokees did not live in metropolitan areas in 1980, but the percentage living in metropolitan areas was much closer to the percentage of the state's population living in metropolitan areas than was the case in North Carolina, as shown in table 31. Forty-six percent of Oklahoma's Cherokee population lived in metropolitan areas, whereas 58.5 percent of Oklahoma's total population did so. Also, this 46.0 percent of Oklahoma's Cherokee population is close to the percentage of American Indians nationally who lived in metropolitan areas—49.8 percent (see table 30).

The Oklahoma Cherokees' age/fertility ratio of 1,603 was very high. However, Oklahoma Cherokees were less likely to be married than Cherokees in general or even individuals in the total United States population; their likelihood of marriage was even further below that of Oklahomans. They also had much higher unemployment rates than did other Oklahomans. Cherokee men had lower incomes than other Oklahoma men, but the opposite was true among women; that is, Cherokee women had higher incomes than other Oklahoma women. Cherokee educational levels were also lower.

California Cherokees

The recently emerged California Cherokee population is similar to the total population of California and distinct from populations in North Carolina and Oklahoma. This was certainly the case with the percentage who live in metropolitan areas and the percentage who were married in 1980. However, the percentage of California Cherokees who lived in metropolitan areas was below the state percentage, and the percentage who were married was above the state percentage. What really seems to distinguish California Cherokees from the total United States population, the total American Indian population, the total United States Cherokee population, and the North Carolina and

Oklahoma Cherokee populations is the very low number of California Cherokee males. As shown in the sex ratios, the percentage of California Cherokees who were female was much higher than the percentage of females in all these other populations.

Cherokees in California were only slightly younger than the total California population; they had a median age of 28.5 years, compared with the state median of 29.9 years. Also, like Californians generally, they had relatively few children. The California Cherokee age/fertility ratio was only 1,590—the lowest of any of the Indian populations identified in tables 30 and 31. And like Californians generally, Cherokees there were relatively less likely to be married than were other Americans. Here again, like other Cherokees, they were much more likely to be unemployed than the general population of the state where they resided. Their educational levels were comparable to those of other Californians, but California Cherokee females had a considerably higher median income than California females in general.

Red-Black Cherokees

Red-Black Cherokees represent a truly unique Cherokee population. As we have seen, some Red-Black Cherokees are descendants of former slaves of the Cherokees—the "freedmen." They are members of the Cherokee tribe but possess no Cherokee ancestry. Other Red-Blacks are the result of admixtures of Cherokees with black and often white ancestry. This latter group surely represents a small segment of the Cherokee population, but it is a unique and important one. These Cherokees have often been forgotten, and they have often been discriminated against by Cherokees and non-Cherokees alike. Their "Indianness" has typically not been accepted to the same degree as that of Indians with white ancestry, even though they might have more Indian blood.

As shown in table 31, 4,588 individuals identified themselves as Cherokee and also as having black ancestry; they represented only 2 percent of the total Cherokee population. As shown in table 32, the Northeast had the largest number of Red-Black Cherokees in 1980, although these particular Cherokees are fairly well distributed among regions of the United States. As shown in table 33, half of the Red-Black Cherokees lived in the Mid-Atlantic and the Pacific

Table 32. Red-Black Cherokees by
Region of the United States, 1980

Region	Number	Percentage
Northeast	1,390	30.3
Midwest	1,026	22.4
South	921	20.1
West	1,251	27.3
Total	4,588	100.1

Source: Unpublished data, U.S. Bureau of the
Census, 1987.

Table 33. Red-Black Cherokees by Division of
the United States, 1980

Division	Number	Percentage
New England[a]	233	5.1
Mid-Atlantic[a]	1,157	25.2
East North Central[b]	751	16.4
West North Central[b]	275	6.0
South Atlantic[c]	275	6.0
East South Central[c]	93	2.0
West South Central[c]	553	12.1
Mountain[d]	130	2.8
Pacific[d]	1,121	24.4
Total	4,588	100.0

Source: Unpublished data, U.S. Bureau of the Census, 1987.
[a] Northeast region.
[b] Midwest region (formerly North Central region).
[c] South region.
[d] West region.

divisions of the United States. This contrasts with the divisional
locations of the total Cherokee population, with its concentration in
the West South Central division (where Oklahoma is located).

Table 34 shows the state distribution of the Red-Black population
in 1980. It is surprising that few of the Red-Black Cherokees were
found in North Carolina, given its large Cherokee and black populations, though large numbers of Red-Black Cherokees lived in the Mid-
Atlantic division of the United States. Comparing this table with
table 28, we see that the proportions of Red-Black Cherokees and
Cherokees in California were virtually identical: 22.8 percent and
22.1 percent, respectively. Wide differences existed vis-à-vis other

states: North Carolina, Oklahoma, and the other forty-seven states and the District of Columbia considered together.

Table 35 shows the percentage of black ancestry in each of the Cherokee population segments. In this instance we see that a far greater proportion of Cherokees in California and all other states have black ancestry than do Cherokees in either Oklahoma or North Carolina.

As shown in tables 30 and 31, Red-Black Cherokees were distinct not only from the total Cherokee population but also from the total United States population, the total American Indian population, and each of the three state Cherokee populations. They were particularly distinct in terms of their low marriage rates, high rates of unemployment, *high* educational levels, *high* incomes for both males and females with incomes, and high percentage living in metropolitan areas. Moreover, as shown in table 31, the Red-Black Cherokees were

Table 34. Red-Black Cherokees in
State Cherokee Populations, 1980

State	Red-Black Cherokees	
	N	%
North Carolina	22	0.5
Oklahoma	428	9.3
California	1,046	22.8
Other	3,092	67.4
Total	4,588	100.0

Source: Unpublished data, U.S. Bureau of the Census, 1987.

Table 35. Percentage of Black Ancestry in
State Cherokee Populations, 1980

State	Percentage Black Ancestry
North Carolina	0.28
Oklahoma	0.72
California	2.04
Other	2.72
Total	1.97

Source: Unpublished data, U.S. Bureau of the Census, 1987.

quite similar to the 1980 total United States black population, except in unemployment, education, and income for females. Interestingly, these Cherokees had an even higher proportion of their population living in metropolitan areas than did blacks in general, and they were better educated though more likely to be unemployed with lower *overall* income. The data on metropolitan residence are surprising because blacks as a population have an extremely high percentage living in metropolitan areas. In fact, nationwide, the Red-Black Cherokees rival the California populations in this regard, and California is a state with extremely high rates of metropolitan living.

The median age of the Red-Black Cherokee population was only slightly higher than the median age of all blacks across the United States. The exception is for Red-Black Cherokee females, who were almost three years older on the average than black females. The median age of Red-Black Cherokees was, however, close to that of American Indians in general and closer still to that of North Carolina and Oklahoma Cherokees. Like blacks in general, the Red-Black Cherokees tended to have relatively large numbers of children, as indicated by their age/fertility ratio of 1,604, which was, however, below that of both the total Cherokee population (1,666) and the total American Indian population (1,687).

Other Cherokees

Although they are not included in table 31, a word may be said about Cherokees in states other than North Carolina, Oklahoma, and California, since they represented 113,867 individuals in 1980, slightly less than half the total Cherokee population. They were scattered throughout the United States, though, as shown in table 28, they lived more frequently in Arkansas, Florida, Michigan, Missouri, Ohio, Texas, and Washington than in any other states. In all our characteristics, they were roughly similar to the total Cherokee population and as such may not be considered a distinct population. Of course, Cherokee populations of some individual states might be distinct. That they were not is partly because, constituting almost half the total Cherokee population, their characteristics weigh heavily in computing those of all Cherokees. The characteristics of these other Cherokees were sex ratio, 92.4; median age, 27.5 (26.4 for males, 28.6 for females); percentage metropolitan, 70.7 (70.3 for males, 71.5 for females); age/fertility ratio, 1,720; percentage married, 63.0 (66.0 for males, 60.5 for females); percentage unemployed, 12.5 (12.1 for males, 13.0 for females); median years of education, 12.3 (12.3 for males, 12.2 for females); and median income, $9,010 ($10,410 for males, $6,310 for females) (unpublished data from U.S. Bureau of the Census, 1987).

Summary of Cherokee Populations

The different Cherokee populations in 1980 may be summarized in terms of these social and demographic characteristics. North Carolina Cherokees were relatively young, were extremely nonmetropolitan, and had moderate marriage rates but high numbers of children. They also had extremely high unemployment rates and low levels of education. Oklahoma Cherokees, in contrast, were relatively older, more likely to be female, and somewhat nonmetropolitan, and they had moderate marriage rates and moderate numbers of children. California Cherokees were extremely metropolitan, very likely to be female, relatively old, and not quite so likely to be married, and they tended to have few children. Red-Black Cherokees were likely to be female, moderately old, and highly metropolitan and were unlikely to be married, but they had high numbers of children. They also tended to be highly educated but had very high rates of unemployment.

CHEROKEE AND INDIAN ANCESTRY

Since in earlier chapters Cherokees of differing degrees of "blood quantum" were discussed using primarily, but not exclusively, published Census Bureau data, and since Red-Black Cherokees have already been singled out, we used unpublished 1980 census data to examine the Cherokees by extent of Indian ancestry.

Measuring Cherokee Ancestry

Questionnaire item 4 of the 1980 United States census obtained information about the racial composition of households. (See Appendix.) It asked respondents to identify themselves as members of a racial group: white, black or Negro, Japanese, Chinese, Filipino, Korean, Vietnamese, American Indian, Asian Indian, Hawaiian, Guamanian, Samoan, Eskimo, Aleut, or other (to be specified by the respondent).[5] Individuals identifying themselves as American Indian were also asked to specify a tribe. It was from responses to this question that the 1,366,676 American Indians and 232,344 Cherokees described above were enumerated.

The 1980 census also contained information about ancestry (or origin or descent) of respondents (see, for example, Lieberson and Waters 1988:6–8). The information was obtained via questionnaire item 14. (See Appendix.) This item asked individuals to specify their ancestry and noted that ancestry might be a nationality group, a lineage, or a country of prior origin. It then noted that those with multiple ancestral origins should so identify themselves—for example, as of English-Irish origin. (For those with more than two ancestries, only the first two were identified by the Census Bureau in most instances.[6]) Whereas the United States census enumerated almost 1.37 million American Indians, almost 7 million Americans indicated some degree of American Indian ancestry through item 14 (U.S. Bureau of the Census 1983a:2; also Lieberson and Waters 1988:18). American Indian ancestry ranked tenth in the total 1980 United States population behind, in descending order, English (50 million), German (49 million), Irish (40 million), Afro-American (21 million), French (13 million), Italian (12 million), Scottish (10 million), Polish (8 million), and Mexican (8 million) (U.S. Bureau of the Census 1983a:2).

Using a combination of responses to the race question (item 4) and the ancestry question (item 14), varying degrees of Indian ancestry within the Cherokee population were ascertained. All those individuals identifying themselves as Cherokee in the race question were subdivided into categories of Indian ancestry, using the first two ancestries indicated. Those Cherokees who listed American Indian as their first and only ancestry were designated "exclusively Indian." (This does not necessarily mean they are full-bloods.) Those listing their first ancestry as American Indian and listing a non-Indian second ancestry were designated "mostly Indian." Those listing a non-Indian first ancestry and American Indian as their second ancestry were designated "mostly non-Indian." Finally, individuals listing first and second non-Indian ancestries, or a non-Indian first ancestry and no second ancestry, were designated "exclusively non-Indian."

Table 36. Ancestry of Cherokee Population, 1980

Ancestry	Number	Percentage
Exclusively Indian	117,750	50.7
Mostly Indian	38,393	16.5
Mostly non-Indian	26,373	11.4
Exclusively non-Indian	36,186	15.6
No response	13,642	5.9
Total	232,344	100.0

Source: Unpublished data, U.S. Bureau of the Census, 1987.

Indian Ancestry

Approximately half of the 232,344 Cherokees enumerated in the 1980 census were designated exclusively Indian; that is, they reported exclusively Indian ancestry (see table 36). Another 16.5 percent reported an American Indian first ancestry and a non-Indian second ancestry. This is the mostly Indian category. Some 11.4 percent of the Cherokees were designated mostly non-Indian, and over 15 percent—some 36,186 individuals—reported no American Indian ancestry, even though they identified themselves as both Indian and Cherokee in the census. Thus only about two-thirds of the Cherokees may be considered either mostly or exclusively Indian.

Directly comparable data on the total American Indian population are not available; however, one analysis (Snipp 1986:242, table 2, 243, table 3) indicated that about 80 percent of the total American Indian population could be considered either mostly or exclusively Indian; that is, they listed Indian as their race and American Indian as their first ancestry (see also Appendix). Therefore about 15 percent less of the Cherokee population could be considered mostly or exclusively Indian in 1980 than was the case for the total American Indian population.

Tables 37 and 38 show variations in the Indian ancestry of the Cherokee population across regions and divisions of the United States in 1980. As is shown in table 37, in only one region—the South —could more than 50 percent of the Cherokee population be considered exclusively Indian. As is shown in table 38, only in the three divisions that constitute the South region of the United States— South Atlantic, East South Central, and West South Central—could over 50 percent of the Cherokee population be defined as exclusively Indian.

Table 37. Cherokee Ancestry by Region of the United States, 1980

	Ancestry												
	Exclusively Indian		Mostly Indian		Mostly Non-Indian		Exclusively Non-Indian		No Response		Total	
Region	N	%	N	%	N	%	N	%	N	%	N	%
Northeast	5,388	45.1	2,164	18.1	1,914	16.0	1,949	16.3	536	4.5	11,951	100.0
Midwest	16,436	46.4	6,340	17.9	4,917	13.9	5,965	16.8	1,784	5.0	35,442	100.0
South	64,950	59.3	14,688	13.4	8,870	8.1	13,748	12.5	7,312	6.7	109,568	100.0
West	30,976	41.1	15,201	20.2	10,672	14.2	14,524	19.3	4,010	5.3	75,383	100.1

Source: Unpublished data, U.S. Bureau of the Census, 1987.

Table 38. Cherokee Ancestry by Division of the United States, 1980

Region	Ancestry											
	Exclusively Indian		Mostly Indian		Mostly Non-Indian		Exclusively Non-Indian		No Response		Total	
	N	%	N	%	N	%	N	%	N	%	N	%
New England[a]	1,096	43.8	396	15.8	452	18.1	440	17.6	119	4.8	2,503	100.1
Middle Atlantic[a]	4,292	45.4	1,768	18.7	1,462	15.5	1,509	16.0	417	4.4	9,448	100.0
East North Central[b]	9,904	44.8	4,022	18.2	3,185	14.4	3,817	17.3	1,153	5.2	22,081	99.9
West North Central[b]	6,532	48.9	2,318	17.3	1,732	13.0	2,148	16.1	631	4.7	13,361	100.0
South Atlantic[c]	13,401	62.4	2,304	10.7	1,545	7.2	2,950	13.7	1,267	5.9	21,467	99.9
East South Central[c]	3,921	57.2	996	14.5	696	10.2	872	12.7	370	5.4	6,855	100.0
West South Central[c]	47,628	58.6	11,388	14.0	6,629	8.1	9,926	12.2	5,675	7.0	81,246	99.9
Mountain[d]	5,005	40.0	2,454	19.6	1,986	15.9	2,419	19.3	662	5.3	12,526	100.1
Pacific[d]	25,971	41.3	12,747	20.3	8,686	13.8	12,105	19.3	3,348	5.3	62,857	100.0

Source: Unpublished data, U.S. Bureau of the Census, 1987.
[a] Northeast region.
[b] Midwest region (formerly North Central region).
[c] South region.
[d] West region.

Ancestry of the State Populations

The American Indian ancestries of the separate 1980 state populations of Cherokees are depicted in table 39. As the table shows, North Carolina Cherokees were overwhelmingly the most "Indian" of the three state populations: 77.7 percent of them were classified exclusively Indian, whereas only 61.3 percent of the Oklahoma Cherokees, the next most Indian Cherokee population, were so classified. Readily apparent is the low Indianness of the California Cherokees: only 40.7 percent were exclusively Indian. Not only are California Cherokees distinct from the North Carolina and Oklahoma Cherokee populations in this regard, they are also distinct from the Cherokees in all other states combined: 47.8 percent of those Cherokees were considered exclusively Indian. In fact, as is shown in table 39, almost one-fifth of the California Cherokees (19.3 percent) may be considered totally non-Indian in terms of ancestry.

*Social and Demographic Characteristics
and Ancestry*

Ancestry was examined in terms of the social and demographic characteristics discussed above, since we thought they might vary by ancestry. To accomplish this, characteristics of Cherokees with exclusively or mostly Indian ancestry were compared with the characteristics of persons with black-Indian or exclusively or mostly non-Indian ancestry. These comparisons are shown in table 40. Some major differences were found. The 154,938 exclusively or mostly Indian Cherokees tended to live in metropolitan areas somewhat less frequently than Cherokees with other ancestries. The percentage of those defined as exclusively or mostly Indian who lived in metropolitan areas was 64.7 (64.0 for males, 65.2 for females), in contrast to 73.4 for Cherokees with exclusively or mostly non-Indian ancestry (72.9 for males, 73.9 for females). These Cherokees also were more likely to be married and had more children: 62.0 percent of them were married (63.8 percent for males, 60.4 percent for females), in contrast to 55.5 percent (54.5 percent for males, 56.3 percent for females) of other Cherokees; and their age/fertility ratio was 1,767, in contrast to 1,561 for other Cherokees. Overall median income was the same, although median incomes for both males and females did

Table 39. Ancestry of State Cherokee Populations, 1980

	North Carolina		Oklahoma		Population California		Other		Total	
Ancestry	N	%	N	%	N	%	N	%	N	%
Exclusively Indian	6,040	77.7	36,365	61.3	20,919	40.7	54,426	47.8	117,750	50.7
Mostly Indian	531	6.8	7,664	12.9	10,810	21.0	19,388	17.0	38,393	16.5
Mostly non-Indian	202	2.6	4,207	7.1	7,017	13.7	14,947	13.1	26,373	11.4
Exclusively non-Indian	613	7.9	6,758	11.4	9,933	19.3	18,882	16.6	36,186	15.6
No response	389	5.0	4,314	7.3	2,715	5.3	6,224	5.5	13,642	5.9
Total	7,775	100.0	59,308	100.0	51,394	100.0	113,867	100.0	232,344	100.0

Source: Unpublished data, U.S. Bureau of the Census, 1987.

Table 40. Social and Demographic Characteristics of Cherokees
by Type of Ancestral Identification

	Exclusively or Mostly Indian		Exclusively or Mostly Non-Indian
	Cherokee	Red-Black Cherokee	
Number	154,938[g]	1,205[h]	62,559[i]
Sex ratio[a]	92.4	68.1	91.8
Median age	27.0	27.3	25.0
Males	26.5	22.5	23.0
Females	27.5	30.5	27.0
Percentage metropolitan	64.7	85.2	73.4
Males	64.0	84.0	72.9
Females	65.2	86.1	73.9
Age/fertility ratio[b]	1,767	1,757	1,561
Percentage married[c]	62.0	49.1	55.5
Males	63.8	46.5	54.5
Females	60.4	50.8	56.3
Median years of education[d]	12.2	12.4	12.0
Males	12.3	12.5	12.0
Females	12.2	12.4	12.0
Median income (dollars)[e]	9,005	9,000	9,005
Males	10,085	9,995	11,005
Females	6,245	8,005	6,830
Percentage unemployed[f]	11.4	13.8	11.4
Males	11.5	16.4	10.9
Females	11.2	11.5	12.0

Source: Unpublished data, U.S. Bureau of the Census, 1987.

[a] Males per 100 females.

[b] Children ever born per 1,000 women aged fifteen to forty-four years.

[c] Aged fifteen years and over; includes separated.

[d] Aged twenty-five years and over.

[e] Aged fifteen years and over with income.

[f] Aged sixteen years and over in civilian labor force.

[g] No response was 13,642; includes Red-Black Cherokees who reported "mostly Indian" ancestry.

[h] No response was zero; none of the Red-Black Cherokees had "exclusive Indian" ancestry by definition.

[i] Includes Red-Black Cherokees who reported mostly non-Indian ancestry.

differ in this regard. Differences in their rates of unemployment were negligible.

Red-Black Cherokees

The same data also permit a further analysis of the Red-Black Cherokee population. Of the 4,588 Red-Black Cherokees, 3,170 listed only their first ancestry as black, 1,404 listed only their second ancestry as black, and almost none listed both first and second ancestries as black.

Perhaps of most significance is the ancestral difference between the Red-Blacks and other Cherokees: 73.7 percent of Red-Black Cherokees are classified as either mostly non-Indian or exclusively non-Indian, whereas only 60.9 percent of other Cherokees *with non-Indian ancestry* were so classified (unpublished data from U.S. Bureau of the Census, 1987). Conversely, 1,205 or 26.3 percent of the Red-Black Cherokees were classified as mostly Indian; none were classified as exclusively Indian (this was by definition). (See table 40.) Unlike the case of other Cherokee populations, there is a relatively large sex difference in Indian ancestry among the Red-Black Cherokees: 22.7 percent of the males were mostly Indian compared with 29.4 percent of the females. Similarly, the sex ratio of these 1,205 Cherokees was a mere 68.1 compared with 92.4 for Cherokees with exclusively or mostly Indian ancestry and 91.2 for Cherokees with exclusively or mostly non-Indian ancestry. As shown in table 40, another important difference was median age. The mostly Indian Red-Black Cherokees tended to be older: their median age was 27.3 years in comparison with a median age of 27.0 for Cherokees with exclusively or mostly Indian ancestry and 25.0 for Cherokees with exclusively or mostly non-Indian ancestry. As shown in the table, an overwhelming proportion of these Cherokees lived in metropolitan areas (85.2 percent compared with only 64.7 percent and 73.4 percent of other Cherokees). They also were somewhat less likely to be married but had higher fertility levels than other Cherokees. Only 49.1 percent (46.5 percent for males, 50.8 percent for females) of them were married, in contrast to 62.0 percent (63.8 percent for males, 60.4 percent for females) for Cherokees with exclusively or mostly Indian ancestry and 55.5 percent (54.5 percent for males, 56.3 percent for females) of other Cherokees. Their age/fertility ratio was 1,757, in contrast to 1,767 and 1,561 for the other Cherokee groups. These mostly Indian Red-Black Cherokees had virtually the same median income as the other Cherokees (but lower for males and higher for females) and higher overall levels of unemployment than the other groups.

ENROLLED CHEROKEES AND
CHEROKEES IN THE 1980 CENSUS

In July 1986 the United States Bureau of Indian Affairs listed 306 American Indian tribes with which it had relations (including one tribe in Alaska and two unorganized tribes). In the early 1980s these tribes totaled some 900,000 members (U.S. Bureau of Indian Affairs 1986; unpublished data provided by Edgar Lister of the Indian Health Service, 1986). This indicates that only about two-thirds of the 1,366,676 American Indians counted in the 1980 United States census were enrolled members of federally recognized American Indian tribes.

As shown in table 41, the three Cherokee tribes—the Eastern Band of Cherokee Indians, the Cherokee Nation of Oklahoma, and the United Keetoowah Band of Cherokee Indians in Oklahoma—had a combined enrollment of 78,381 about 1980. Comparing these enrollment figures with the 1980 census enumeration indicates that probably only about one-third of the 232,344 Cherokees listed in the 1980 census were actually enrolled in one of the three Cherokee tribes. The Navajo tribe, in contrast, had over 150,000 enrolled members about 1980 (U.S. Bureau of Indian Affairs 1986; unpublished data provided by Edgar Lister of the Indian Health Service, 1986). Hence, unlike the Cherokees, most of those who identified themselves as Navajo in the 1980 census were likely enrolled members of the Navajo Tribe.

In 1970, as indicated in chapter 6, about 35 percent of all Cherokees identified in the census were enrolled. Thus the proportion of Chero-

Table 41. Population of the Three Cherokee Tribes about 1981

Tribe	Population
Eastern Band of Cherokees	8,381
Cherokee Nation of Oklahoma	63,400
United Keetoowah Band of Cherokee Indians in Oklahoma	7,000
Total	78,781

Source: U.S. Bureau of Indian Affairs (1986).

Table 42. American Indian Population of Eastern
Cherokee Reservation by Enrollment Status, 1980

	Population					
	Cherokees		Other American Indians		Total	
Enrollment Status	N	%	N	%	N	%
Enrolled	4,546	97.6	165	58.8	4,643	96.3
Not enrolled	84	1.8	45	27.3	129	2.6
Not reported	27	0.6	23	13.9	50	1.0
Total	4,657	100.0	165	100.0	4,822	99.9

Source: U.S. Bureau of the Census (1985:18, table 4).

Table 43. American Indian Population of
Historic Cherokee Areas of Oklahoma by
Enrollment Status, 1980

	Population	
Enrollment Status	N	%
Enrolled	17,638	46.2
Not enrolled	18,680	48.8
Not reported	1,925	5.0
Total	38,243	100.0

Source: U.S. Bureau of the Census (1985:99, table 13).
Note: Population reported as American Indian, but presumably only Cherokee; excludes urbanized areas.

kees identified in the United States census who were enrolled in a
Cherokee tribe more or less remained constant from 1970 to 1980.
Both the self-identified Cherokee populations in the 1970 and 1980
census and the enrolled Cherokee populations grew at tremendous
rates during the decade 1970–80. Comparing Cherokee enrollment
with the approximately two-thirds figure for tribal enrollment of all
American Indians enumerated in the 1980 census indicates that the
Cherokees are about half as likely to be enrolled in a tribe as are other
American Indians, despite the tremendous growth in the enrolled
members of the Cherokee Nation of Oklahoma.

The 1980 census also collected information on those Cherokees
living on the Eastern Cherokee reservation in North Carolina and
in the "historic Cherokee area" of Oklahoma (the area of Cherokee lands in Indian Territory dating from the removal period). As is
shown in table 42, only about 4,600 Cherokees lived on the Eastern

Cherokee reservation in 1980 and almost all were enrolled, whereas a total of 8,381 individuals were enrolled in the Eastern Band of Cherokee Indians at about this time. Table 43 presents similar information for the "historic Cherokee area" of Oklahoma.[7] These data show, in contrast to the Eastern Band of Cherokees, that although 38,243 Cherokees lived in this historic area, only about 50 percent of them were actually enrolled. Also, only about 25 percent of the total enrollment about 1980 of the Cherokee Nation of Oklahoma (about 63,000) and the United Keetoowah Band of Cherokee Indians in Oklahoma (about 7,000) were actually living on former Cherokee lands.

THE "CHEROKEE GRANDMOTHER" PHENOMENON

Overlapping rather than coinciding with those who are of Cherokee ancestry and reported it in the 1980 census are a large, undetermined number of people with some degree of Cherokee lineage. Many say they have a "Cherokee grandmother"; fewer say they have a "Cherokee grandfather." Although no data are available, one hears much about these individuals, either informally or through the media, when one or another prominent person is reported to have Cherokee ancestry. Indeed, this might be described as a phenomenon of the twentieth century. These people typically do not consider themselves American Indian or Cherokee; rather, they consider themselves, and in fact are, white, black, or other Americans. They probably would not appear in the data presented above on the Cherokees, since it was derived only from those identified racially as American Indian. The primary "pool" of these people lies outside those 1,366,676 individuals identifying themselves as American Indian but within the almost 7 million Americans stating some American Indian ancestry. Why, though, do so many Americans have or claim Cherokee grandmothers?

Perhaps one reason is that the Cherokees traditionally traced their descent along matrilineal lines (as did many other American Indian peoples). Children born of Cherokee women were Cherokee, whether the father was Cherokee or non-Cherokee, American Indian or non-Indian; children of a non-Cherokee mother were non-Cherokee, again regardless of paternal ancestry. Therefore one could not be a Cherokee without a Cherokee grandmother (or mother or great-grand-mother, etc.), but one could be a Cherokee without a Cherokee grand-father (or father or great-grandfather, etc.). Another reason perhaps is that the early history of the United States was characterized by a demographic imbalance between American Indian women and men and non-Indian women and men. There were, relatively speaking, more American Indian women than men and more non-Indian men than women. A surplus of American Indian women was created by the mortality of American Indian men in warfare, particularly with the Europeans. The surplus of non-American Indian men occurred because the first Europeans and Africans on this land were soldiers, traders, or black slaves (male slaves were typically brought here earlier and in larger numbers than female slaves). Given the demographic imbalance, the two groups combined and produced offspring.

When Cherokees mixed with these Europeans and Africans, offspring were typically Cherokee, since the union was likely to be between Cherokee women and non-Indian men and it was the mother who determined Cherokee lineage. One frequently hears, for example, in early American history about the "squaw man" (a non-Indian with an Indian wife), but not about the "buck woman" (a non–American Indian woman with an American Indian husband). Perhaps, too, American Indian women were frequently raped by non-American Indians. And as we have pointed out, the Cherokees have intermarried with non-Indians to a greater extent than have most other American Indian groups. Given such circumstances, it is not surprising that a large number of non–American Indians—white and black alike—have a "Cherokee grandmother." They seem proud of it, and so they should be.

A related issue is that many Americans without an actual Cherokee grandmother claim one. There are also explanations for this. Such "lineage" might be from another, non-Cherokee tribe or it might be totally non-Indian. The Cherokees have grown to be a very large American Indian population, greatly mixed with non-Indians. Thus the Cherokees are well known, and individual Cherokees often have a large amount of non-Indian blood. As we have seen as well, the Cherokee population has become very dispersed geographically; concentrations are scattered throughout the United States, from North Carolina to Oklahoma to California, although many Cherokees in California are of marginal Indian ancestry. The Cherokees are probably the best known of all contemporary American Indian people. People believing they have Indian ancestry might simply define it as Cherokee for this reason.

Also, the Cherokees adopted many of the ways of Euro-Americans earlier than most Indian tribes; they are a "civilized" tribe. In this sense Cherokee lineage might be more acceptable to many Americans than lineage from other American Indian peoples. As Wahrhaftig (1968) indicated, it is not only acceptable but desirable for Oklahomans to have some slight degree of Cherokee ancestry, probably because early in Oklahoma history the Cherokees established themselves as an elite. They were sophisticated in military organization, experienced in plantation agriculture, and created a public school system superior to the schools attended by non-Indians at the time.

WHO ARE THE CHEROKEES?

Cherokees today are diverse. Geographically, they encompass widely distributed populations—from North Carolina to Oklahoma to California, the last group having a particularly distinctive set of "Indian" characteristics. Cherokees also encompass the Red-Black Cherokees, a small but unique population segment concentrated in California and in states other than North Carolina or Oklahoma where important, traditional concentrations of Cherokees have been located.

Cherokees today also encompass population segments with varying degrees of tribal membership as well as Indian self-identification and ancestry. Only about one-third of the Cherokee population are members of one of the three formal Cherokee "tribes." Similarly, only about half of the Cherokee population may be considered exclusively Indian (by self-definition), and over one-fourth may be considered mostly or exclusively non-Indian (again by self-identification).

Who, then, are the Cherokees? The best answer seems to be that there are many different Cherokee populations. As we have seen, however, the Cherokees have never been a clearly defined population. Differences have always existed. Initially these differences were defined culturally and linguistically. They represented the geographical populations—the different towns—that gave rise to cultural and linguistic differences. Historical events, to which the Cherokees responded and ultimately adapted, produced other differences in the

Cherokee population. Cultural and linguistic differences still exist. Some Cherokees actively participate in Cherokee cultural life; some speak the Cherokee language, often as their "mother tongue." This notwithstanding, Cherokee differences might today be best defined as social and demographic ones. Many of these also stem from geographic location or are at least related to location; others may be traced to the biological mixing with white and black populations. Such mixing has produced varying degrees of "Indianness" within the contemporary self-defined Cherokee population: a significant population segment—over 36,000, or more than 15 percent—is self-defined as *exclusively* non-Indian, using our ethnicity criteria.

But common to all the Cherokees is an identity as Cherokee. All of the 232,344 individuals described here—fully 17 percent of all American Indians in the United States in 1980, according to the census definition and resulting enumeration—identified themselves as Cherokee. So they are. They are distinct from the total United States population; they are distinct from the total United States American Indian population. Like all peoples of the world, they are the products of history, response to history, and adaptation to history. Yet few other groups in American society today seem shaped by a *demographic* history to the same extent as the Cherokees.

A NOTE ON THE FUTURE

Future Cherokee populations will undoubtedly become demographically more like the total United States population and those of the states where they live. The keys to such demographic change will likely be the same as they have been for several centuries: geographic dispersion (including movement to metropolitan areas) and racial mixing. Other factors will certainly be important; some are included in this analysis. They are social factors that tend to influence demographic ones. Encompassed here are education, income, and employment. As Cherokees' social characteristics are similar to those of the total United States population, so are their demographic characteristics.

Conclusion

Cherokee population history and recent trends allow me to make some predictions about the demographic future of American Indians.

Cherokee history has been unique, as have the histories of other American Indian peoples. Nevertheless common forces, even common events, have impinged on Cherokees and on all American Indians. As I have shown elsewhere (Thornton 1987a), American Indians throughout the United States were subjected to the same forces of depopulation to one degree or another. These may be summarized as disease, warfare and genocide, removal and relocation, and destruction of lifeways. Virtually all American Indians suffered from each of these at times in their history.

Cherokees adapted to these forces, as did most other American Indians. Through adaptation American Indians were changed, demographically and otherwise. The Cherokees adapted earlier than many American Indian peoples: along with the Chickasaws, the Choctaws, the Creeks, and the Seminoles, they constituted the Five Civilized Tribes; that is, they adopted Euro-American ways rather quickly. Now, all American Indian peoples in the United States have adopted such ways, though to greatly varying degrees. A key to the rapidity, and perhaps even extent, of their adoption seems to be whether the particular American Indian group continued on tribal lands—reservations, rancherias (in California), or pueblos (in the Southwest) or had lands that were eventually all taken away or allotted. Even with tribal lands, geographical dispersion has occurred, since there has been much out-migration to non-Indian areas, particularly metropolitan ones, and considerable intermarriage has taken place (see Thornton 1987a: chaps. 7, 8, and 9).

Data show, for example, that during the past few decades the movement of American Indians to metropolitan areas has greatly accelerated: only about one-quarter of all American Indians lived in such areas in 1960; about half did so in 1980 (see Thornton 1987a:227, table 9-1; Snipp 1989).

Data also show that in 1980 over half of all American Indians were married to non-Indians (see Sandefur and McKinnell 1985). The United States Bureau of the Census reported: "In 1980, 119,448 out of 258,154 married American Indian, Eskimo, and Aleut couples were married within the same racial group; 130,256 Indian individuals were married to either whites, blacks, Filipinos, Japanese, or Chinese; and 8,450 Indians were married to individuals of other races" (U.S. Congress 1986:74). This intermarriage rate has increased from about one-third in 1970, and it is higher in metropolitan than non-metropolitan areas (Thornton 1987a:236–37).

These two pronounced trends of American Indians—increased metropolitan residence and increased intermarriage—will produce a profound change in the nature of the American Indian population. One projection is that it will increase to about 4 million by the year 2020 and almost 16 million by the year 2080. The projection also indicates that the percentage of American Indians with half or more Indian blood quantum will decline from about 87 percent in 1980 to about 8 percent by 2080. Conversely, the percentage with less than one-fourth Indian blood quantum will increase from about 4 percent in 1980 to about 59 percent in 2080 (U.S. Congress 1986:78). Thus American Indians will become racially more like the non-Indian population.

As with the Cherokees, changes in social factors such as education, income, and employment will also influence the demographic future of the total American Indian population. As these and other social characteristics of American Indians and non-Indians become more similar, we can expect the basic demographic characteristics of the two populations to become more alike. These too, of course, are influenced by metropolitan residence and intermarriage.

Do Cherokees today represent a prototype for the demographic future of American Indians? If the recent trend continues, the answer is yes. Perhaps ultimately most, if not all, Indian blood, to quote the Cherokee John Ridge, "will win[d] its courses in beings of fair complexions."

Appendix:
Cherokees in the
1980 Census

The issues surrounding the content and quality of census data for American Indians in general and the Cherokees in particular are highly complex. This appendix will acquaint interested readers with the procedures used to generate data about the Cherokees and other American Indians as well as problems that may exist in these data.

The 1980 census data for the Cherokees presented here and in chapter 7 are based on special tabulations done under a program funded jointly by the American Statistical Association, the National Science Foundation, and the United States Bureau of the Census. The 1980 census data for the total American Indian population presented here are based on a 5 percent sample of the Public-Use Microdata Sample (PUMS) and a 1 percent sample (20 percent of the 5 percent PUMS) of the 1980 census. Sampling errors cause the population data presented here to differ somewhat from published population figures of the United States Bureau of the Census.

COUNTING CHEROKEES AND OTHER
AMERICAN INDIANS

The United States Bureau of the Census made an unprecedented effort to identify and enumerate American Indians in the 1980 decennial census. Among the efforts was an extensive outreach

C. Matthew Snipp and Nancy Breen are coauthors with me of the Appendix.

program in conjunction with American Indian tribal governments and urban American Indian organizations to encourage American Indians to return their census questionnaires with their Indian race so identified. As a result of these efforts, 1980 census data for American Indians, though not flawless, are surely more accurate and complete than data from previous censuses. As we have seen, in 1980 the Census Bureau enumerated 1,366,676 American Indians, of whom 232,344, or 17.0 percent, indicated they were Cherokee.

Cherokees in the 1980 Census

The data for the 232,344 Cherokees in the 1980 census are based solely on persons who identified their *race* as American Indian. The number does not include persons who list a race other than American Indian (e.g., white) yet report one or more Cherokee (Indian) ancestors. Furthermore, all Cherokees were persons who identified themselves as such on the line asking persons to reveal their tribal affiliation if they identified their race as American Indian.

Although the overwhelming majority of Cherokees identified in the 1980 census listed their tribe as "Cherokee," this was not the only response identified as Cherokee by the Census Bureau. For example, persons who identified themselves as "Western Cherokee" or "Eastern Cherokee" were also counted as Cherokee. Table 44 shows the distribution of responses recognized as variations of Cherokee.

As the table shows, the Census Bureau recognized six Cherokee responses. The most common was simply the tribal identification "Cherokee"; this accounted for 99.4 percent of the enumerated Cherokees. The second largest response category was for the 1,104 persons who identified themselves as "Eastern Cherokee"; most resided in North Carolina and throughout parts of the Southeast. Others did not reside in the East, nor were there only 1,104 Cherokees in the East in 1980. And many Cherokees residing in the eastern United States reported their tribal affiliation simply as "Cherokee." Other categories of Cherokee identification, referring to historic Cherokee groups, though recognized by the Census Bureau, represented such small numbers as to be hardly more than a residual grouping.

In viewing these data on the Cherokees, one should remember that they are based entirely on self-identification and are not necessarily linked to blood quantum or other standards used by either the

Table 44. Persons Identifying Themselves as
Cherokee in the 1980 United States Census

Cherokee Identification	Number	Percentage
Cherokee	230,924	99.4
Eastern Cherokee	1,104	0.5
Western Cherokee	85	0.0
Etowah Cherokee	43	0.0
United Keetoowah	110	0.0
Tuscola	78	0.0
Total	232,344	99.9

Source: Unpublished data, U.S. Bureau of the Census, 1987.
Note: These figures differ slightly from those first available
from the 1980 census (1981, 1985:B-17). The original total
was 232,080.

Cherokee tribes or the Bureau of Indian Affairs to determine who
is (and is not) a Cherokee. In fact, as shown in chapters 6 and 7,
all census figures on race and ethnicity are now based on unverified
self-reports about racial identity and tribal affiliation. This procedure
has a number of implications about the content and interpretation
of such census data; thus it is helpful to understand the procedures
used to count Cherokees and other American Indians in the 1980
census.

Background

Since the first United States census in 1790, as provided for in the Constitution, and until 1870, most American Indians
(those "not taxed") were not officially included in decennial censuses.
This was because of the separateness of American Indians and American Indian tribes from larger society as well as the resulting sovereign
tribal rights: most American Indians were not United States citizens. Also, the nomadic lifeways of some American Indian tribes and
even the hostility of some tribes, along with the logistics of finding
American Indian settlements in otherwise unsettled territories, were
undoubtedly considerations in not enumerating American Indians in
the various decennial censuses until 1870.

Historically, to 1960 the Census Bureau depended on platoons
of enumerators, mostly temporary employees, to conduct house-by-
house interviews to collect census data. These interviews were intended to discover the number of persons in each residence as well

as such additional information as sex, age, race, education, employment, and income. Information about the residence per se, such as the number of rooms, also was typically recorded.

The Census Bureau depended on United States marshals to conduct the 1870 census, as had been customary since the first census in 1790. In the 1870 census, however, the federal marshals were assigned for the first time the task of enumerating American Indians, except those on reservations, who were not included until the 1890 census. The marshals and their assistants were instructed to record the presence of any American Indian in a household as part of information collected about race. They also were instructed to distinguish "Indians taxed" from "Indians not taxed": "Indians not taxed" were defined as "Indians living on reservations under the care of Government agents, or roaming individually, or in bands, over unsettled tracts of country" (U.S. Bureau of the Census 1979:22); "Indians taxed" were those living in or near settlements of whites. Needless to say, the enumeration of "Indians not taxed" was undoubtedly a haphazard operation at best.

The distinction between Indians taxed and not taxed was crucial because those not taxed were considered ineligible for inclusion in the regular United States census and were not included in official census figures. Nevertheless, the federal marshals were instructed to record the number of Indians not taxed and to submit this information separately. The reason for this distinction bore directly on the citizenship status of American Indians. Indians taxed (regardless of whether they actually paid taxes) were United States citizens and were thus to be included in the census. Citizenship for them, however, was achieved only by giving up tribal lifeways and settling in white communities; American Indians who became landowners by virtue of the allotment acts of the late 1800s also were confirmed as United States citizens. Indians not taxed, in contrast, were those who refused to abandon their American Indian communities and traditional cultures or who were exempt from land allotments.

In 1924 all American Indians were granted United States citizenship regardless of their residence or life-style; consequently, the distinction between Indians taxed and Indians not taxed ceased to appear in Census Bureau documents. Also, beginning in 1890 United States marshals were no longer used to conduct the census enumerations. With the granting of citizenship, the Census Bureau counted American Indians in the 1930 to 1950 censuses in much the same way as it counted other Americans. However, in both 1930 and 1950 the Census Bureau made a special effort to collect and report specific information about American Indians. This information was later published in special reports intended to update earlier special reports dealing with American Indians derived from the 1890 and 1910 censuses (see U.S. Bureau of the Census 1937, 1953). As used in chapter 6, the special reports based on the 1910 and 1930 censuses contain particularly detailed information about Cherokees and other American Indians.

The quality of the data from the 1950 and earlier censuses is difficult to judge. In the 1950 report on American Indians, the quality of the data was estimated to be reasonably good in areas where many American Indians lived and therefore were easily identified by enumerators. The data for American Indians in other areas were believed to be less reliable (U.S. Bureau of the Census 1953:4–5). This meant, for example, that the enumeration of American Indians in the 1950 census was likely to be more accurate in areas such as the Southwest and Oklahoma than east of the Mississippi River, but it probably was poor in most urban areas no matter where they were.

There is little evidence of systematic efforts to document the quality of United States census data before 1950. To the extent that the federal marshals, and later the Census Bureau enumerators, were diligently committed to their work, the accuracy and completeness of the data were probably good. In the absence of committed enumerators, the data were probably inaccurate and incomplete. In any case, it seems impossible to determine with any precision the degree of error in these early censuses. By modern standards, the data in all early United States censuses are probably flawed in many ways, as are data derived from most historical sources. Historians generally agree, however, that American Indian population figures from sources such as the Annual Reports of the Commissioners of Indian Affairs are more accurate than those from early United States census enumerations (see Thornton and Marsh-Thornton 1981).

The 1960 and 1970 Censuses

In the 1960 census, as we saw in previous chapters, the Census Bureau made a landmark change in its procedures for enumerating racial groups, one that profoundly altered the way American Indians were counted in this and subsequent censuses. The reliance

Table 45. American Indian Population in
the United States, 1910 to 1980

Date	Population	Change from Previous Census	
		N	%
1900	237,196		
1910	276,927	39,731	16.8
1920	244,437	−32,490	−11.7
1930	343,352	98,915	40.5
1940	345,252	1,900	0.6
1950	357,499	12,247	3.5
1960	523,591	166,092	46.5
1970	792,730	269,139	51.4
1980	1,366,676	573,946	72.4

Source: U.S. Bureau of the Census (1973b:xi, table II;
1984, 2, table 4).

on enumerators in earlier censuses meant that the numbers of American Indians counted depended mainly on the census enumerators' ability to recognize someone visually as American Indian. If in doubt whether someone was an Indian, particularly for later censuses, enumerators were instructed to inquire if the person was recognized in his or her community as an American Indian. But in all likelihood there were many, especially in urban areas, who were mistakenly identified as white, black, or another race. New procedures made in the 1960 census changed this with dramatic effect.

The procedures adopted for the 1960 census resulted in the Census Bureau's giving up the use of enumerators as its primary vehicle of data collection. Instead, it implemented a system of mailing questionnaires to occupied dwellings. Residents were asked to complete the questionnaires and then retain them until they were picked up by an enumerator. One of the most significant changes this system brought about was that information about race no longer depended on enumerators' judgments. Instead, a self-reported racial identification of respondents replaced their reports. The impact of this change on the American Indian population seems readily apparent in table 45. For most of this century until 1950, the American Indian population experienced slow but steady growth. With the introduction of racial self-identification in the 1960 census, the number of American Indians counted skyrocketed from 357,499 in 1950 to 523,591 in 1960, an increase of 46.5 percent. This unprecedented increase in the American Indian population of the United States suggests that many persons who considered their race to be American Indian in 1960 were not identified as such by Census Bureau enumerators in 1950. In other words, the growth in the American Indian population between 1950 and 1960 is so large that it surely cannot be accounted for by an excess of births over deaths, making the introduction of self-identification the most plausible explanation.

The events of the 1960s, especially the political turmoil arising from the civil rights movement and subsequent "ethnic pride" movements, probably had a large, albeit unmeasurable, impact on the growth of the American Indian population between 1960 and 1970 as measured in census enumerations. During this decade, the American Indian population grew by 51.4 percent to reach 792,730. The political upheavals of the 1960s are most notable because during this time it became acceptable, if not actually popular, to claim a distinctive ethnic heritage—American Indian or otherwise. This was a marked departure from earlier times in the history of the United States, when ethnic minorities such as American Indians often sought to assimilate and otherwise "pass" into white society as a way of avoiding the racial discrimination prevalent in the larger American society. The civil rights movement, the rise of the counterculture and ecology movements, and political protests by American Indians such as the occupation of Alcatraz Island in 1968 doubtless imbued many individuals with pride in their American Indian heritage and produced the upsurge in the 1970 census (see, for example, Passel 1976).

Like the American Indian population growth between 1950 and 1960, the sheer magnitude of the growth from 1960 to 1970 cannot be explained by differences in fertility and mortality rates; however, unlike the case in the 1950 and 1960 censuses, the 1970 census enumeration procedures were not markedly different from those in the 1960 census. In the 1970 census, respondents were asked to mail their completed questionnaires to the United States Bureau of the Census rather than having them picked up by enumerators as in 1960. Yet both the 1960 and 1970 censuses obtained information about race from the self-reports of respondents. The only other significant difference regarding identification of race between the 1960 and 1970 censuses was that in the latter census respondents reporting their race as American Indian were asked to indicate a tribal affiliation. It is doubtful if this change produced a significant increase in the numbers of persons listing American Indian as their race. However, the fact that questionnaires were returned by mail in 1970 likely increased the number of returns from areas undercounted in 1960, when enumerators still picked up the questionnaires. Census agents are less likely to pick up returns in isolated areas or areas they perceive as unwelcoming or unimportant to count.

Although the 1970 census question about tribal affiliation was probably not consequential for American Indian population growth in the 1960s, the change was significant for what is known about American Indians. Compared with earlier censuses that collected information about blood quantum and tribal membership, the 1960 census was an extreme departure in that it asked only if persons considered their race to be American Indian. The 1960 census did not inquire about either blood quantum or tribal membership. As a result this census is a relatively poor source of information about American Indians; needless to say, it is impossible to single out Cherokees in these data. The addition once again of tribal identification in the 1970 census was a decided improvement in this regard, and most of the information about American Indians, including Cherokees, from the 1970 census is available from a special subject report published in 1973 (U.S. Bureau of the Census 1973b). Unlike censuses before 1960, however, the 1970 census did not collect information about blood quantum; besides this limitation, the Census Bureau estimated that it undercounted the American Indian population by 10 to 15 percent. There are no estimates in this regard, but it seems likely that the undercount was even higher in the 1960 census than in the 1970 census.

The 1980 Census

Race

Responses to item 4 in figure 7 are the basis of reports about the racial composition of the United States population. The race item shows that the Census Bureau recognized fifteen racial groups, including a residual category for "other" races: whites, blacks, and nine types of Asian and Pacific islanders are represented in this classification; Hispanics can belong to any racial group, including American Indian, but they are separately identified by the question about Hispanic origins, shown as item 7 in figure 7. Three categories were allotted to the Native American United States population: American

Facsimile of questionnaire item 4.

| 4. Is this person —

Fill one circle | ○ White
○ Black or Negro
○ Japanese
○ Chinese
○ Filipino
○ Korean
○ Vietnamese

○ Indian (Amer.)
   Print
   tribe → -- | ○ Asian Indian
○ Hawaiian
○ Guamanian
○ Samoan
○ Eskimo
○ Aleut
○ Other — *Specify*
               ↓ |

Facsimile of questionnaire item 7.

| 7. Is this person of Spanish/Hispanic
   origin or descent?

Fill one circle | ○ No (not Spanish/Hispanic)
○ Yes, Mexican, Mexican-Amer., Chicano
○ Yes, Puerto Rican
○ Yes, Cuban
○ Yes, other Spanish/Hispanic |

Facsimile of questionnaire item 14.

> **14.** What is this person's ancestry? *If uncertain about how to report ancestry, see instruction guide.*
>
> ---
>
> *(For example: Afro-Amer., English, French, German, Honduran, Hungarian, Irish, Italian, Jamaican, Korean, Lebanese, Mexican, Nigerian, Polish, Ukrainian, Venezuelan, etc.)*

Facsimile of instructions to the respondent for questionnaire item 14.

> **14.** Print the ancestry group with which the person *identifies*. Ancestry (or origin or descent) may be viewed as the nationality group, the lineage, or the country in which the person or the person's parents or ancestors were born before their arrival in the United States. Persons who are of more than one origin and who cannot identify with a single group should print their multiple ancestry (for example, German-Irish).
> Be specific; for example, if ancestry is 'Indian', specify whether American Indian, Asian Indian, or West Indian. Distinguish Cape Verdean from Portuguese, and French Canadian from Canadian.
> A religious group should not be reported as a person's ancestry.

Figure 7. Items used to ascertain race, Hispanic origin, and ancestry in the 1980 Census. Source: U.S. Bureau of the Census (1979:81–82).

Indian, Eskimo, and Aleut. American Indians were asked to also note their tribal identification.

An important limitation of item 4 is that it did not allow individuals to identify more than one race: the categories of classification were mutually exclusive, so it was not possible to respond that one was multiracial. For instance, people could not respond that they were American Indian and white; they were either American Indian or white, but not both.

Information from those reporting more than one race on the questionnaire was handled with special procedures. Individuals giving multiracial responses were assigned to their mothers' race if it could be ascertained. However, this was possible only when the mothers of multiracial offspring resided in the same household as their children; this is most likely true for younger persons. When their mothers' race could not be ascertained, multiracial individuals were assigned to the first race they indicated.

These procedures have significant consequences for how the American Indian population was counted, especially younger children of racially mixed marriages. In particular, the procedures in which the mother's race was assigned to multiracial offspring causes sex-specific mate selection patterns to have an effect on the number of American Indian children. For example, if more American Indian men than women were married to non-Indians, there would be a smaller number of American Indian children enumerated than if more Indian women than men were married to non-Indians: children with American Indian fathers who reported more than one race were not counted as American Indians, and this would decrease the number of enumerated American Indian children. Likewise, children who reported more than one race and had American Indian mothers were counted as Indian, and this would increase the number enumerated. Census procedures therefore increase or decrease the count of American Indian children, depending on the extent of multiracial reports for children of Indian–non-Indian marriages and on the preferences of American Indian men and women for non-Indian mates. The degree to which Census Bureau methods affect population estimates cannot be investigated. Data are available for studying sex-specific patterns of racial intermarriage, but not patterns of multiracial reporting. From a policy standpoint, American Indian leaders and federal authorities should be concerned about this problem because it represents a potential undercount of persons who as American Indians would be eligible for federal and tribal services yet are otherwise identified as white in Census Bureau data.

Ancestry

Independent of their status as racial groups, American Indians, Eskimos, and Aleuts were also recognized as ethnic or ancestral groups in the 1980 census. Information about this was obtained from item 14 (see fig. 7). This item had two significant features. Perhaps most important, the Census Bureau used *ancestry* as the operational characteristic of ethnicity. The instructions for the ancestry item are shown below it and are very general. Persons were asked to report the nationality, lineage, or national origin of themselves or their ancestors—to identify their ethnic origins in terms of their heritage. Also important, respondents were not asked to choose among a set of predetermined categories, as they did in item 4. Instead, individuals in the household freely responded with as many different ancestries as they pleased.

For reporting purposes, the Census Bureau generally used only the first two responses if individuals gave several ancestries, ignoring third and subsequent ones. Persons who reported a single ancestry such as "Indian" were counted as "Indian." But individuals, for example, who reported their ancestry as "Irish-French-Indian" were counted as "Irish-French"; others who responded as "Indian-French-Irish" were counted as "Indian-French." Census Bureau procedures did recognize a few cases of frequently reported triple ancestries: Four recognized triple ancestries were frequently reported by individuals with American Indian ancestry. The combinations and the number of individuals reporting each combination were: Indian-English-French, 77,537; Indian-English-German, 169,207; Indian-English-Irish, 246,842; and Indian-German-Irish, 328,295 (U.S. Bureau of the Census 1983a:6, table 6).

1980 Racial and Ethnic Ancestry Data

The race and ancestry questions used in the 1980 census are strikingly different in important ways. Racial data were based on a question forcing the respondent to make a single choice from among a set of preselected categories. Ethnic ancestry data, in contrast, were elicited via a question allowing freely chosen responses from the

Table 46. Population Estimates of American Indians by Sex and
Category of Race and Ancestry, 1980

	Persons Reporting American Indian Race [a]		Persons Reporting American Indian Ancestry	
Sex	N	%	N	%
Male	760,520	49.4	3,259,600	48.3
Female	779,300	50.6	3,495,200	51.7
Total	1,539,820	100.0	6,754,800	100.0

Source: Estimates for persons reporting American Indian race are based on a 5 percent sample of the 1980 census (5 percent PUMS). Estimates for persons reporting
American Indian ancestry are based on a 1 percent sample of the 1980 census (20
percent sample of 5 percent PUMS).
[a] Includes Eskimos and Aleuts.

repertoires of personal memory and self-identification. These differences resulted in sharply discrepant coverage for the American Indian
population, reflected in two remarkably different estimates derived
from samples for the size of the United States American Indian population.

Table 46 shows sex-specific estimates of the American Indian
population based on race and ethnic ancestry definitions. Using race
to define population boundaries results in an estimate of 1,539,820
American Indians. Ethnic ancestry produces a dramatically different
figure. Including everyone who reported American Indian ancestry
yields a population estimate of 6,754,800, over four times larger than
the estimate based on racially defined population boundaries. Sheer
magnitude makes it difficult to reconcile the differences in these
estimates.

Social scientists generally agree that there is little variation in the
racial composition of most ethnic groups. That is, most do not include more than one race, and members of the same ethnic group
usually share certain physical appearances. This is evidently not
true for those who indicated in the 1980 census that their ancestry
included American Indians. Table 47 shows the sex-specific racial
profile of all who reported American Indian ancestry in the 1980
census. Of the estimated 6,754,800 persons generated by our sample
who reported American Indian ancestry, 5,173,500 (76.6 percent) also
identified their race as white. A much smaller group of 1,217,200 persons (18.0 percent) of American Indian ancestry also reported their
race as American Indian. Blacks and other races made up the small
(5.4 percent) remaining balance of persons who reported American

Table 47. Race of Persons Reporting American Indian Ancestry by Sex, 1980

Race	Male N	%	Female N	%	Total N	%
American Indian	599,200	18.4	618,000	17.7	1,217,200	18.0
Black	108,000	3.3	148,700	4.3	256,700	3.8
White	2,497,100	76.6	2,676,400	76.6	5,173,500	76.6
Hispanic and other	38,200	1.2	37,400	1.1	75,600	1.1
Asian	17,100	0.5	14,700	0.4	31,800	0.5
Total	3,259,600	100.0	3,495,200	100.1	6,754,800	100.0

Source: One percent sample of 1980 census data (20 percent sample of 5 percent PUMS data).

Table 48. First Ancestry of Persons Reporting American Indian Race by Sex, 1980

Ancestry	Male N	%	Female N	%	Total N	%
American Indian	554,680	72.9	572,080	73.4	1,126,760	73.2
African	1,700	0.2	1,340	0.2	3,040	0.2
European	79,380	10.4	82,260	10.6	161,640	10.5
Hispanic	25,840	3.4	24,980	3.2	50,820	3.3
Asian and Pacific Islanders	2,440	0.3	2,540	0.3	4,980	0.3
Other	22,880	3.0	23,440	3.0	46,320	3.0
Unknown	73,600	9.7	72,660	9.3	146,260	9.5
Total	760,520	99.9	779,300	100.0	1,539,820	100.0

Source: Five percent sample of 1980 census data (PUMS).
Note: Includes Eskimos and Aleuts.

Indian ancestry. The most significant finding in this table seems to be that the vast majority of persons claiming American Indian ancestry consider their race to be not Indian, but white.

Using the same format as in table 47, a parallel analysis can be made of the distribution of ethnic ancestors among persons in the sample reporting American Indian as their race. Table 48 presents a profile, based on "first" ancestries, that is, the first ancestry listed in a series of ancestries for persons of multiethnic background, or the only ancestry of persons reporting a single ethnic background. Table 48 shows that most (73.2 percent) of the 1,539,820 people who identified their race as American Indian also reported their ancestry as American Indian. However, about 161,640, or 10.5 percent, indicated a European group as their first or only ethnic ancestry. Although they said their race was American Indian, these individuals identified their ethnic ancestry in terms such as Irish-Indian, German-Indian, English-Indian, Italian-Indian, or simply as Irish, German, French, English, Italian, or any one of the large number of other European nationality or ethnic groups. Even smaller proportions reported Hispanic (3.3 percent), African (0.2 percent), and other ethnic (3.0 percent) ancestries. The category of "unknown" is for persons who did not report an ancestry, for whatever reason. One possible reason for such nonreporting is that once people reported their race, they viewed the question about ancestry as redundant and did not bother to respond. Of the racially defined American Indian population, 9.5 percent responded in this manner. Ordinarily this would not be significant, but this category represented the third most common response for American Indians.

These data suggest several important conclusions. One is that there is significant overlap between race and ethnic backgrounds among American Indians. Such overlap is not peculiar to American Indians, since the linkage between race and ethnicity is repeatedly mentioned in the race relations literature. There is, however, considerable racial heterogeneity among those identifying an American Indian ancestry. But it is striking that the reported race of most persons reporting American Indian ancestry is *white*, not Indian. In contrast, the ethnic background composition of those reporting American Indian race is relatively homogeneous. In other words, most persons who claim American Indian ancestry do not identify their race as American Indian, but most persons who identify their race as American Indian also claim American Indian ancestry.

American Indian Population Levels

Using the information about race and ethnicity ancestry, several levels of American Indian population, broadly defined and not restricted by Census Bureau definitions, may be constructed. The first level includes persons who disclosed their race *and* ethnic background as American Indian. There is no doubt that they are members of a basic American Indian population; the consistency of their responses makes them the core group of the American Indian population: they may be classified as simply "American Indians." Another level of American Indian population consists of persons who reported

Table 49. Population Estimates for Type of American Indians by Sex, 1980

Type	Male		Female		Total	
	N	%	N	%	N	%
American Indians	466,100	14.3	481,400	13.8	947,500	14.0
American Indians of multiple ancestry	133,100	4.1	136,600	3.9	269,700	4.0
Americans of Indian descent	2,660,400	81.6	2,877,200	82.3	5,537,600	82.0
Total	3,259,600	100.0	3,495,200	100.0	6,754,800	100.0

Source: One percent sample of 1980 census data (20 percent sample of 5 percent PUMS data).

their race as American Indian but included non-Indian ancestry in their ethnic background. In the jargon of an earlier era, these individuals would be known as "mixed-bloods" or in some cases "half-breeds," "quarter-breeds," or simply "breeds." "American Indians of multiple ancestry" is a more accurate designation. These two population levels constitute the Census Bureau's definition of the American Indian population. A third level, primarily one of American Indian identity, consists of those persons who cited a non-Indian race yet claimed American Indian ancestry in their ethnic background. They may be considered "Americans of Indian descent."

Each of these American Indian population levels defines a distinct population or subpopulation, as shown in table 49. In 1980, thus, 6,754,800 persons reported their race or ethnic ancestry or both as Indian, and 82.0 percent of them were "Americans of Indian descent." "American Indians" and "American Indians of multiple ancestry" constituted the second and third largest levels. It is only the population defined by the category "American Indians," however, that is both racially and ethnically homogeneous.

These three levels of the American Indian population derived from 1980 census data accent the complex factors involved in personal perceptions of racial and ethnic identity, which give rise to definitions of a population. As the data demonstrate, race and ethnic ancestry are distinct yet intricately related. The relationship between them, moreover, has fundamental implications for the way the total American Indian population—or for that matter any racial or ethnic population—is defined and enumerated, at least for the purpose of demographic analysis.

Cherokee Ancestry

Because the Census Bureau coded only the first two reported ethnic ancestries in their order of appearance, it was possible to cross-classify first-reported ancestries with second-reported ancestries. The results were revealing about the Cherokee population. The ethnic ancestries of those who identified themselves as Cherokee (or one of the variations shown in table 44) are shown in table 50. As the data show, Cherokees in the 1980 census claimed a diverse mixture of ethnic ancestries.

In reading table 50, one must remember that many people did not report any ancestry; in fact 14,751 persons did not respond to the ancestry question, as shown in the table. Also, those who did not report a first ancestry by definition did not have a second ancestry. (This explains the row of zeros at the bottom of table 50.) And one could not have the same first and second ancestry; therefore no one had an American Indian first and second ancestry. (However, one could have European first and second ancestries, e.g., French-Irish.) Finally, many people reported only one ancestry. This led to possibly the most significant finding reported in table 50—that, of the 164,428 Cherokees who reported their first ancestry as American Indian, over 76 percent did not report a second ancestry. This indicates to us that a very substantial number of Cherokees have a consistent image of their race and ethnic ancestry and that these Cherokees did not consider themselves descended from any group except American Indians.

For Cherokees who reported a second ancestry, a European one was most frequently reported: about 20 percent of the Cherokees who reported American Indian as their first ancestry also reported a group such as German, Irish, French, or Italian as their second ancestry. Very small numbers of Cherokees reported African or Hispanic ancestries. This information coupled with the preceding information shows that among Cherokees who reported their first ancestry as American Indian, over 96 percent claimed either European ancestry or no ancestry other than American Indian.

Although an overwhelming majority of Cherokees reported American Indian as their first ancestry, about a quarter of the Cherokee population—67,916 to be exact—did not do so. Instead, most of these Cherokees identified a European first ancestry. Out of the total number of Cherokees who *did not* report American Indian as

Table 50. Distribution of First and Second Ancestries Reported by Cherokees in the 1980 Census

First Ancestry	Second Ancestry							
	American Indian	European	Hispanic	African	Asian and Pacific Islander	Other United States	Not Reported	Total
American Indian								
Number	0	32,804	1,423	254	356	3,338	124,253	164,428
Percentage	0.0	20.2	0.9	0.2	0.2	2.1	76.4	100.0
European								
Number	22,985	13,402	321	50	83	289	7,342	44,472
Percentage	51.7	30.1	0.7	0.1	0.2	0.7	16.5	100.0
Hispanic								
Number	1,245	224	37	0	30	44	548	2,128
Percentage	58.5	10.5	1.7	0.0	1.4	2.1	25.8	100.0

								Total
African[a]								
Number	211	96	0	0	0	27	150	484
Percentage	43.6	19.8	0.0	0.0	0.0	5.6	31.0	100.0
Asian and Pacific Islander								
Number	352	125	29	13	32	38	202	791
Percentage	44.5	15.8	3.7	1.6	4.1	4.8	25.5	100.0
Other United States[b]								
Number	1,580	263	19	8	28	222	5,170	7,290
Percentage	21.7	3.6	0.3	0.1	0.4	3.1	70.8	100.0
Not Reported								
Number	0	0	0	0	0	0	14,751	14,751
Percentage	0.0	0.0	0.0	0.0	0.0	0.0	100.0	100.0
Total								232,344

Source: Unpublished data, U.S. Bureau of the Census, 1987.
[a] Includes West Indians.
[b] Includes Eskimos and Aleuts.

Appendix

their first ancestry, 44,472, or 65.5 percent, identified themselves as
of German, Irish, or other European ancestry. (Relatively few Cherokees [2.3 percent] reported non-European ancestries.) However, the
majority, 51.7 percent, identified American Indian as their second ancestry. Nevertheless, a considerable number of Cherokees, 13,402, or
30.1 percent, identified a European first *and* second ancestry, while
a smaller percentage (16.5 percent) revealed no ancestry other than
their European first ancestry.

Several conclusions can be drawn from these data. First, there
is a large core group within the Cherokee population that strongly
identifies with an American Indian heritage: over half of the Cherokee population reported no ancestry other than American Indian. A
second conclusion, on the other hand, is that a very large number
of Cherokees—over 50,000—claim mixed ancestries of American
Indian and other, mostly European, heritage. The size of this group
is hardly surprising in view of the extensive intermarriage between
Cherokees and other ethnic groups, notably European ones. Even the
great Cherokee leader John Ross claimed Scottish ancestry and only
about one-eighth Cherokee blood quantum.

Finally, within the total Cherokee population there is a relatively
small, yet distinct, group of about 27,000 who appear to identify
weakly with their American Indian heritage. They listed no American Indian ancestry. Some members of this group may have failed to
reveal an American Indian background because they misunderstood
the question on the census form. Yet many of them probably were
children of extensive intermarriages between Cherokees and non-
Indians who were highly assimilated into the mainstream American
population. As a group, these Cherokees who identify so weakly with
their American Indian heritage may have few links with traditional
tribal culture or have life-styles associated with the American Indian
population at large or a Cherokee tribe in particular.

In conclusion, these varying degrees of ethnic identification reveal
that the Cherokee population is characterized by a diverse membership that differs considerably in strength of American Indian ethnic
identification.

COMPONENTS OF GROWTH

Between 1970 and 1980 the American Indian population, as enumerated in censuses of those decades (and not including Alaska Natives), grew from 792,730 to 1,366,676. This represented an increase of over 72 percent in the number of persons identifying themselves as American Indian in the two censuses. This growth cannot be explained only by an excess of births over deaths in the 1970s. Procedural improvements in the way American Indians were counted in 1980 may explain some growth, but it is unlikely that they account for very much of it. It seems more likely that a sizable number of individuals who did not report themselves as American Indian in the 1970 census (or earlier censuses) did so in the 1980 census. There are many reasons this may have occurred, as we have indicated. The "ethnic activism" by American Indian organizations during the 1970s was probably an inducement for many to identify themselves as American Indian. Others may have been encouraged to assert their Indian identity by diminished racial discrimination and increased career opportunities made available through affirmative action and related government policies and legal rulings. No explanation can be established beyond doubt, but unquestionably a tidal shift in racial self-identification produced much of the growth in American Indian population during the 1970s.

For example, Passel and Berman (1985) examined data for American Indians from the 1980 census and explored possible reasons for the explosive population growth between 1970 and 1980. They voiced concerns about the increase in the Cherokee population but did not closely examine the Cherokee data in the way they did for data on the total American Indian population. In the remainder of this appendix, we examine the growth of the Cherokee population in a way that parallels Passell and Berman's analysis of the total population of American Indians.

Population growth (and decline) of a constantly defined population is the result of only two processes: migration and an excess of births over deaths (or the reverse in the case of population decline). For the Cherokee population (and for all American Indians), immigration from outside the United States can be ruled out as a source of population growth. This leaves only vital events—births and deaths—as the source of growth for the Cherokee population as

Table 51. Annual Estimates of the Cherokee Population and Components
of Change, 1970 to 1980

Year or Period	Population (January 1 or Census Date)	Estimated Births (Calendar Year)	Estimated Deaths (Calendar Year)	Natural Increase
1970 census	66,150	2,149	454	1,695
1971	67,421	2,486	516	1,970
1972	69,391	2,737	590	2,147
1973	71,538	2,868	670	2,198
1974	73,736	3,109	696	2,413
1975	76,149	3,445	751	2,694
1976	78,843	3,867	820	3,047
1977	81,890	4,317	894	3,423
1978	85,313	4,966	1,022	3,944
1979	89,257	5,411	1,044	4,367
1980	93,624	6,109	1,132	4,977
1980 (April 1)	94,868	NA	NA	NA
1980 census	232,344	NA	NA	NA
Intercensal period	NA[a]	36,345	7,627	27,586
Errors of closure	137,476	NA	NA	NA

Sources: Passel and Berman (1985); unpublished data, U.S. Bureau of the Census, 1987.
[a] Not applicable.

defined in the 1970 census. However, the 1980 Cherokee population
was not defined only by the 1970 population, since persons changed
their racial identification from one census to another. This resulted
in what are known as "errors of closure." Between 1970 and 1980,
errors of closure in the Cherokee population indicated that significant numbers of people decided to switch their racial identification
from non-Indian, such as white, to American Indian, with Cherokee
as their tribal affiliation.

Although the exact sources of shifts in racial self-identification
are not clear, it is possible to demonstrate that the errors of closure
resulting from these shifts were primarily responsible for the massive population growth in the Cherokee population between 1970
and 1980. Annual estimates for the Cherokee population between
1970 and 1980 are shown in table 51. These estimates are based
on the difference between estimated births and estimated deaths
(natural increase) for each year between 1970 and 1980. Births and
deaths for the Cherokee population were estimated from data for

the total American Indian population, but vital statistics reports do not provide information separately for individual tribes, Cherokee or otherwise. To estimate births and deaths, we assumed that Cherokee births and deaths were proportional to Cherokee representation in the total American Indian population. In 1970 Cherokees constituted about 8.7 percent of the total American Indian population; by 1980 this had risen to 17.0 percent. Assuming a linear increase, this meant that the Cherokees increased their representation in the total American Indian population at the rate of about 0.8 percent per annum. Based on these assumptions, we estimated annual births and deaths for the Cherokee population from available vital statistics data.

Table 51 shows that as of April 1, 1970, the Census Bureau enumerated 66,150 American Indians who reported their tribe as Cherokee. In 1970 Cherokee births exceeded deaths by 2,149 to 454, resulting in an increase of the population by about 1,700 persons. Births continued to exceed deaths throughout the decade, with larger numbers of births and deaths in each successive year. Changes in racial self-identification notwithstanding, by January 1, 1980, the 1970 Cherokee population would have grown to about 94,000 on the basis of natural increase. This number increased slightly through the first quarter of 1980, so that the Cherokee population would have numbered 94,868 as of April 1, 1980, the date of the 1980 census.

Thus the yearly population estimates in table 51 suggest that, in the absence of changes in self-identification, the expected growth in the Cherokee population between 1970 and 1980 would have been 28,718, an increase of about 43 percent. While this level of population growth is extraordinarily high, it is modest compared with the increase registered by the 1980 census.

In fact, the 1980 census enumerated 232,344 Cherokees, of whom 137,476 represented errors of closure according to our analysis. Instead of an expected growth rate of 43 percent, the actual growth rate, as recorded in the 1980 census, was a nearly unbelievable 251 percent. Thus errors of closure accounted for nearly 83 percent of the increase between 1970 and 1980. Likewise, numbers of "new" Cherokees due to errors of closure were approximately five times greater than the numbers of new Cherokees due to natural increase.

By definition, errors of closure could have arisen from at least two sources. One source could have been gross undercounting of the 1970 Cherokee population. With a better enumeration in 1980, it is conceivable, though we think unlikely, that thousands of new Cherokees were "discovered" and that this produced the massive increase in the Cherokee population between 1970 and 1980. A second, much more likely source of the errors of closure was a tidal shift in racial identification, with record numbers of individuals who claimed for the first time in 1980 that their race was American Indian and their tribe was Cherokee. In other words, a large number of persons counted as Cherokees in 1980 identified their race as something other than American Indian in 1970.

Passel and Berman (1985) argued, as we have noted, that such changes in racial self-identification were probably the result of emerging ethnic pride movements during the 1970s. Declining racial discrimination, perceived opportunities through affirmative action programs, and greater awareness of resources for American Indians such as Bureau of Indian Affairs' scholarships also were factors that probably induced many people to change their racial self-identification. Added to these reasons is another, more or less specific to the Cherokees: the resurgence of the Cherokee Nation of Oklahoma during the 1970s, as noted in chapter 7, and the consequent large increase in the number enrolled in the Cherokee Nation during that decade.

Although impossible to isolate directly, it is possible to observe the effects of such developments in the distribution of errors of closure across age cohorts. For example, if job opportunities through affirmative action and educational assistance from the Bureau of Indian Affairs were significant incentives to identify oneself as an American Indian, then younger persons, such as those in their twenties and early thirties, would have been the most likely to have switched their racial identification in order to take advantage of these benefits. On the other hand, a decline in discrimination, an easing of assimilationist pressures, and a greater ethnic pride may have had a more pronounced effect on older persons who, in earlier years, denied their American Indian background in order to avoid discrimination and to gain access to the economic opportunities of mainstream white society. (Remember, a large segment of the Cherokee population claims a measure of European ancestry.)

To examine such possible age-specific changes in racial identification, we constructed table 52, which shows the distribution of errors in closure across five-year age cohorts. The data show that, with a single exception, every age group displayed a large discrepancy between expected and observed population sizes. The single exception is for children under five years of age, who appeared to have been

Table 52. Comparisons of Age-Specific Cherokee Population Estimates from 1970 and 1980 Data

Age		1970 Census (or Births)	Estimated Cohort Deaths 1970–80	Estimated 1980 Population	1980 Census	Difference	
1970	1980					N	%
Births 1975–80	0–4	19,495	356	19,139	17,017	−2,122	−12.5
Births 1970–75	5–9	16,850	413	16,437	18,768	2,331	12.4
0–4	10–14	5,470	113	5,357	22,084	16,727	75.7
5–9	15–19	6,385	150	6,235	25,268	19,033	75.3
10–14	20–24	7,025	304	6,721	23,593	16,872	71.5
15–19	25–29	6,754	390	6,364	20,883	14,519	69.5
20–24	30–34	5,393	371	5,022	20,507	15,485	75.5
25–29	35–39	4,599	360	4,239	17,274	13,035	75.5
30–34	40–44	4,069	381	3,688	13,879	10,191	73.4
35–39	45–49	3,607	398	3,209	11,345	8,136	71.7
40–44	50–54	4,016	435	3,581	11,063	7,482	67.6
45–49	55–59	3,722	460	3,262	9,004	5,742	63.8
50–54	60–64	3,433	492	2,941	6,827	3,886	56.9
55–59	65–69	3,124	528	2,596	5,467	2,871	52.5
60–64	70–74	2,704	541	2,163	3,959	1,796	45.4
65+	75+	5,849	1,935	3,914	5,406	1,492	27.6
Total		102,495	7,627	94,868	232,344	137,476	59.2

Source: Passel and Berman (1985); unpublished data, U.S. Bureau of the Census, 1987.

undercounted by about 13 percent in the 1980 census. In contrast, the errors of closure suggest that the largest overcounts cover a wide age range. Large errors of closure begin with youths aged ten to fourteen years in 1980 and include successively older cohorts through adults who were forty-five to forty-nine years of age in 1980. For these age groups, the errors of closure range from 70 to 76 percent and do not exhibit any systematic variation with respect to age. After age fifty, the errors of closure diminish in each older cohort and reach a low for persons who were seventy-five or older in 1980.

The absence of highly distinctive age-specific differences in the errors of closure probably indicates that changes in racial self-identification arose from a variety of sources. Opportunities for jobs and education may have melded to produce the largest errors of closure among peak working-age adults and among youths beginning to contemplate their future education. From this perspective, declining discrimination and greater ethnic pride may have been lesser factors in changing racial self-identification, at least among persons over the age of fifty, for whom the errors of closure are smaller. Nevertheless, even for the oldest cohort, the error of closure of nearly 28 percent is striking. Overall, the errors of closure suggest that changes in racial self-identification, regardless of the cause, were primarily responsible for population growth among all ages of Cherokees.

CONCLUDING REMARKS

As we have attempted to show, interpreting census data for American Indians is a complex task. This is no less true for data about the Cherokee population, and perhaps is even more true. The key to understanding Census Bureau data about the Cherokees, as about American Indians in general, is that it relies on the information respondents provide on racial background and tribal affiliation. Neither the Census Bureau nor any other organization has the time and resources to check the accuracy of information provided on over 225 million Americans in the 1980 decennial census. As a result, racial data published by the Census Bureau is necessarily the result of subjective views about the meaning of race and of prevailing social and political conditions that affect the desirability of identifying with one race or another. Changing social conditions related to declines in discrimination, growing ethnic pride, affirmative action policies, and tribal resurgence appear to have had a dramatic impact on how Cherokees identified themselves.

Because Census Bureau data is based on self-identification, it cannot be directly compared with data from such sources as the Bureau of Indian Affairs or individual tribal enrollments. Tribal enrollments for the Cherokees, for example, require some Cherokee ancestry based on blood quantum documentation. The Census Bureau, on the other hand, recognizes as Cherokee anyone who reports this tribal affiliation, regardless of ancestry or the ability to document lineage. To complicate matters, it is also limiting to use Census Bureau data for making detailed comparisons over time. The Cherokee population of 1980 was much larger than and very different from the Cherokee population of 1970. As a result of the influx of new Cherokees between 1970 and 1980, there were changes in the composition of the

Cherokee population that cannot be distinguished from changes due to factors not related to shifts in racial self-identification.

One of the most important, yet not directly answerable, questions raised is the degree to which the growth in the self-identified Cherokee population represented an increase in the population recognized as Cherokee by the membership and governing authorities of one of the Cherokee tribes. Undoubtedly many changes in self-identification reflected a return to tribal roots, or simply a more accurate characterization of one's racial identity. However, it is equally likely that some, and perhaps many, individuals who identified themselves as Cherokee in 1980 knew virtually nothing about Cherokee tribal culture, were descended from distant and possibly unverifiable Cherokee ancestors, and probably would have difficulty obtaining tribal membership. Unfortunately, it is impossible in census data to distinguish these persons from bona fide tribe members. As we mentioned earlier, however, only about one-third of the self-identified Cherokees in the 1980 census actually held Cherokee tribal membership. This is a surprisingly small proportion given that two-thirds of all American Indians reported tribal membership.

These problems exist mainly because objective criteria have never been established for deciding who is and is not an American Indian, and who is and is not a Cherokee; any such criterion is controversial. Nevertheless, this is a matter that all American Indian tribes should resolve for themselves. Deciding who is and is not a Cherokee will be a profoundly complex and controversial process. It will have equally profound implications, since it will influence more than matters of data collection; it will affect who is entitled to share tribal resources in the near future and how the tribes will be constituted in the more distant future.

Notes

Introduction

1. Readers are referred to the following for Cherokee histories: Washburn (1910), Adair ([1775] 1930), Foreman (1934), Brown (1938), Gilbert (1943), Starkey (1946), Malone (1956), Woodward (1963), Starr ([1922] 1967), Reid (1970, 1976), Wilkins (1970, 1986), Royce ([1887] 1975), Carter (1976), Hudson (1976), Goodwin (1977), Wardell ([1938] 1977), Hewes (1978), King (1979), Perdue (1979), Swanton ([1946] 1979), Mooney ([1900, 1891] 1982), and Finger (1984). See also Fogelson (1978) for a bibliography of writings on the Cherokees.

Chapter One

1. "Going to water" refers to ritualized Cherokee bathing in running streams, after fasting and typically at daybreak.

2. The Cherokees also likely had seven "mother towns." Mooney (1907: 247) noted that according to the explorer Cuming in 1730, each had a hereditary chief in the female line. According to Samuel G. Drake, the seven towns were Tannassie, Kettooah, Ustenary, Telliquo, Estootowie, Keyowee, and Noyohee. Drake (1872:9) also stated: "These towns had each their king, but at this time [1730] the kings of but three of the towns were alive, namely, those of Tannassie in the upper settlements; of Kettooah in the middle; and of Ustenary in the lower. Besides a king, or head man, each town had a head warrior." (Reports of Cherokee "kings" may not be accurate [see Reid 1970].) In any event, these towns in turn were probably related to the seven Cherokee clans: Ani-waya (Wolf), Ani-Kawi (Deer), Ani-Tsiskwa (Bird), Ani-wadi ([Red] Paint), Ani-Sahani (Blue?), Ani-Gatagewi (Wild Potatoes?), and Ani-Gilahi (Twisters?). Mooney (1907:247) concluded there may have originally been fourteen clans, but "by extinction or absorption" they were reduced to seven; he also noted that the Wolf clan was the most important as well as the largest.

3. Witthoft (1947:304) asserted further: "The second group preceded the first into the East, and the two divisions seem to represent the middle and Western Cherokee dialect groups."

4. For discussions of Cherokee origin, see Mooney (1889, [1900] 1982:17–22); Corkran (1957); Coe (1961); Dickens (1976, 1979); Keel (1976); Goodwin (1977:32–36); Fogelson (1978:10–11); Swanton ([1946] 1979:68, 110–15); Oliver (1985); and Thomas ([1894] 1985:718).

5. Recent scholarship has focused on De Soto's route; see DePratter, Hudson, and Smith (1985) and Hudson et al. (1985).

6. John Swanton ([1946] 1979:110) noted: "It has usually been assumed that the 'province of Chalaque or Xalaque' of which the De Soto chroniclers speak was inhabited by these [the Cherokee] Indians, but the name may be the Muskogee term signifying 'people of a different speech,' and only one town in this region mentioned in the De Soto narratives, Guasili, near the present Murphy, North Carolina, may be identified as perhaps occupied by real Cherokee Indians."

7. The 1980 census enumerated 42,162 Eskimos and 14,205 Aleuts as well, for a grand total of 1,423,043 Native Americans (U.S. Bureau of the Census 1984:2, table B).

8. James Mooney did not necessarily consider his estimates to refer to aboriginal population size; they may have related to the date of first extensive white contact in an area (Ubelaker 1976b:288). Accordingly, aboriginal population sizes could have been reduced, particularly by new diseases introduced by Europeans and Africans, before the dates Mooney used.

9. According to the same contemporary scholars, this made the Gulf states region the most heavily, though not the most densely, populated area, about 1492, of what is now the United States. For an examination of the early archaeological record in this regard see Smith (1984); see also Ramenofsky (1987).

Chapter Two

1. In 1708 over half of the Charleston population of 9,580 was said to have been composed of slaves: 1,400 American Indian slaves and 4,100 black slaves. In addition, Indian slaves were being exported from Charleston to colonies to the north as well as to the West Indies. Some of these were undoubtedly Cherokees, though most were perhaps from tribes closer to the colony (Thomas 1903:94–96).

2. See Krzywicki (1934:318) and Cook (1976:5–6) for discussions of the ratio of "warriors" to total American Indian population.

3. It was here that the sacred Cherokee town of Kituhwa was situated (on the Tuckasegee River near present-day Bryson City, North Carolina).

As I mentioned, it is to Kituhwa that the Cherokees trace themselves; it is Kituhwa that is the Cherokee "mother town"; and it is as Ani-Kituhwagi, the "people of Kituhwa," that the Cherokees sometimes refer to themselves on ceremonial occasions. The town was perhaps the first "Cherokee" settlement, the original nucleus of the Cherokee tribe, according to James Mooney ([1900] 1982:15).

4. Adair also asserted that "all the magi and prophetic tribe broke their old consecrated physic-pots, and threw away all the other pretended holy things they had for physical use, imagining they had lost their divine power by being polluted; and shared the common fate of their country" (Adair [1775] 1930:245).

5. See Louis DeVorsey, Jr.'s, *The Indian Boundary in the Southern Colonies, 1763–1775* (1961) for further discussion of Cherokee land cessions and boundary lines during part of the eighteenth century.

6. Chief Bowl was the child of a full-blood Cherokee mother and a Scottish trader father who was killed when Bowl was about twelve (Foreman 1930:21).

7. At least for a time, some Cherokees emigrated to St. Augustine and to Pensacola in Florida (see, for example, Anderson and Lewis 1983:157, 450, 527, 594, 613, 659).

8. Mooney ([1900] 1982:83) argued: "Most of this white blood was of good stock, very different from the 'squawman' element of the western tribes." Reid (1976:141–50), however, seems to disagree.

9. For a fuller discussion of Indian-white intermixing, see Nash (1982: 275–80).

10. For a fuller discussion of Indian-black intermixing, see Nash (1982: 285–91, esp. 290).

Chapter Three

1. Howard (1970:74) further noted that cholera also affected groups of Cherokees journeying on their own that spring.

2. These numbers total 16,406, not 16,542, the total census enumeration, seemingly as a result either of incomplete data or of some non-Cherokees' being included in the data. Also, mixed-bloods referred only to those of Cherokee-"white" admixture, not those of Cherokee-black or even Cherokee-Spanish admixture (see McLoughlin and Conser 1977:682, table 3).

3. This was somewhat of a decrease from earlier numbers of intermarried whites: 341 in 1809, 211 in 1826, and 205 in 1828 (McLoughlin and Conser 1977:681, table 1).

4. It is estimated that some 100,000 American Indians were removed from

eastern homelands to west of the Mississippi River during the first half of the nineteenth century (see Blue 1974:iii; Doran 1975–76:496–97). Most relocations took place in the decade following the passage of the Indian Removal Act, though some occurred both earlier and later. Most of the total number removed were members of five tribes: Cherokees, Chickasaws, Choctaws, Creeks, and Seminoles, along with remnants of other southeastern Indian groups joined with them.

5. Charles Royce ([1887] 1975:169) gave the figure of 2,103 for those removed by 1838, "of whom 1,282 had been permitted to remove themselves."

6. James Mooney ([1900] 1982:131) asserted that the number rounded up approached 17,000. This seems an exaggeration if his earlier statement was correct that some 2,000 of the 17,000 had previously "voluntarily" emigrated.

7. The author of this quotation was referring to the removal of all of the Five Civilized Tribes, not only the Cherokees.

8. This was reported in 1837 (see Doran 1975–76:498); apparently it thus refers to emigrants soon after the treaty of 1835.

9. Such an estimate would place Cherokee mortality about midway in the mortality losses of the other four major southeastern tribes, as nearly as can now be ascertained. The Choctaws are said to have lost 15 percent of their population, 6,000 out of 40,000 (Allen 1970:62), and the Chickasaw removal is said to have been "a comparatively tranquil affair" (Foreman 1932:226), though they surely had severe losses as well. By contrast, the Creeks and Seminoles are said to have suffered about 50 percent mortality. For the Creeks this came primarily in the period immediately after removal: for example, "of the 10,000 or more who were resettled in 1836–37, . . . an incredible 3,500 . . . died of 'bilious fevers.'" The high Seminole mortality seems to have resulted not primarily from postremoval disease but from "the terrible war of attrition that had been required to force them to move" (Doran 1975–76:497–500).

10. This contrasts sharply with population estimates for the period: one, in 1841, asserted there were 18,000 Cherokees in Indian Territory alone (*New American State Papers*, [1789–1860] 1972, 11:13).

Chapter Four

1. The epidemic was characterized by a severe rash; it was perhaps measles or smallpox (Pulte and Altom 1984:35).

2. Doran (1978:341) noted: "The greatest efforts in the salt trade seem to have gotten under way in 1838 after Lewis Ross of the Cherokee Nation brought in several hundred slaves to the 'Saline District' specifically for employment on the farms and salt works there."

3. Mooney noted of the Catawbas among the Cherokees: "In 1840 about

one hundred Catawba, nearly all that were left of the tribe, being dissatisfied with their condition in South Carolina, moved up in a body and took up their residence with the Cherokee. Latent tribal jealousies broke out, however, and at their own request negotiations were begun in 1848, through Thomas and others, for their removal to Indian Territory. The effort being without result, they soon after began to drift back to their own homes, until, in 1852, there were only about a dozen remaining among the Cherokee" (Mooney [1900] 1982:165).

4. Some have asserted that the Keetoowahs were the same as the "Pin Indians," named because they used crossed pins on their coat lapels for identification. This is not correct: Hendrix writes that "the Pins were a separate organization of activists that started among the militants of Goingsnake District, and while most of them were Keetoowahs it was not a requirement and there were many Keetoowahs who were not Pins" (1983a:24).

5. It has even been suggested that White Path's rebellion of 1828 was a Keetoowah movement (Hendrix 1983a:25).

6. The sickness was reportedly pneumonia (S. Thornton 1937).

Chapter Five

1. There was a small immigration of Eastern Cherokees into the Cherokee Nation in 1867, organized by D. M. Morris. Some seventy-five North Carolina Cherokees voluntarily emigrated from Valley River in Cherokee County, far from the two other concentrations of Cherokees. They sought an improvement not only in their economic situation but in their political situation as well, since they were afraid the Qualla settlement would still dominate Cherokee affairs, depriving them of benefits (Perdue 1982:69).

2. There were 5,175 females and 5,169 males over eighteen years of age, a total of 10,344, and the total number under eighteen was 9,391 (Cherokee Nation 1881:6, table A).

3. This and the preceding statement refer not only to the Cherokees but also to the other four of the Five Civilized Tribes: Creeks, Choctaws, Chickasaws, and Seminoles.

4. Two other groups were also mentioned: those claiming citizenship but denied it, and intruders into Indian Territory. The latter group was subclassified: "Those innocently coming into the county, not knowing that it is unlawful; those fraudently [sic] pretending to be of Indian blood; those persistently and willfully defying and evading the authorities simply for the privilege of living in the Indian county; escaped criminals and felons from the States seeking refuge here" (U.S. Department of the Interior 1885:106).

5. A description of the different geographical locations of segments of the Cherokee population, particularly full-bloods and mixed-bloods, in Indian

Territory may be found in the 1886 *Annual Report of the Commissioner of Indian Affairs* (U.S. Department of the Interior 1886:148).

6. It was also reported that there were fifty-six families of white intruders on their tract, "occupying and farming 6,000 acres, most of it good land" (U.S. Bureau of the Census 1894b:501).

7. There was a plan in 1893 to merge some Chiricahua Apache "prisoners" with the Eastern Cherokees; it did not materialize, and the Apaches were relocated to Fort Sill, Oklahoma Territory. In 1913, "after twenty-seven years in captivity they were sent to join the Mescalero Apaches on a reservation in Otero County, New Mexico" (Williams 1977:244).

Chapter Six

1. A general discussion of the Dawes Act may be found in Washburn (1975).

2. This enabled the women to have the following characteristics: "(1) They were of child-bearing age; (2) had been married long enough to have children; and (3) were living in the married state at the time of the enumerations" (U.S. Bureau of the Census 1915:157).

3. From the reported data on married women in the Indian population, marriage rates were calculated between and among full-bloods, mixed-bloods, and whites, as shown in the accompanying table. These data indicate that, overwhelmingly, full-bloods were married to full-bloods: 90.6 percent of the full-blood women and 94.8 percent of the full-blood men. Also, most of the approximately 45 percent of the mixed-blood men and women not married to other mixed-bloods were married to whites, not to full-bloods.

| | Husband | | | | | | | |
| | Full-Blood | | Mixed-Blood | | White | | | |
Wife[a]	N	%	N	%	N	%	Total	%
Full-blood	10,780[b]	90.6 (94.8)	914	7.7 (12.7)	208	1.7 (7.1)	11,902	100.0
Mixed-blood	594	8.1 (5.2)	3,970	54.4 (55.0)	2,730	37.4 (92.9)	7,294	99.9
White	—	—	2,336	100.0 (32.4)	NA[c]	NA (NA)	2,336	100.0
Total	11,374	(100.0)	7,220	(100.1)	2,938	(100.0)	21,532	

Source: U.S. Bureau of the Census (1915:157, table 53).
[a] For women aged fifteen to forty-four years, married at least one year and neither divorced, widowed, nor married more than once.
[b] Includes 401 polygamous marriages; husband and wives probably full-bloods (U.S. Bureau of the Census 1915: 157, table 53).
[c] Not applicable.

4. It was further noted: "The census of 1910 was probably more accurate than that of 1930 in the enumeration by tribe and blood of those Indians whose tribal organization had broken down, and who were living as a part of the white community, or scattered through mountain areas. In North Carolina, and also in many other areas, the proportion of Indians shown in the census of 1930 as of full blood is much too high. This is particularly true of those tribes in which there is a large Negro admixture" (U.S. Bureau of the Census 1937:1).

5. According to the Department of the Interior (1941:13, table 3, n. 6), this estimate "was made by adding to the 1930 population as reported by the Bureau of the Census, a proportionate increase similar to that reported by the remaining agencies in Oklahoma."

6. The Department of the Interior (1943:13, table 11, n. 4) noted of this estimate: "Not carried on annual census roll. Estimated on basis of last available census."

7. According to this same author, this is considerably fewer than the number identified as Cherokees in the 1960 census enumeration (Wahrhaftig 1968:512, table 3).

8. It has been estimated that in the early 1960s only about 10,000 people could speak Cherokee (Chafe 1962:165).

9. In July 1986 the United States Bureau of Indian Affairs listed 306 American Indian tribes with which it had relations (including one American Indian tribe in Alaska and two unorganized tribes) (U.S. Bureau of Indian Affairs 1986).

10. In 1981 6,210 individuals were enrolled as formal members of the Confederated Salish and Kootenai Tribes (unpublished data provided by Edgar Lister of the Indian Health Service). In 1980, however, only 2,760 people identified as Salish or Kootenai lived on the Flathead reservation: 2,112 were enrolled in the tribes, and 303 did not report their enrollment status (U.S. Bureau of the Census 1985:19).

Chapter Seven

1. The 1980 census also counted 42,162 Eskimos and 14,205 Aleutian Islanders for a grand total of 1,423,043 Native Americans (Swagerty and Thornton 1982:92; U.S. Bureau of the Census 1984:2, table B).

2. This procedure of self-identification has been used by the Census Bureau since the 1960 census.

3. Most American Indians in North Carolina are identified with the Lumbee tribe. See Blu (1980) for a discussion of North Carolina's Lumbee Indians, a recently organized group of largely Indian-white-black mixed descendants of various American Indian peoples indigenous to the area.

4. Metropolitan areas, as defined by the Census Bureau, are somewhat more exclusive than urban areas. They include both rural and urban areas within a metropolitan radius but do not include small urban places. Consequently, percentage metropolitan is typically somewhat lower than percentage urban.

5. The 1980 census asked a separate question to identify individuals of Spanish/Hispanic origin or descent. (See Appendix.) Those specifying more than one race in item 4 were assigned the race of their mothers if this could be ascertained; if not, they were assigned the first race they listed (Snipp 1986:238).

6. The Census Bureau reported seven combinations of triple ancestry, including four for American Indians: Indian-English-French, Indian-English-German, Indian-English-Irish, and Indian-German-Irish (U.S. Bureau of the Census 1983a:6, table 6; Snipp 1986:240, 251, n. 2). (See also Appendix.)

7. This comprised Adair, Cherokee, Craig, Delaware, McIntosh, Mayes, Muskogee, Nowata, and Ottawa counties and portions (urbanized area was excluded) of Rogers, Sequoyah, Tulsa, Wagoner, and Washington counties (U.S. Bureau of the Census 1985:99, table 13).

References

Abel, Annie Heloise
1915   *The American Indian as slaveholder and secessionist.* Vol. 1 of *The slaveholding Indians.* Cleveland: Arthur W. Clark.
1919   *The Indian as a participant in the Civil War.* Vol. 2 of *The slaveholding Indians.* Cleveland: Arthur W. Clark.
1925   *The Indian under Reconstruction.* Vol. 3 of *The slaveholding Indians.* Cleveland: Arthur W. Clark.

Adair, James
1930   *Adair's history of the American Indians.* Edited by Samuel Cole Williams. Johnson City, Tenn.: Watauga Press. Originally published 1775.

Allen, Virginia R.
1970   Medical practices and health in the Choctaw Nation, 1831–1885. *Chronicles of Oklahoma* 48:60–73.

Alterman, Hyman
1969   *Counting people: The census in history.* New York: Harcourt, Brace and World.

Anderson, William L., and James A. Lewis
1983   *A guide to Cherokee documents in foreign archives.* Metuchen, N.J.: Scarecrow Press.

Axtell, James, ed.
1981   *The Indian peoples of eastern America: A documentary history of the sexes.* New York: Oxford University Press.

Baker, Jack D.
1977   *Cherokee emigration rolls, 1817–1835.* Oklahoma City: Baker.

Bartram, William
1958   *Travels of William Bartram.* Edited by Francis Harper. New Haven: Yale University Press. Originally published 1791.

Berlandier, Jean Louis
1969   *The Indians of Texas in 1830.* Edited and introduced by John C. Ewers. Washington, D.C.: Smithsonian Institution Press.

Blankenship, Bob
1978   *Cherokee roots.* Cherokee, N.C.

Blasingham, Emily
  1956   The depopulation of the Illinois Indians. *Ethnohistory* 3, pt. 1,
          193–224; pt. 2, 361–412.
Blu, Karen I.
  1980   *The Lumbee problem: The making of an American Indian
          people.* New York: Cambridge University Press.
Blue, Brantly
  1974   Foreword. In *The Indian removals*, 1:iii–v. New York: AMS Press.
Bolton, Herbert Eugene
  1987   *The Hasinais: Southern Caddoans as seen by the earliest Euro-
          peans.* Edited and with an introduction by Russell M. Magnaghi.
          Norman: University of Oklahoma Press.
Brown, John P.
  1938   *Old frontiers: The story of the Cherokee Indians from earliest
          times to the date of their removal to the West, 1838.* Kingsport,
          Tenn.: Southern Publishers.
Burnett, John G.
  1978   The Cherokee removal through the eyes of a private soldier. *Jour-
          nal of Cherokee Studies* 3:180–85.
Callender, Charles
  1978   Shawnee. In *Northeast*, ed. Bruce G. Trigger, 622–35. Vol. 15
          of *Handbook of North American Indians.* Washington, D.C.:
          Smithsonian Institution Press.
Callender, Charles, Richard K. Pope, and Susan M. Pope
  1978   Kickapoo. In *Northeast*, ed. Bruce G. Trigger, 656–67. Vol. 15
          of *Handbook of North American Indians.* Washington, D.C.:
          Smithsonian Institution Press.
Canouts, Veletta, and Albert C. Goodyear III
  1985   Lithic scatters in the South Carolina Piedmont. In *Structure and
          process in southeastern archaeology*, ed. Roy S. Dickens, Jr., and
          H. Trawick Ward, 180–94. University: University of Alabama
          Press.
Carter, Samuel, III
  1976   *Cherokee sunset: A nation betrayed.* Garden City, N.Y.: Double-
          day.
Chafe, Wallace L.
  1962   Estimates regarding the present speakers of North American
          Indian languages. *International Journal of American Linguistics*
          28:162–71.
Cherokee Nation
  1881   *Summary of the census of the Cherokee Nation, 1880.* Washing-
          ton, D.C.: Gibson Brothers.

Coe, Jeffre L.

1961   Cherokee archeology. In *Symposium on Cherokee and Iroquois
        culture*, ed. William N. Fenton and John Gulick, 51–60. Bureau of
        American Ethnology Bulletin 180. Washington, D.C.: U.S. Gov-
        ernment Printing Office.

*Constitution and by-laws of the United Keetoowah Band of Cherokee Indi-
ans, Oklahoma*

1950

*Constitution and Laws of the Cherokee Nation: Passed at Tahlequah,
Cherokee Nation, 1839–51*

1852

Constitution of the Cherokee Nation of Oklahoma

1976

Cook, Sherburne F.

1976   *The Indian population of New England in the seventeenth cen-
        tury*. Berkeley: University of California Press.

Corkran, David H.

1952   A Cherokee migration fragment. *Southern Indian Studies* 4:27–
        28.

1957   Cherokee pre-history. *North Carolina Historical Review* 34:
        455–66.

1962   *The Cherokee frontier: Conflict and survival, 1740–62*. Norman:
        University of Oklahoma Press.

Crane, Verner W.

1959   *The southern frontier: 1670–1732*. Ann Arbor: University of
        Michigan Press. Originally published 1929.

Debo, Angie

1951   *The Five Civilized Tribes of Oklahoma: Report on social and
        economic conditions*. Philadelphia: Indian Rights Association.

DePratter, Chester, Charles Hudson, and Marvin Smith

1985   The Hernando de Soto Expedition: From Chiaha to Mobila. In
        Alabama and its borderlands, from prehistory to statehood, ed.
        Reid Badger and Lawrence A. Clayton, 108–26. University: Uni-
        versity of Alabama Press.

DeVorsey, Louis, Jr.

1961   *The Indian boundary in the southern colonies, 1763–1775*.
        Chapel Hill: University of North Carolina Press.

Dickens, Roy S., Jr.

1976   *Cherokee prehistory: The Pisgah phase in the Appalachian Sum-
        mit region*. Knoxville: University of Tennessee Press.

1979   The origins and development of Cherokee culture. In *The Chero-
        kee Indian Nation: A troubled history*, ed. Duane H. King, 3–32.
        Knoxville: University of Tennessee Press.

Dobyns, Henry F.
  1966   Estimating aboriginal American population: An appraisal of
          techniques with a new hemispheric estimate. *Current Anthro-
          pology* 7:395–449.
  1983   *Their number become thinned: Native American population dy-
          namics in eastern North America.* With the assistance of Wil-
          liam R. Swagerty. Knoxville: University of Tennessee Press.
Doran, Michael F.
  1975–76 Population statistics of nineteenth century Indian Territory.
          Chronicles of Oklahoma 53:492–515.
  1978   Negro slaves of the Five Civilized Tribes. *Annals of the Associa-
          tion of American Geographers* 68:335–50.
Drake, Samuel G.
  1872   *Early history of Georgia embracing the embassy of Sir Alexan-
          der Cuming to the country of the Cherokees, in the year 1730:
          With a map of the Cherokee country, from a draft made by the
          Indians.* Boston: David Clapp.
Duffy, John
  1951   Smallpox and the Indians in the American colonies. *Bulletin of
          the History of Medicine* 25:324–41.
1835 residences of Cherokees who avoided removal
  1979   *Journal of Cherokee Studies* 4:240.
Emigration detachments
  1978   *Journal of Cherokee Studies* 3:186–87.
Englund, Donald Ralph
  1974   A demographic study of the Cherokee Nation. Ph.D. diss., Uni-
          versity of Oklahoma.
Evans, E. Raymond, ed.
  1981   Jedediah Morse's report to the secretary of war on Cherokee
          Indian affairs in 1822. *Journal of Cherokee Studies* 6:60–78.
Everett, Dianna
  1985   Ethnohistory of the Western Cherokees in Texas. Ph.D. diss.,
          Texas Tech University.
Fernow, Berthold
  1890   *The Ohio Valley in colonial days.* Albany, N.Y.: Joel Munsell's
          Sons.
Finger, John R.
  1980   The North Carolina Cherokees, 1838–1866: Traditionalism, pro-
          gressivism, and the affirmation of state citizenship. *Journal of
          Cherokee Studies* 5:17–29.
  1984   *The Eastern Band of Cherokees, 1819–1900.* Knoxville: Univer-
          sity of Tennessee Press.

Fogelson, Raymond D.
  1978   *The Cherokees: A critical bibliography.* Bloomington: Indiana University Press.
  1984   Who were the Ani-Kutani? An excursion into Cherokee historical thought. *Ethnohistory* 31:255–63.
Foreman, Grant
  1930   *Indians and pioneers: The story of the American Southeast before 1830.* New Haven: Yale University Press.
  1932   *Indian removal.* Norman: University of Oklahoma Press.
  1934   *The Five Civilized Tribes.* Norman: University of Oklahoma Press.
Foreman, Grant, ed.
  1934   The Murder of Elias Boudinot. *Chronicles of Oklahoma* 12:19–25.
Gilbert, William Harlen, Jr.
  1943   *The Eastern Cherokees.* Bureau of American Ethnology Bulletin 133. Washington, D.C.: U.S. Government Printing Office.
  1957   The Cherokees of North Carolina: Living memorials of the past. In *Smithsonian report for 1956,* 529–55. Washington, D.C.: U.S. Government Printing Office.
Goddard, Charles
  1978   Delaware. In *Northeast,* ed. Bruce G. Trigger, 213–39. Vol. 15 of *Handbook of North American Indians.* Washington, D.C.: Smithsonian Institution Press.
Goodwin, Gary C.
  1977   *Cherokees in transition: A study of changing culture and environment prior to 1775.* Chicago: Department of Geography, University of Chicago.
Gulick, John
  1960   *Cherokees at the crossroads.* Chapel Hill: University of North Carolina Press.
Haas, Mary R.
  1961   Comment on Floyd G. Lounsbury's "Iroquois-Cherokee linguistic relations." In *Symposium on Cherokee and Iroquois culture,* ed. William N. Fenton and John Gulick, 21–23. Bureau of American Ethnology Bulletin 180. Washington, D.C.: U.S. Government Printing Office.
Halliburton, R., Jr.
  1977   *Red over black: Black slavery among the Cherokee Indians.* Westport, Conn.: Greenwood Press.
Heizer, Robert F., and Albert B. Elsasser
  1980   *The natural world of the California Indians.* Berkeley: University of California Press.

Hendrix, Janey E.
  1983a Redbird Smith and the Nighthawk Keetoowahs. *Journal of Cherokee Studies* 8:22–39.
  1983b Redbird Smith and the Nighthawk Keetoowahs. *Journal of Cherokee Studies* 8:73–86.
Hewes, Leslie
  1978 *Occupying the Cherokee country of Oklahoma.* University of Nebraska Studies, N.S. 57. Lincoln: University of Nebraska Press.
Hitchcock, Ethan Allen
  1930 *A traveler in Indian Territory: The journal of Ethan Allen Hitchcock, late major-general in the United States Army.* Edited and annotated by Grant Foreman. Cedar Rapids, Iowa: Torch Press.
Hodge, Frederick Webb, ed.
  1907–10 *Handbook of American Indians North of Mexico.* Bureau of American Ethnology Bulletin 30. 2 pts. Washington, D.C.: U.S. Government Printing Office.
Howard, R. Palmer
  1970 Cherokee history to 1840: A medical view. *Oklahoma State Medical Association Journal* 63:71–82.
Howard, R. Palmer, and Virginia E. Allen
  1975 Stress and death in the settlement of Indian Territory. *Chronicles of Oklahoma* 53:492–515.
Hudson, Charles
  1976 *The southeastern Indians.* Knoxville: University of Tennessee Press.
  1987 Juan Pardo's Excursion beyond Chiaha. *Tennessee Anthropologist* 12:74–87.
Hudson, Charles, Marvin T. Smith, and Chester B. DePratter
  1984 The Hernando De Soto Expedition: From Apalachee to Chiaha. *Southeastern Archaeology* 3:65–77.
Hudson, Charles, Marvin Smith, David Hally, Richard Polhemus, and Chester DePratter
  1985 Coosa: A chiefdom in the sixteenth-century southeastern United States. *American Antiquity* 4:723–37.
Institute for the Development of Indian Law
  n.d.a *Treaties and agreements of the eastern Oklahoma Indians.* Washington, D.C.
  n.d.b *Treaties and agreements of the Five Civilized Tribes.* Washington, D.C.
Kappler, Charles J., ed. and comp.
  1904–79 *Indian affairs: Laws and treaties.* 7 vols. Washington, D.C.: U.S. Government Printing Office.

Keel, Bennie C.
  1976   *Cherokee archaeology: A study of the Appalachian Summit.*
          Knoxville: University of Tennessee Press.
King, Duane H., ed.
  1979   *The Cherokee Indian Nation: A troubled history.* Knoxville:
          University of Tennessee Press.
Knight, Oliver
  1954–55 Cherokee society under the stress of removal, 1820–1846.
          Chronicles of Oklahoma 32:414–28.
Kroeber, Alfred L.
  1939   *Cultural and natural areas of native North America.* University
          of California Publications in American Archaeology and Ethnol-
          ogy 38. Berkeley: University of California Press.
Krzywicki, Ludwik
  1934   *Primitive society and its vital statistics.* London: Macmillan.
Kupferer, Harriet J.
  1968   The isolated Eastern Cherokee. In *The American Indian today,*
          ed. Stuart Levine and Nancy Oestreich Lurie, 87–97. Delano,
          Fla.: Everett/Edwards.
Latorre, Felipe, and Dolores T. Latorre
  1976   *The Mexican Kickapoo Indians.* Austin: University of Texas
          Press.
Lawson, John
  1709   *A new voyage to Carolina.* London.
Lewis, Thomas M. N., and Madeline Kneberg
  1946   *Hiwassee Island: An archaeological account of four Tennessee
          Indian peoples.* Knoxville: University of Tennessee Press.
  1958   *Tribes that slumber: Indian times in the Tennessee region.* Knox-
          ville: University of Tennessee Press.
Lieberson, Stanley, and Mary C. Waters
  1988   *From many strands: Ethnic and racial groups in contemporary
          America.* New York: Russell Sage Foundation.
Lillybridge, C.
  1931   Journey of a party of Cherokee emigrants. Edited by Grant Fore-
          man. *Mississippi Valley Historical Review* 18:232–45.
Littlefield, Daniel F., Jr.
  1971   Utopian dreams of the Cherokee fullbloods, 1890–1934. *Journal
          of the West* 10:404–27.
  1978   *The Cherokee freedmen: From emancipation to American citi-
          zenship.* Westport, Conn.: Greenwood Press.
Litton, Gaston
  1940   Enrollment records of the Eastern Band of Cherokee Indians.
          North Carolina Historical Review 17:199–231.

Lounsbury, Floyd G.
    1961   Iroquois-Cherokee linguistic relations. In *Symposium on Chero-
            kee and Iroquois culture*, ed. William N. Fenton and John Gulick,
            11–17. Bureau of American Ethnology Bulletin 180. Washington,
            D.C.: U.S. Government Printing Office.
McLoughlin, William G.
    1975   Thomas Jefferson and the beginning of Cherokee nationalism,
            1806–1809. *William and Mary Quarterly* 32:547–80.
    1984   *The Cherokee ghost dance: Essays on the southeastern Indi-
            ans 1789–1861*. With Walter H. Conser, Jr., and Virginia Duffy
            McLoughlin. Macon, Ga.: Mercer University Press.
McLoughlin, William G., and Walter H. Conser, Jr.
    1977   The Cherokees in transition: A statistical analysis of the federal
            Cherokee census of 1835. *Journal of American History* 64:678–
            703.
Malone, Henry T.
    1956   *Cherokees of the Old South*. Athens: University of Georgia Press.
Milner, George R.
    1980   Epidemic disease in the postcontact Southeast: A reappraisal.
            Midcontinental Journal of Archaeology 5:39–56.
Momeni, Jamshid A.
    1984   *Demography of racial and ethnic minorities in the United
            States: An annotated bibliography with a review essay*. West-
            port, Conn.: Greenwood Press.
Mooney, James
    1889   Cherokee mound-building. *American Anthropologist* 2:167–71.
    1907   Cherokee. In *Handbook of American Indians north of Mexico*,
            ed. Frederick Webb Hodge, pt. 1, 245–49. Bureau of Ameri-
            can Ethnology Bulletin 30. Washington, D.C.: U.S. Government
            Printing Office.
    1910   Population. In *Handbook of American Indians north of Mexico*,
            ed. Frederick Webb Hodge, pt. 2, 286–87. Bureau of Ameri-
            can Ethnology Bulletin 30. Washington, D.C.: U.S. Government
            Printing Office.
    1911   The passing of the Delaware Nation. *Proceedings of the Missis-
            sippi Valley Historical Association for the Year 1909–10* 3:329–
            40.
    1928   The aboriginal population of America north of Mexico. Edited by
            John R. Swanton. *Smithsonian Miscellaneous Collections* 80:1–
            40.
    1982   *Myths of the Cherokee* and *Sacred formulas of the Cherokees*.
            Nashville: Charles and Randy Elder. Originally published 1900
            and 1891.

Mooney, Thomas G.

1987   *Exploring your Cherokee ancestry: A basic genealogical research guide.* Tahlequah, Okla.: Cherokee National Historical Society.

Morris, John W., Charles R. Goins, and Edwin C. McReynolds

1986   *Historical atlas of Oklahoma.* 2d ed., rev. and enl. Norman: University of Oklahoma Press.

Morse, Jedediah

1970   *A report to the secretary of war of the United States on Indian Affairs.* New York: Augustus M. Kelley. Originally published 1822.

Moses, L. G.

1984   *The Indian man: A biography of James Mooney.* Urbana: University of Illinois Press.

Muller, Jon D.

1978   The Southeast. In *Ancient Native Americans,* ed. Jesse D. Jennings, 281–325. San Francisco: W. H. Freeman.

Nash, Gary B.

1982   *Red, white, and black: The peoples of early America.* 2d ed. Englewood Cliffs, N.J.: Prentice-Hall.

The New American State Papers, 1789–1860

1972   Edited by Thomas C. Cochran. 13 volumes. Wilmington, Del.: Scholarly Resources. Originally published 1789–1860.

O'Donnell, James H., III

1973   *Southern Indians in the American Revolution.* Knoxville: University of Tennessee Press.

Oliver, Billy L.

1985   Tradition and typology: Basic elements of the Carolina projectile point sequence. In *Structure and process in southeastern archaeology,* ed. Roy S. Dickens, Jr., and H. Trawick Ward, 195–211. University: University of Alabama Press.

Passel, Jeffrey S.

1976   Provisional evaluation of the 1970 census count of American Indians. *Demography* 13:397–409.

Passel, Jeffrey S., and Patricia A. Berman

1985   An assessment of the quality of 1980 census data for American Indians. Unpublished paper presented at the 1985 annual meetings of the American Statistical Association, Las Vegas.

Perdue, Theda

1979   *Slavery and the evolution of Cherokee society, 1540–1866.* Knoxville: University of Tennessee Press.

1982   Remembering removal, 1867. *Journal of Cherokee Studies* 7:69–72.

Price, John A.

  1968   The migration and adaption of American Indians to Los Angeles. *Human Organization* 27:168–75.

Prucha, Francis Paul

  1975   *Documents of the United States Indian policy.* Lincoln: University of Nebraska Press.

Pulte, William, and Kathy Altom

  1984   The Mexican Cherokees and the Kickapoo of Nacimiento, Mexico: A previously unreported relationship. *Journal of Cherokee Studies* 9:35–36.

Ramenofsky, Ann F.

  1987   *Vectors of death: The archaeology of European contact.* Albuquerque: University of New Mexico Press.

Reagan, John H.

  1897   The expulsion of the Cherokees from east Texas. *Quarterly of the Texas State Historical Association* 1:38–46.

Reid, John Phillip

  1970   *A law of blood: The primitive law of the Cherokee Nation.* New York: New York University Press.

  1976   *A better kind of hatchet: Law, trade, and diplomacy in the Cherokee Nation during the early years of European contact.* University Park: Pennsylvania State University Press.

Royce, Charles C.

  1975   *The Cherokee Nation of Indians.* Chicago: Aldine. Originally published 1887.

Sandefur, Gary D., and Trudy McKinnell

  1985   Intermarriage among blacks, whites, and American Indians. Unpublished paper presented at the 1985 annual meetings of the American Sociological Association, Washington, D.C.

Siler, David W.

  1972   *The Eastern Cherokees: A census of the Cherokee Nation in North Carolina, Tennessee, Alabama and Georgia in 1851.* Cottonport, La.: Polyanthos. Originally published 1851.

Smith, Betty Anderson

  1979   Distribution of eighteenth-century Cherokee settlements. In *The Cherokee Indian Nation: A troubled history,* ed. Duane H. King, 46–60. Knoxville: University of Tennessee Press.

Smith, Marvin

  1984   Depopulation and cultural change in the early historic period interior Southeast. Ph.D. diss., University of Florida.

Snipp, C. Matthew

  1986   Who are American Indians? Some observations about the perils and pitfalls of data for race and ethnicity. *Population Research and Policy Review* 5:237–52.

1989   *American Indians: The First of this land.* New York: Russell
        Sage Foundation.
Starkey, Marion L.
    1946   *The Cherokee Nation.* New York: Alfred A. Knopf.
Starr, Emmet McDonald
    1967   *Starr's history of the Cherokee Indians.* Edited by Jack Gregory
            and Rennard Strickland. Fayetteville, Ark.: Indian Heritage Asso-
            ciation. Originally published 1922.
Stearn, E. Wagner, and Allen E. Stearn
    1945   *The Effect of smallpox on the destiny of the Amerindian.* Boston:
            Bruce Humphries.
Sturtevant, William C., ed.
    1981   John Ridge on Cherokee civilization in 1826. *Journal of Cherokee
            Studies* 6:79–91.
Swagerty, William R., and Russell Thornton
    1982   Preliminary 1980 census counts for American Indians, Eskimos
            and Aleuts. *American Indian Culture and Research Journal*
            6:92–93.
Swanton, John R.
    1979   *The Indians of the southeastern United States.* Washington,
            D.C.: Smithsonian Institution Press. Originally published 1946.
    1985   *Final report of the United States De Soto Expedition Commis-
            sion.* Washington, D.C.: Smithsonian Institution Press. Origi-
            nally published 1939.
Tanner, Helen Hornbeck
    1978   Cherokees in the Ohio country. *Journal of Cherokee Studies*
            3:95–101.
Tax, Sol
    1960   *Map of the American Indians: 1950 distribution of descendants
            of the aboriginal population of Alaska, Canada and the United
            States.* Chicago: Department of Anthropology, University of Chi-
            cago.
Thomas, Cyrus
    1891   The story of a mound; or, The Shawnees in pre-Columbian times.
            American Anthropologist 4, pt. 1:109–59; pt. 2:237–73.
    1903   *The Indians of North America in historic times.* Vol. 2 of *The
            History of North America.* Edited by Guy Carlton Lee. Philadel-
            phia: George Barrie.
    1985   *Report on the mound explorations of the Bureau of Ethnology.*
            Introduction by Bruce D. Smith. Washington, D.C.: Smithsonian
            Institution Press. Originally published 1894.
Thornton, Russell
    1978   Implications of Catlin's American Indian population estimates

for revision of Mooney's estimate. *American Journal of Physical Anthropology* 49:11–14.

1984   Cherokee population losses during the Trail of Tears: A new perspective and a new estimate. *Ethnohistory* 31:289–300.

1987a   *American Indian holocaust and survival: A population history since 1492*. Norman: University of Oklahoma Press.

1987b   Tribal history, tribal population, and tribal membership requirements: The cases of the Eastern Band of Cherokee Indians, the Cherokee Nation of Oklahoma, and the United Keetoowah Band of Cherokee Indians in Oklahoma. Paper presented at the Newberry Library Conference toward a Quantitative Approach to American Indian History, Chicago.

1989   Beyond violence and resistance: Native American responses to the demography of conquest. Paper presented at the Smithsonian Institution–University of Maryland Quincentenary Symposium, Violence and Resistance in the Americas: The Legacy of Conquest, College Park, Md., and Washington, D.C.

Thornton, Russell, and Joan Marsh-Thornton

1981   Estimating prehistoric American Indian population size for United States area: Implications of the nineteenth century population decline and nadir. *American Journal of Physical Anthropology* 55:47–53.

Thornton, Smith

1937   WPA interview with Smith Thornton. Vian, Okla., September 16, 1937.

Thornton, Wallace

1937   WPA interview with Wallace Thornton. Vian, Okla., May 21, 1937.

Thwaites, Reuben Gold, ed.

1905   *Nuttall's travels into the Arkansas Territory, 1819. Vol. 13 of Early western travels, 1748–1848*. Cleveland: Arthur H. Clark.

Trimble, William

n.d.   Census of Indian tribes. Unpublished papers, Ohio Historical Society.

Trosper, Ronald L.

1976   Native American boundary maintenance: The Flathead Indian reservation, Montana, 1860–1970. *Ethnicity* 3:256–74.

Tyner, James W.

1974   *Those who cried: The 16,000*. n.p.:Chi-ga-u.

Ubelaker, Douglas H.

1976a   Prehistoric New World population size: Historical review and current appraisal of North American estimates. *American Journal of Physical Anthropology* 45:661–66.

1976b   The sources and methodology for Mooney's estimates of North American Indian populations. In *The Native population of the Americas in 1492*, ed. William M. Denevan, 243–88. Madison: University of Wisconsin Press.

1988   North American Indian population size, A.D. 1500 to 1985. *American Journal of Physical Anthropology* 77:289–94.

U.S. Bureau of Indian Affairs

1986   Tribal leaders list. Mimeographed.

U.S. Bureau of the Census

1892   *Indians. Eastern Band of Cherokee. Extra census bulletin. Eleventh census of the U.S.* Washington, D.C.: U.S. Government Printing Office.

1894a   *Extra census bulletin. The Five Civilized Tribes in Indian Territory: The Cherokee, Chickasaw, Choctaw, Creek and Seminole nations.* Washington, D.C.: U.S. Government Printing Office.

1894b   *Report on Indians taxed and Indians not taxed in the United States (except Alaska) at the eleventh census: 1890.* Washington, D.C.: U.S. Government Printing Office.

1907   *Population of Oklahoma and Indian Territory: 1907.* Bulletin 89. Washington, D.C.: U.S. Government Printing Office.

1915   *Indian population in the United States and Alaska: 1910.* Washington, D.C.: U.S. Government Printing Office.

1937   *The Indian population of the United States and Alaska.* Washington, D.C.: U.S. Government Printing Office.

1953   *U.S. census of population: 1950.* Vol. 4. *Special reports.* Part 3, chapter B. *Nonwhite population by race.* Washington, D.C.: U.S. Government Printing Office.

1971   *1970 census of population. Number of inhabitants. United States summary.* PC(1)-A1. Washington, D.C.: U.S. Government Printing Office.

1973a   *1970 census of population. Detailed characteristics. United States summary.* PC(1)-D1. Washington, D.C.: U.S. Government Printing Office.

1973b   *1970 census of population. Subject reports: American Indians.* PC(2)-1F. Washington, D.C.: U.S. Government Printing Office.

1979   *Twenty censuses: Population and housing questions, 1790–1980.* Washington, D.C.: U.S. Government Printing Office.

1982a   *1980 census of population: Characteristics of the population. Number of inhabitants: California.* PC80-1-A6. Washington, D.C.: U.S. Government Printing Office.

1982b   *1980 census of population: Characteristics of the population. Number of inhabitants: North Carolina.* PC80-1-A35. Washington, D.C.: U.S. Government Printing Office.

1982c   *1980 census of population: Characteristics of the population. Number of inhabitants: Oklahoma.* PC80-1-A38. Washington, D.C.: U.S. Government Printing Office.

1983a   *Ancestry of the population by state: 1980.* Supplementary report PC80-SI-10. Washington, D.C.: U.S. Government Printing Office.

1983b   *1980 census of population. General population characteristics.* Pt. 1. *United States summary.* PC80-1-B1. Washington, D.C.: U.S. Government Printing Office.

1983c   *1980 census of population. General social and economic characteristics.* Pt. 1. *United States summary.* PC80-1-C1. Washington, D.C.: U.S. Government Printing Office.

1984   *1980 census of population. American Indian areas and Alaska Native villages: 1980.* Supplementary report PC80-S1-13. Washington, D.C.: U.S. Government Printing Office.

1985   *1980 census of population.* Vol. 2. *Subject reports. American Indians, Eskimos and Aleuts on identified reservations and in the historic areas of Oklahoma (excluding urbanized areas).* Document Number PC80-2-1D, pt. 1. Washington, D.C.: U.S. Government Printing Office.

U.S. Congress

1867   *Condition of the Indian tribes. Report of the joint special committee, appointed under joint resolution of March 3, 1865, with an appendix.* Washington, D.C.: U.S. Government Printing Office.

1986   *Indian health care.* OTA-H-290. Washington, D.C.: U.S. Government Printing Office.

U.S. Department of the Interior

1855   *Annual report of the commissioner of Indian affairs, transmitted with the message of the president at the opening of the second session of the thirty-third Congress, 1854.* Washington, D.C.: A.O.P. Nicholson.

1856   *Annual report of the commissioner of Indian affairs, transmitted with the message of the president at the opening of the first session of the thirty-fourth Congress, 1855.* Washington, D.C.: A.O.P. Nicholson.

1861   *Report of the commissioner of Indian affairs, accompanying the annual report of the secretary of the interior for the year 1861.* Washington, D.C.: U.S. Government Printing Office.

1864   *Report of the commissioner of Indian affairs for the year 1863.* Washington, D.C.: U.S. Government Printing Office.

1865   *Report of the commissioner of Indian affairs for the year 1865.* Washington, D.C.: U.S. Government Printing Office.

1866   *Report of the commissioner of Indian affairs for the year 1866.* Washington, D.C.: U.S. Government Printing Office.

1868   *Report on Indian affairs by the acting commissioner for the year 1867.* Washington, D.C.: U.S. Government Printing Office.

1872a   *Report of the commissioner of Indian affairs to the secretary of the interior for the year 1871.* Washington, D.C.: U.S. Government Printing Office.

1872b   *Annual report of the commissioner of Indian affairs to the secretary of the interior for the year 1872.* Washington, D.C.: U.S. Government Printing Office.

1874a   *Annual report of the commissioner of Indian affairs to the secretary of the interior for the year 1873.* Washington, D.C.: U.S. Government Printing Office.

1874b   *Annual report of the commissioner of Indian affairs to the secretary of the interior for the year 1874.* Washington, D.C.: U.S. Government Printing Office.

1876   *Annual report of the commissioner of Indian affairs to the secretary of the interior for the year 1876.* Washington, D.C.: U.S. Government Printing Office.

1878   *Annual report of the commissioner of Indian affairs to the secretary of the interior for the year 1878.* Washington, D.C.: U.S. Government Printing Office.

1879   *Annual report of the commissioner of Indian affairs to the secretary of the interior for the year 1879.* Washington, D.C.: U.S. Government Printing Office.

1880   *Annual report of the commissioner of Indian affairs to the secretary of the interior for the year 1880.* Washington, D.C.: U.S. Government Printing Office.

1881   *Annual report of the commissioner of Indian affairs to the secretary of the interior for the year 1881.* Washington, D.C.: U.S. Government Printing Office.

1882   *Annual report of the commissioner of Indian affairs to the secretary of the interior for the year 1882.* Washington, D.C.: U.S. Government Printing Office.

1883   *Annual report of the commissioner of Indian affairs to the secretary of the interior for the year 1883.* Washington, D.C.: U.S. Government Printing Office.

1884   *Annual report of the commissioner of Indian affairs to the secretary of the interior for the year 1884.* Washington, D.C.: U.S. Government Printing Office.

1885   *Annual report of the commissioner of Indian affairs to the secretary of the interior for the year 1885.* Washington, D.C.: U.S. Government Printing Office.

1886   *Annual report of the commissioner of Indian affairs to the secretary of the interior for the year 1886.* Washington, D.C.: U.S.
Government Printing Office.

1887   *Annual report of the commissioner of Indian affairs to the secretary of the interior for the year 1887.* Washington, D.C.: U.S.
Government Printing Office.

1888   *Fifty-seventh annual report of the commissioner of Indian affairs
to the secretary of the interior, 1888.* Washington, D.C.: U.S.
Government Printing Office.

1889   *Fifty-eighth annual report of the commissioner of Indian affairs
to the secretary of the interior, 1889.* Washington, D.C.: U.S.
Government Printing Office.

1892   *Sixty-first annual report of the commissioner of Indian affairs
to the secretary of the interior, 1892.* Washington, D.C.: U.S.
Government Printing Office.

1896   *Annual report of the commissioner of Indian affairs, 1895.* Washington, D.C.: U.S. Government Printing Office.

1898   *Annual report of the Department of the Interior for the fiscal
year ended June 30, 1898. Indian affairs.* Washington, D.C.: U.S.
Government Printing Office.

1903   *Annual reports of the Department of the Interior for the fiscal
year ended June 30, 1902. Indian affairs. Part 2. Commission to
the Five Civilized Tribes. Indian inspector for Indian Territory.
Indian contracts.* Washington, D.C.: U.S. Government Printing
Office.

1904   *Annual report of the commissioner of Indian affairs to the secretary of the interior, 1904.* Washington, D.C.: U.S. Government
Printing Office.

1906   *Annual reports of the Department of the Interior for the fiscal
year ended June 30, 1905: Indian affairs. Part 2.* Washington,
D.C.: U.S. Government Printing Office.

1907a   *Annual report of the Department of the Interior. 1906. Indian
affairs: Report of the commissioner and appendixes. Report of
the commissioner to the Five Civilized Tribes. Report of the
mine inspector for Indian Territory. Report of the Indian inspector for Indian Territory.* Washington, D.C.: U.S. Government
Printing Office.

1907b   *Reports of the Department of the Interior for the fiscal year
ended June 30, 1907. Indian affairs. Territories.* Vol. 2 of *Admin-
istrative reports.* Washington, D.C.: U.S. Government Printing
Office.

1941   *Indian population in continental United States and Alaska. Supplement to the annual report of the commissioner of Indian
affairs.* Washington, D.C.: U.S. Department of the Interior.

1943   *Statistical supplement to the annual report of the commissioner of Indian affairs for the fiscal year ended June 30, 1943.* Washington, D.C.: U.S. Department of the Interior.

1945   *Statistical supplement to the annual report of the commissioner of Indian affairs for the fiscal year ended June 30, 1945.* Washington, D.C.: U.S. Department of the Interior.

Wahrhaftig, Albert

1968   The tribal Cherokee population of eastern Oklahoma. *Current Anthropology* 9:510–18.

Walker, Robert S.

1931   *Torchlights to the Cherokees.* New York: Macmillan.

Wardell, Morris L.

1977   *A political history of the Cherokee Nation, 1838–1907.* Norman: University of Oklahoma Press. Originally published 1938.

Washburn, Cephas

1910   *Cherokees "West," 1794 to 1839.* Claremore, Okla.: Emmet Starr.

Washburn, Wilcomb E.

1975   *The assault on Indian tribalism: The General Allotment Law (Dawes Act) of 1887.* Philadelphia: J. B. Lippincott.

Weslager, C. A.

1974   Enrollment list of Chippewa and Delaware-Munsies living in Franklin County, Kansas, May 31, 1900. *Kansas Historical Quarterly* 40:234–40.

Wilkins, Thurman

1970   *Cherokee tragedy: The story of the Ridge family and of the decimation of a people.* New York: Macmillan.

1986   *Cherokee tragedy: The Ridge family and the decimation of a people.* 2d ed., rev. Norman: University of Oklahoma Press.

Williams, Walter T.

1977   The merger of Apaches with Eastern Cherokees: Qualla in 1893. *Journal of Cherokee Studies* 2:240–45.

Wilms, Douglas C.

1974   Cherokee settlement patterns in nineteenth century Georgia. *Southeastern Geographer* 14:46–53.

Witthoft, John

1947   Notes on a Cherokee migration story. Communicated by W. N. Fenton. *Journal of the Washington Academy of Sciences* 37:304–5.

Wood, Peter

1988   Re-counting the past. *Southern Exposure* 16:30–37.

1989   The changing population of the colonial South: An overview by race and region, 1685–1790. In *Powhatan's mantle,* ed. Peter

Wood, Gregory A. Waselkov, and M. Thomas Hatley, 35–103. Lincoln: University of Nebraska Press.

Woodward, Grace Steele

    1963   *The Cherokees*. Norman: University of Oklahoma Press.

Wright, Muriel H.

    1951   *A guide to the Indian tribes of Oklahoma*. Norman: University of Oklahoma Press.

Young, Mary

    1975   Indian removal and the attack on tribal autonomy: The Cherokee case. In *Indians of the lower South: Past and present*, ed. John K. Mahon, 125–42. Pensacola: Fla.: Gulf Coast History and Humanities Conference.

Index

Other volumes in the Indians of the Southeast
series include:

CREEKS AND SEMINOLES
*The Destruction and Regeneration of
the Muscogulge People*
By J. Leitch Wright, Jr.

THE SOUTHEASTERN CEREMONIAL
COMPLEX
Artifacts and Analysis
Edited by Patricia Galloway
Exhibition Catalog by David H. Dye and Camille Wharey

POWHATAN'S MANTLE
Indians in the Colonial Southeast
Edited by Peter H. Wood, Gregory A. Waselkov, and
M. Thomas Hatley

CHEROKEE AMERICANS
*The Eastern Band of Cherokees in the
Twentieth Century*
By John R. Finger